Safeguarding and Protecting Children in the Early Year

This book provides a comprehensive guide to safeguarding and child protection in the early years. Aimed at students and practitioners, it offers insight into contemporary developments in early years and safeguarding practice, and sets out the legal and policy foundations for effective practice before exploring areas of contemporary concern.

Drawing on the everyday dilemmas and experiences of early years professionals, the book focuses on helping you to seek solutions to both practical and moral issues in a context of legal duties and responsibilities. Covering a broad range of issues, chapters consider:

- how to identify physical and/or emotional neglect;
- consequential abuse that can occur as a result of parental behaviours;
- safeguarding children's health and wellbeing;
- safeguarding against the misuse of technology;
- communication with parents, carers and the 'team around the child' alongside examples of real-life issues and consequences that have arisen when communication has broken down;
- safeguarding as a member of a team;
- safeguarding through inter-professional and multidisciplinary work.

Written by a multidisciplinary team with a wealth of experience in safeguarding and child protection, the Early Years Foundation Stage, health visiting, social work, the police, and in leading and managing services, this timely new text is essential reading for all those working with young children.

James Reid is a Senior Lecturer in Childhood Studies within the Department of Community and International Education at the University of Huddersfield, UK.

Steven Burton is a Senior Lecturer at the University of Huddersfield, lecturing in the areas of early years, educational leadership and management, and safeguarding.

Safeguarding and Protecting Children in the Early Years

Edited by James Reid with
Steven Burton

Routledge
Taylor & Francis Group

LONDON AND NEW YORK

First published 2014
by Routledge
2 Park Square, Milton Park, Abingdon, Oxon OX14 4RN

and by Routledge
711 Third Avenue, New York, NY 10017

Routledge is an imprint of the Taylor & Francis Group, an informa business

British Library Cataloguing in Publication Data
A catalogue record for this book is available from the British Library

Library of Congress Cataloging in Publication Data
A catalog record for this book has been requested

ISBN: 978-0-415-52749-1 (hbk)
ISBN: 978-0-415-52750-7 (pbk)
ISBN: 978-1-315-88376-2 (ebk)

Typeset in Palatino
by Wearset Ltd, Boldon, Tyne and Wear

Printed and bound by CPI Group (UK) Ltd, Croydon, CR0 4YY

Contents

Contributors

Steven Burton, in his early career, worked for a UK police force within its Force Intelligence unit, which gave him his first introduction to the world of online safeguarding. He began his teaching career in the fields of management and public services. His keen interest in e-learning has developed throughout his career, as demonstrated by his taking part in a project with a Finnish college to investigate how e-learning has proliferated in Finnish culture. He has also managed a national Learning and Skills Development Agency sponsored project to investigate the potential use of e-learning in initial teacher training. He is a Senior Lecturer at the University of Huddersfield, lecturing in the areas of early years, educational leadership and management, and safeguarding. He has contributed significantly to the development of this book.

Sharon Frankland has worked since 2007 as a Senior Lecturer in Early Years at the University of Huddersfield, where she teaches modules on safeguarding children, children's health and wellbeing, and work-based learning. Previously she has worked as a registered nurse, health visitor and practice educator, undertaking a number of roles within hospital and community settings. She was involved in the initial launch of the Sure Start local programme in a deprived area of South Yorkshire, where she worked with other professionals and agencies to provide a range of services for children and their families. She is currently undertaking a professional doctorate in nursing and is exploring how professionals from different backgrounds work together to promote family wellbeing.

Frances Marsden is a Senior Lecturer in the School of Education and Professional Development at the University of Huddersfield. She is a programme leader for the BA (Hons) Educational Management and Administration and the International BA (Hons) Human Resource Development courses. She is also a module leader for Early Years, Childhood Studies BA (Hons) programmes and the Postgraduate Certificate in Higher Education. She is a personal tutor to a range of diverse students in the School of Education and Professional Development, from full-time undergraduates to part-time mature professionals. Her current doctoral research aims to investigate the role of empathy and emotional labour from the higher education personal tutor's perspective. She has presented papers at a number of conferences in the United Kingdom and elsewhere in Europe with Andrew Youde on the topic of transactional distance and work-based learning. She has also co-authored a range of papers and book chapters.

Samantha McMahon has ten years' experience of nursery, primary and further education, and her key experiences include a pilot study of the Foundation Stage curriculum and work on seamless integrated provision for children from the nursery to Reception. Her role at the University of Huddersfield has included the development and growth of early years provision and the subsequent progression routes. She works closely with practitioners and providers in enhancing early years provision, including developing in-service training in child development for practitioners or teachers in children's centres.

Nigel Parton graduated with a BA (Hons) in Applied Social Studies/CQSW from Bradford University in 1974 and worked as a social worker in Bradford Social Services until 1976. He joined the then Polytechnic of Huddersfield in 1977 as a Lecturer in Social Work, teaching primarily on the Non-Graduate Diploma in Social Work and Certification of Qualification in Social Work courses, and also teaching social policy on the BSc (Hons) Behavioural Sciences, the Certificate in Health Visiting and the Diploma in District Nursing courses. He became Professor in Child Care Studies at Keele University in 1993 before returning to the University of Huddersfield in 1994 to become Professor in Child Care and Director of the Centre of Applied Childhood Studies. As the author of numerous articles, reports and books he has a reputation of international significance. He is currently the Foundation NSPCC Chair in Applied Childhood Studies at the University of Huddersfield.

Julie Percival joined the University of Huddersfield in 2007 and is course leader for the postgraduate routes to Early Years Professional Status within the School of Education and Professional Development. She has been teaching (and learning) for over 20 years and has supported children in a variety of contexts, including special schools, maintained schools, pre-school play groups and private day nurseries. She has supported adults in their learning and development of practice, informally in the workplace and as part of a team of advisory teachers offering centrally and locally devised programmes. She has collaborated with families and a variety of agencies, including psychological services, health and Sure Start, to devise packages of care and learning for the very youngest people in society. She has been a member of a team researching children's development and learning as part of a Sure Start evaluation project and is co-author of a book on assessment for learning in the Foundation Stage.

James Reid, main editor of this book, joined the University of Huddersfield in September 2008 and is a Senior Lecturer in Childhood Studies in the Department of Education and Community Studies, where he teaches child protection and safeguarding. He advises on safeguarding in the School of Education and Professional Development and is responsible for a significant increase in childhood studies, early years, initial teacher training and youth and community work students gaining employer-recognised certificates in safeguarding and child protection. He is regularly invited to offer seminars, lectures and talks to other professionals by organisations such as the Consortium for Post-Compulsory Education and Training. Subsequently to engaging in social work practice with children and their families and working as a social work manager, he spent four years as a staff development officer with a local authority children's department. He then took up a post with the University of Teesside, where he taught social work before managing the social work programmes at that university. He has experience in developing social work provision in Central Asia with UNICEF, is a member of the Centre of Applied Childhood Studies at Huddersfield and has contributed to international texts on vulnerable children and the law.

Neil Ventress comes from a background of almost 30 years of social work practice with children and their families as a social worker, a manager and an inter-agency trainer. After starting his career with a short period as a residential social worker, he moved to fieldwork in 1977 and he gained his Certificate of Qualification in Social Work in 1982. From 2007 to 2011 he enjoyed a post as a Senior Lecturer at Teesside University, where he taught on both the undergraduate and post-qualifying social work programmes and was Programme Leader for the university's post-qualifying programme for social workers working with children, young people, their families and carers. He is currently an independent trainer and consultant, and he continues to focus on safeguarding children. His principal research and writing interests are around the field of child neglect, although he also has an interest in inter-professional safeguarding education, and in 2007–2009 he was an active member of the Project Advisory Group for a large-scale piece of research funded by the Department of Health and the Department for Children, Schools and Families on the effectiveness of inter-agency safeguarding training. He writes regularly for *Community Care Inform*.

Andrew Youde is Head of Division within the Department of Education and Community Studies at the University of Huddersfield. He has particular research interests in the skills and qualities of online tutors, and his doctoral research involves exploring the relationship between emotional intelligence and success in blended learning environments. He lectures on various programmes, including MSc Multimedia and E-learning, BA (Hons) Educational Management and Administration and BA (Hons) Leading in the Children's Workforce.

Acknowledgements

The editor and authors would like to thank their family, friends and colleagues for their encouragement and support in writing this book. Thanks also to Annamarie Kino at Routledge for her encouragement and comments. Most of all, we are indebted to the early years practitioners who graciously gave up their time and their experience to enhance the credibility of the text.

Thank you:
Gilly Milner, Rising Stars Children Centre, Worsborough Common Primary
    School, and
Margaret Smelt
Donna Pendergast
Gillian Turner
Andrea Wyles
Rachel Coburn
Gill Holden
Lauren Butterworth

Abbreviations

ACPC	Area Child Protection Committee
BME	black and minority ethnic
CAMHS	Child and Adolescent Mental Health Services
CEOP	Child Exploitation and Online Protection Centre
CWDC	Children's Workforce Development Council
DCSF	Department for Children, Schools and Families (2007–2010)
DfE	Department for Education (2010 to date)
DfEE	Department for Education and Employment (1995–2001)
DfES	Department for Education and Skills (2001–2007)
DH	Department of Health (1988 to date)
DHSS	Department of Health and Social Security (1968–1988)
ECHR	European Convention for the Protection of Human Rights and Fundamental Freedoms
EYFS	Early Years Foundation Stage
EYPS	Early Years Professional Status
HRA	Human Rights Act 1998
ICT	information and communications technology
JAR	Joint Area Review
LSCB	Local Safeguarding Children Board
NCMP	National Child Measurement Programme
NHS	National Health Service
OECD	Organisation for Economic Co-operation and Development
PVI	private, voluntary and independent
RoSPA	Royal Society for the Prevention of Accidents
SPOC	single point of contact
UKCCIS	United Kingdom Council for Child Internet Safety
UNCRC	United Nations Convention on the Rights of the Child

I want to begin with an admission.
The state is currently failing in its duty to keep our children safe.
It may seem hard to believe – after the killing of Victoria Climbié, after the torture of Peter Connelly, after the cruel death of Khyra Ishaq – surely as a society, as a state, we must have got the message.
But, I fear, we haven't.

Michael Gove
Secretary of State for Education
16 November 2012

1

Introduction

James Reid

The epigraph quotation from Michael Gove may seem like a startling admission, but of course any message that the state is 'failing' depends on the vested interests of those providing and receiving the message! The key question is why might a Secretary of State make such an admission? The answer, in part, is that it is true to a particular political ideology, and of course previous Secretaries of State have been mired in child death tragedies as they are ultimately responsible for legislation, policy and guidance for safeguarding and child protection. This quotation underlines the fact that definitions and understanding of safeguarding and child protection are based on social constructions – that is, they are not fixed but change and develop over time; they are fluid. The child-rearing and working practices of the Victorian era are not acceptable today. In the contemporary context, our understanding of the dangers of information and communication technologies and child exploitation is continuing to develop; and there are cultural and societal influences, including the media and a political desire not to be associated with negative headlines. Beliefs and practices about children, women and families differ around the world; there are patriarchal societies and societies based on community. Some countries treat children as adults when it comes to crime or immigration, and in many places corporal punishment is acceptable. Nor is it necessary to look around the world for variations in law, policy and understanding, since there are important differences between the devolved states of the United Kingdom. In Scotland, for example, physical chastisement of a child is not permitted, whereas in England, section 58 of the Children Act 2004 permits 'reasonable punishment' (which may include smacking).

Even the terms 'safeguarding' and 'child protection' have been used differently over time. The statutory guidance *Working Together to Safeguard Children: A Guide to Inter-agency Working to Safeguard and Promote the Welfare of Children* (DH *et al.* 1999) alongside the *Framework for the Assessment of Children in Need and Their Families* (DH *et al.* 2000b) reinforced the then government's view that children in need of protection from harm represented only one of a range of needs. Indeed, a child's need to be safe was one of five outcomes enshrined in the 2003 Green Paper *Every Child Matters* (DfES 2003a). While not always using the lexicon of the previous administration, Michael Gove (current Secretary of State for Education) and the Coalition government that came to power in the United Kingdom in 2010 continue to emphasise the need to safeguard and promote the welfare of all children. However, 'child protection' has again gained prominence as a specific professional activity undertaken with children who are suffering or likely to suffer significant harm. That is, all childcare professionals continue to have responsibilities and duties to safeguard children but it is social workers in particular whose duties extend to child protection. The Department for Education defines the difference between safeguarding and child protection like this:

> Safeguarding and promoting the welfare of children is defined as:
>
> - protecting children from maltreatment
> - preventing impairment of children's health or development
> - ensuring children are growing up in circumstances consistent with the provision of safe and effective care.
>
> Child protection is a part of safeguarding and promoting welfare. It refers to the activity that is undertaken to protect specific children who are suffering, or are likely to suffer, significant harm.
>
> Effective child protection is essential as part of wider work to safeguard and promote the welfare of children. However, all agencies and individuals should aim to proactively safeguard and promote the welfare of children so that the need for action to protect children from harm is reduced.
>
> (DfE 2013: online)

It is important, therefore, for the early years practitioner to be aware of two aspects of professional activity: child protection and safeguarding. Consequently, this book covers these two areas of practice, with an overall aim of enabling and being an aid to the practitioner in meeting their safeguarding responsibilities and duties. It is divided into two parts. Following this introductory chapter, Part 1 provides an overview of the contemporary context for child protection, with a focus on a number of key areas of child protection and safeguarding concern for *all* children, their families and the professionals who work with them. Content includes consideration of the history and social constructions of child abuse before deliberation on the expectations and requirements as stated in policy, guidance and by Local Safeguarding Children Boards. Understanding the historical, legal and policy context is crucial, since we can only seek to support and safeguard children and intervene in family life because there are laws and policies that require and enable us to do so.

Subsequent to discussion in Chapters 2 and 3 of the historical and legal context, Chapters 4 and 5 focus on areas of particular concern for safeguarding practitioners, including child neglect, consequential abuse and the 'toxic trio' of parental mental health problems, substance misuse and domestic violence. We have decided not to focus on other concerns such as physical, sexual and emotional abuse, as these are covered in great detail elsewhere and in staff development programmes. The focus in this book is on those issues that have been identified by practitioners as requiring further exploration in the literature.

In this vein, Part 2 develops the overview from the macro contemporary knowledge for child protection that is relevant to all childcare practitioners to focus explicitly on the early years context, and specifically on those everyday issues that confront staff. Importantly, the chapters draw upon early years workers' real experiences in practice and reveal some of the 'grey' areas that frustrate and confront them. The first chapter in this part sets the scene for safeguarding in early years settings and consideration of the need for risky practice. Discussion in the next chapter considers proactive practice focused on children's health and well-being. The following chapter deals with an area of contemporary risk highlighted by the Vanessa George case in an early years setting in Plymouth in 2006: risks arising from the use of ICT.

Focus then moves to the crucial task of communicating with parents and carers, and highlights the knowledge and skills required in working in partnership with parents and carers to ensure their continued participation in the safeguarding process. Consideration is also given to the task of maintaining effective communication in difficult and at times conflictual circumstances, and readers are asked to reflect on their own approaches to communication. Effective safeguarding practice also requires practitioners to be aware of their role as a member of a multi-agency team. Consequently, consideration is given to power dynamics within teams and teams within teams. The concept of 'team' is further explored in a multidisciplinary context, including the critical 'team around the child'. The book concludes with a chapter on the reflective practitioner which aims to enable workers to consider their continuing professional development, including the need for effective supervision.

Safeguarding and child protection: moral, legal and professional obligations

Michael Gove's remark alludes to the fact that the safeguarding and protection of children are both moral and legal expectations of all of those who work with children. The topic continually exercises practitioners and policy makers, and is of interest to the wider public, particularly through the media. Successive governments have sought to improve child protection services, and the current government continues to recognise the role that early years professionals have in safeguarding children. Continuing emphasis is being placed on early intervention and face-to-face work with children and their families.

This book aims to help early years practitioners to understand their roles and responsibilities in keeping children safe from harm. This is particularly necessary for those practitioners who are perhaps recently qualified or unqualified, or inexperienced, or daunted by the thought of safeguarding and child protection. However, the content of this book is constructed in the knowledge that practitioners are not a homogeneous group and it is written with all early years practitioners in mind.

As I have already pointed out, safeguarding and child protection are not fixed concepts, and successive governments seek to improve and to enhance the structures and policies already in place. The UN Convention on the Rights of the Child, the Children Act 1989, the Children Act 2004 and the current Working Together to Safeguard Children (HM Government 2013) guidance provide the statutory basis for child protection in England and Wales. (Similar legislation exists in the other devolved regions of the United Kingdom.) All early years practitioners have moral and legal duties and responsibilities to ensure the protection of children. It is essential, therefore, that practitioners, whatever their status, experience or knowledge, keep up to date with policy and legal developments. Whereas child protection relates to those children who are suffering or likely to suffer significant harm, safeguarding applies to all children and encompasses the need to protect all children from maltreatment, to prevent impairment of their health or development, and to ensure that children are growing up in circumstances consistent with the provision of safe and effective care. Safeguarding is therefore a core element of the content of all government policy and guidance relating to children and their families.

Soon after coming to power, the Coalition government set in motion a number of reviews into children's and families services all of which considered safeguarding as an important and critical issue. The most relevant of these reviews for the early years sector was Dame Clare Tickell's work *The Early Years: Foundations for Life, Health and Learning: An Independent Report on the Early Years Foundation Stage to Her Majesty's Government* (2011), which, in part, led to the government's vision for early years services in *Supporting Families in the Foundation Years* (DfE 2011a). This, in particular, recognises the need for early intervention and good early years services when we seek to achieve a successful and healthy life for our children. A separate review by Professor Eileen Munro, *The Munro Review of Child Protection* (2011a, b), called for the introduction of a duty on all local services to co-ordinate an early offer of help to families that do not meet the criteria for social care services, to address problems before they worsen to become child protection issues. The focus is therefore very much on early years practitioners in engaging with children and their families in safeguarding their future prospects.

The government is clear that early help and intervention are crucial in supporting children and their families. This means that early years practitioners need to be clear how they can best support child development, including through safeguarding and protection, so that children reach school age ready to take advantage of all the opportunities available to them. In paragraph 4.1 of her review report, Tickell writes:

> Children learn and develop best when they are safe, happy and healthy. For all those working with young children, *safeguarding is everyone's responsibility and must be their first and foremost consideration.* Regardless of their level or experience within the workforce, everyone working with young children must know how and when to raise any concerns. They must be aware of the warning signs and alert to acting on any concerns. This is one area of the EYFS [Early Years Foundation Stage] which cannot be compromised and where the evidence shows wide support for the current welfare requirements. There is a shared view amongst practitioners that regulation is needed and essential to support good practice.
>
> (2011: 37; emphasis added)

Working to protect, safeguard and promote the welfare of children is not optional; it is a core duty and responsibility of the early years practitioner. However, child protection and safeguarding is much more than a cerebral activity; it also involves emotions and deep-seated feelings, perhaps even including our own prejudices! It is important too, therefore, that early years practitioners are also aware of the need to look after themselves. Much of this need could be met in effective supervision. Tickell (2011: 46–47) recognises that supervision is an opportunity for early years practitioners 'to receive support to help them deal with difficult or challenging situations at work'. Although Tickell overemphasises the management function of supervision, a good practitioner will also use supervision effectively to learn and develop more broadly. It is in recognition of the importance of supervision as a professional obligation that the final chapter of the book focuses on this activity.

Chapters and their focus

This book is an essential text for all early years practitioners as it provides an overview of developments in early years and safeguarding practice, and. importantly, considers some of the grey areas experienced by practitioners, such as the power relations in early years practice, either between young, inexperienced staff and more senior staff, or in the unconditional regard children have for staff, and therefore the powerful practitioner in children's lives. Drawing on the everyday experiences and dilemmas of early years professionals in seeking to safeguard and protect young children, the book focuses on helping them to seek solutions to both practical and moral issues in a context of legal duties and responsibilities. The book is written by authors with close connections to early years practice and with a wealth of experience, including in safeguarding and child protection, the Early Years Foundation Stage, health visiting, social work, the police, and in leading and managing services. The authors are able therefore to draw upon their own contemporary professional experience in constructing chapters that are relevant to the early years sector.

However, this rich mix of experience and knowledge goes beyond the contemporary legislative and policy context to offer meaningful and practical insight into the issues faced by practitioners on a day-to-day basis. Content deals with issues on both the macro and the micro levels. For example, Chapter 8, 'Safeguarding children from online danger', explores the potential for harm that can come from the improper or illegal use of technology around children (macro), whereas Chapter 9, 'Communicating through a crisis', highlights some of the issues in face-to-face communication with children (micro). Similarly, Chapter 7, 'Safeguarding children's health and wellbeing', highlights the macro interface between parental responsibility and state accountability and makes the direct links between social exclusion, poverty and ill health and the need for early help and intervention. The chapter then moves forward to offer practical tips in implementing policy by suggesting a role for parenting education classes.

Thus, this book is focused on the real experiences of practitioners, not just on safeguarding and child protection as an academic subject for study. The book deals with the gaps in the understanding of policy and guidance and the grey areas of practice that hinder or confound good practice. For example, if a member of staff loses their temper with young children, is this a safeguarding issue? In this regard it is also important to explore how practitioners feel about safeguarding and managing their own feelings.

In Chapter 2, Nigel Parton and James Reid consider the recent history of central government guidance about child protection. The purpose of this chapter is to describe and outline the growth of government guidance on child protection from 1974 to date, with particular consideration of the period since the late 1990s. This analysis provides important insights into the changing nature of child protection policy and practice during the period in terms of its priorities, focus and organisation. It also reminds us that ideas of safeguarding and protection are not fixed but fluid, and contingent upon both societal norms and practices and the ideology of the day. It brings the development of policy and guidance up to date by incorporating discussion of key policy and practice reviews.

In Chapter 3, James Reid focuses on the social, legal and practice context for protecting and safeguarding children. There is an acknowledgement that safeguarding and child protection are social constructions and a recognition of how child deaths, changing understandings of the family and legislation all shape practice. Crucially, the chapter also considers the basis for empowering practice in safeguarding and child protection and thus provides a significant link with the later chapter 'Communicating through a crisis'.

The next two chapters, by Neil Ventress, deal with significant safeguarding and protection concerns. In Chapter 4 he highlights the difficulties in identifying and working with neglect. It is notable, therefore, that this chapter seeks to enhance practitioner understanding of the range of experiences which constitute neglect in the early years, their impact on the developing child, and the necessary legal and procedural requirements that apply when neglect is identified. In Chapter 5, Ventress considers, among other things, the consequences of domestic violence. Significantly, in England and Wales the Adoption and Children Act 2002 amended the definition of significant harm provided by the Children Act 1989, adding a new category of 'impairment suffered from seeing or hearing the ill-treatment of another'. Domestic violence takes several forms and has the potential to significantly blight children's lives. Of consequence in both chapters is the acknowledgement that neglect and domestic violence can be present pre-natally.

Chapters 2–5 constitute Part 1 of the book and deal largely with macro issues. Part 2 begins with Chapter 6 by Julie Percival, which begins to deal in greater depth on the micro context of early years practice and experience – that is, there is significant reference to practitioners' views and experiences. In 'Safeguarding within the Early Years Foundation Stage', Percival considers how practitioners can interpret the EYFS so that they can support children's learning about themselves and their world. Safeguarding relies on each practitioner's sense of both personal and professional responsibility for the holistic care of children and takes into account theories that see children as co-constructors in learning when choosing how to implement the EYFS. Percival highlights the key aspects of early years practice that contribute to the safeguarding of children as part of everyday practice.

The mantle is then taken by Sharon Frankland, who in Chapter 7 discusses the centrality of safeguarding children's health and wellbeing. Frankland explores the inextricable link between the role of the children's workforce in safeguarding children, and the holistic positive promotion of their health and wellbeing. There have been many changes in the way that children's health services have been delivered over the past decades, including the change in focus from a state-led health educating model to one of an empowering 'promotional model'. In this context, Frankland considers the interface between parental responsibility and state accountability. There are direct links between social exclusion, poverty and ill health, and it is now very clear that early help and intervention are crucial if families are to be empowered to break out of a cycle of poor outcomes.

Steven Burton contributes Chapters 8 and 9, where he considers online dangers and communication respectively. Significantly, the models he puts forward are based on conversations and feedback from early years practitioners and managers. Information and communication technologies, including the capabilities of smartphones and similar devices, have particular safeguarding and protection resonance for the early years sector following the exposure and conviction of Vanessa George and her associates. He develops our appreciation of the types of potential online danger and offers guidance on how to construct an appropriate online safeguarding policy for an early years setting. His 'model of online danger' is an important contribution to the discussion. In Chapter 9, Burton looks at the imperative of effective communication. It is here that we begin to highlight the fact that working with safeguarding and child protection is much more than a cerebral process; it can affect the practitioner. He raises aspects of theory underpinning communication and relates this to examples of communication during safeguarding episodes. The outcome is an initial framework of communication with children for practitioners to utilise if involved in a safeguarding episode.

Frances Marsden, Samantha McMahon and Andrew Youde further the discussion on communication and raise the inter-agency approach to safeguarding children in Chapter 10. Their contribution considers the knowledge and skills necessary for protecting children in light of the Common Assessment Framework, including the importance of their communications and relationships in professional roles. Furthermore, they emphasise the essential practice of observations and assessing children's needs to provide evidence that then informs the team around the child. In this context the role of advocate for the child is considered.

The final chapter, by Samantha McMahon and Julie Percival, deals with the essential issue of reflective practice. Having acknowledged the need for effective management of practice, Dame Clare Tickell's report recognises the importance of supervision as a learning and developmental opportunity. That is why practitioners are required to be proactive in their engagement with supervision and in their continuing professional development. Concluding with this chapter reminds us that early years practitioners are active agents in the care and development of children and themselves. A good practitioner is one who is willing to learn, acknowledges mistakes and is unafraid to ask questions.

The guidance relating to child protection and safeguarding is vast. It includes a good deal that relates to children in specific circumstances, some of which, such as parental mental health problems, substance misuse and domestic violence, parental learning disability, and the misuse of ICT, are discussed in this book. There are many other areas of concern, including female genital mutilation or fabricated or induced illness, and abuse linked to spiritual or religious beliefs, for which you are advised to access the procedures (usually available online) of your Local Safeguarding Children Board. This is important since cultural or religious practices may be used to defend certain actions that harm children. Female genital mutilation, for example, has no religious or cultural defence, and indeed is a criminal offence in the United Kingdom – a reminder that UK law and policy have precedence in all safeguarding or child protection concerns in that country.

We need to be aware also that children can be harmed because of their ethnic background. While racism is not a category of child abuse, it can cause significant harm. Children and families from black and minority ethnic groups are likely to have experienced harassment and racial discrimination, yet we must not assume that their experience is common. Attention should be paid to the needs of all children, and practices must be inclusive and respectful to all, addressing any issues of racism, culture and religion whether it concerns the child or family. In this regard it is appropriate to highlight findings of the Macpherson Inquiry Report (Home Office 1999):

> 6.4 Racism in general terms consists of conduct or words or practices which disadvantage or advantage people because of their colour, culture, or ethnic origin. In its more subtle form it is as damaging as in its overt form.

> 6.34 [I]nstitutional racism consists of: [t]he collective failure of an organisation to provide an appropriate and professional service to people because of their colour, culture, or ethnic origin. It can be seen or detected in processes, attitudes and behaviour which amount to discrimination through unwitting prejudice, ignorance, thoughtlessness and racist stereotyping which disadvantage minority ethnic people.

We all have a responsibility to challenge such 'unwitting prejudice, ignorance, thoughtlessness and racist stereotyping'.

As the Macpherson Inquiry Report shows, the consequences of individual, organisational, collective or governmental failure can be horrendous. It would be too easy, however, to accept Michael Gove's admission of state failure in child protection and safeguarding at face value and to overlook the wider inherent purpose in his statement. Politicians no longer want to be in a position where they can be held responsible for or negatively associated with any future tragedy or poor practice. The onus is clearly on the practitioner to assure the protection and safeguarding of children, with concomitant consequences for failure in that regard. This book serves to support early years practitioners in meeting their responsibilities and duties.

Legal and policy foundations and key safeguarding concerns

2

The recent history of central government guidance about child protection

Nigel Parton and James Reid

The purpose of this chapter is to describe and outline the growth of government guidance on child protection from 1974 to date, with particular consideration of the period since the late 1990s. This analysis provides important insights into the changing nature of child protection policy and practice during the period in terms of its priorities, focus and organisation.

By the end of the chapter you will:

- discover that the guidance has grown enormously in length, detail and complexity during this period;
- understand that the object of concern has shifted from 'non-accidental injury' to 'child abuse' to 'safeguarding and promoting the welfare of children' and more recently to 'child protection';
- appreciate government moves to decrease bureaucracy and regulation.

Child protection, like childhood, is a social construction and as such is subject to the social, political, economic and cultural vagaries of the day. Understandings and explanations of abuse are not fixed or culturally specific and as a consequence they develop over time. It is unsurprising, therefore, that child protection guidance and policy are in a state of constant change. Parton (2006a) has identified three significant periods of concern regarding child maltreatment in the United Kingdom: from the 1870s to the beginning of the First World War, from the mid-1960s to the 1980s, and now. In Chapter 3 you will discover further some of the influential events that have shaped our understanding of childhood and child protection and safeguarding policy and practice. In contemporary society the focus on safeguarding and protection has moved beyond the home to include other aspects of children's lived experiences that may give rise to harm. Later in this book, for example, you will read about concern over new technologies, the need for safeguarding health and wellbeing, and the potential for abuse by practitioners. Consideration in this chapter is given to specific influences and the development of government guidance from 1974.

The beginnings of the contemporary child protection system

The contemporary child protection system in England was effectively inaugurated with the issue of the DHSS circular entitled *Non-accidental Injury to Children* (DHSS 1974) in the wake of the public inquiry into the death of Maria Colwell (Secretary of State 1974) and followed earlier guidance in relation to 'battered babies' (DHSS 1970, 1972). The system was refined in a series of further guidance throughout the decade (DHSS 1976a, b, 1978), and the problem being addressed had been officially re-named as child abuse which was made up of physical [...] emotional abuse but did not [...]

[...] that a range of key professionals [...] accidental injury to children [...] mechanisms were established so that [...]. Co-ordination between agencies [...] children was seen as key to [...] paediatricians, GPs, health visitors [...] However, it was social service departments [...] 'key agency' and local authority social [...] the statutory professionals for co-ordinating [...]

The [...] Review Committees', subsequently [...] Protection Committees' (ACPCs) (DHSS 1988), were established [...] local authority areas as policy-making bodies in order to co-ordinate the work of the local agencies, develop interprofessional training and produce detailed procedures to be followed where it was felt a child had been abused or might be at risk of abuse. In such situations there was to be a system of case conferences so that the relevant professionals could share information about a particular child and family, make decisions on what to do and provide an ongoing mechanism for monitoring progress. Where it was felt that a child protection plan was required, the child's name and details would be placed on a child protection register. The register could then be consulted by other professionals to establish whether the child was currently known.

Non-accidental Injury to Children (DHSS 1974) was circulated in the form of a memorandum. It was just seven pages long and had one footnote, which included four references, three of which were to previous DHSS circulars, plus reference to an article from the *British Medical Journal* entitled 'Non-accidental Injury to Children: A Guide to Management' (Working Party in the Department of Child Health, University of Newcastle upon Tyne 1973).

Working Together guidance

The first central government guidance had the title *Working Together* and was published in 1988 (DHSS 1988) on the same day as the publication of the public inquiry into the events in Cleveland the previous year (Secretary of State 1988). While it explicitly built on the consultation document published two years previously (DHSS 1986), it had been considerably redrafted to take account of the Cleveland Inquiry, where a major concern had been the inappropriate and possibly excessive intervention of state welfare professionals into the privacy of families on the basis of uncertain and questionable evidence of sexual abuse (see Parton 1991: 121–135). While the guidance broadened the definition of child abuse to include sexual abuse, it was primarily concerned to ensure that professionals maintained a balance in their work between protecting children from abuse and protecting the privacy of the family from unnecessary and unwarranted intrusion – the issue that was to lie at the heart of the 1989 Children Act (Parton 1991). The 1988 *Working Together* was 72 pages long, made up of 48 pages of guidance plus nine appendices of 24 pages. Appendix 1 consisted of references to 11 items of 'related Guidance'. There were no other notes or references in the document. Clearly, however, this was a much more substantial document than the DHSS circular *Non-accidental Injury to Children* (DHSS 1974), which had begun the process of establishing the contemporary child protection system.

In addition, it established a new element to the system and something that would grow in significance 20 years later. Part 9 of the guidance introduced a system of 'case reviews' to be carried out by the senior management of the relevant agencies, conducted under the auspices of the Area Child Protection Committee (ACPC) (which would become Serious Case Reviews in the 2006 guidance). The case review was introduced to try to pre-empt and perhaps avert the need for time-consuming, expensive and high-profile public inquiries, such as the Cleveland Inquiry, in the future. The case review by management in each involved agency would be instigated in all cases that involved the death of, or serious harm to, a child where child abuse was confirmed or suspected. These cases in particular cause distress within the family, create distress and anxiety among the staff of the agencies, and arouse public concern. Agencies need to respond quickly and positively to ensure that their services are maintained and are not undermined by the incident, that public concern is allayed and media comment is answered in a positive manner (DHSS 1988: para. 9.1).

From 'The Protection of Children from Abuse' to the 'Safeguarding and Promotion of Children's Welfare'

Government guidance in *Working Together* was revised on two occasions during the 1990s. A brief comparison of the two documents clearly demonstrates how official thinking about the nature of the problem to be addressed and the best way of responding changed significantly during the decade. The 1991 *Working Together* (Home Office *et al*. 1991) was published to coincide with the implementation of the Children Act 1989 and very closely followed the 1988 version of *Working Together* (DHSS 1988). It was framed in terms of responding to child abuse and improving the child protection system. This was very evident in the document's subtitle: *A Guide to Arrangements for Inter-agency Co-operation for the Protection of Children from Abuse*. The focus was upon the need to identify 'high-risk' cases so that these could be differentiated from the rest. Thereby, children could be protected from abuse while ensuring that family privacy was not undermined and scarce resources could be directed to where, in theory, they were most needed. While working in partnership with the parents and child was seen as important, the focus was 'children at risk of significant harm', such that the whole document was framed in terms of when and how to carry out an 'investigation' pursuant to section 47 of the Children Act 1989. The key 'threshold' criterion to be addressed was whether the child was 'suffering or likely to suffer significant harm' (s. 31(1)(9)). While the essential principles of the Children Act 1989 provided the legal framework, the focus of the child protection system was quite specific. For:

> The starting point of the process is that any person who has knowledge of, or suspicion, that a child is *suffering significant harm, or is at risk of suffering significant harm*, should refer their concern to one or more of the agencies with statutory *duties and/or powers to investigate or intervene* – the social services departments, the policy or the NSPCC.
>
> (Home Office *et al*. 1991, para. 5.11.1; emphasis added)

There was no mention of any of the more wide-ranging preventive duties that local authorities had in terms of section 17(1) of the Children Act 1989 'to safeguard and promote the welfare of children in their area who are in need'. As the title indicated, the 1999 *Working Together* guidance was very different: *Working Together to Safeguard Children: A Guide to Inter-agency Working to Safeguard and Promote the Welfare of Children* (DH *et al*. 1999). Not only was this the first time that the word 'safeguarding' was used in official guidance about child abuse, but also the subtitle explicitly framed the issues in terms of section 17(1) of the Children Act.

Working Together following Messages from Research: the introduction of the Framework for the Assessment of Children in Need and Their Families

The 1999 *Working Together* was revised in the light of *Child Protection: Messages from Research* (DH 1995), the refocusing debate (Parton 1997) and research on the implementation of the Children Act 1989 – particularly that concerning the difficulties that local authorities were having in developing their 'family support' services (DH 2001). The guidance underlined that local authorities had a clear responsibility than simply responding to concerns about 'significant harm' and was explicitly located in the wider agenda for children's services being implemented in the early years of the New Labour government which had been elected in 1997 (see Parton 2006, particularly chapters 5 and 6). While the 1999 guidance continued to make it clear that if anyone believed a child might be suffering 'significant harm' they should always refer these concerns to the social services department, it also stressed that these should be responded to by social services in the context of their much wider 'responsibility towards all children whose health or development may be impaired without the provision of support services, or who are disabled (described by the Children Act 1989 as children "in need")' (para. 5.5). In order to develop such a more holistic approach to assessment was introduced.

The publication of the 1999 edition of *Working Together* was combined with the publication of *Framework for the Assessment of Children in Need and Their Families* (Lord *et al.* 2000b), and the two documents needed to be read and used together. The *Framework* 2000a 'Assessment Framework', like *Working Together*, was issued as guidance under section 7 of the Local Authority Social Services Act 1970, which meant that it 'must be followed' by local authority social services departments unless there were exceptional circumstances that justified a variation. It thus had the same legal status as, and was incorporated into, *Working Together*.

The 'Assessment Framework' replaced the previous guidance, *Protecting Children: A Guide for Social Workers Undertaking a Comprehensive Assessment* (DH 1988), which had only been concerned with comprehensive assessment for long-term planning where child abuse had been confirmed or strongly suspected. In contrast, the 'Assessment Framework' moved the focus from the assessment of risk of child abuse and 'significant harm' to concern regarding possible impairment to a child's development. Both the safeguarding and the promotion of a child's welfare were seen as intimately connected aims for intervention, so that it was important that access to services was via a common assessment route. The critical task was to ascertain whether a child was 'in need' and how the child and the parents, in the context of their family and community environment, might be helped. While primarily a practice tool for social services departments, the 'Assessment Framework' also aimed to provide a common language, shared values and commitment among a much wider range of agencies and professionals.

[handwritten margin note: Local authority have more responsibility]

This comparison of the 1991 *Working Together* and the 1999 *Working Together* demonstrates that the 1990s witnessed a significant broadening of focus in government guidance. For while the concept of 'safeguarding' was an important idea in the Children Act 1989, particularly the rationale for section 17, it was only in the 1999 *Working Together* that it was made central to government guidance in relation to child protection. When considering the development of government guidance at this time, it is also important to include the 'Assessment Framework' (DH *et al.* 2000b), which was incorporated in the 1999 *Working Together* (DH *et al.* 1999).

In addition, the 'Assessment Framework' was also supported by the publication of a range of other material, which included practice guidance (DH 2000a), assessment record forms (DH and Cleaver 2000), a family assessment pack of questionnaires and scales (DH *et al.* 2000a), a summary of studies that informed the development of the framework (DH 2000b), and a training pack consisting of a video, guide and reader (NSPCC and University of Sheffield 2000). While these did not carry the same statutory status as the 'Assessment Framework' itself, they did demonstrate the growing expectations being placed upon social workers and other professionals. Taken together, the 1999 *Working Together* (DH *et al.* 1999) and the assessment framework guidances were much more substantial and complex documents than the 1991 *Working Together* (Home Office *et al.* 1991). Not only were the objects of concern broadened, but also the demands made of agencies and practitioners were increased.

Working Together in the context of *Every Child Matters*

There was a clear attempt in the 1999 *Working Together* (DH *et al.* 1999) to reframe the object of concern away from a narrow, forensically driven conception of child protection towards the much broader notion of safeguarding, to the point where some commentators argued that child protection had got lost altogether (Munro and Calder 2005; Smith 2008). However, the document did not provide a clear definition of safeguarding and its relationship with child protection. In fact, a report produced jointly by eight chief inspectors argued that while the idea of safeguarding children had become a major government priority, the term 'safeguarding has not been defined in law or government guidance' (DH 2002a: para. 1.5).

This was to change with the publication of the 2006 *Working Together* (HM Government 2006), where

> [s]*afeguarding and promoting the welfare of children* is defined for the purposes of this guidance as:
>
> - protecting children from maltreatment
> - preventing impairment of children's health or development

■ ensuring that children are growing up in circumstances consistent with the provision of safe and effective care; and undertaking that role so as to enable those children to have optimum life chances and to enter adulthood successfully.

(para. 1.18; original emphasis)

While the 2006 *Working Together* had the same title as the 1999 version, this was the first guidance that was authored by HM Government (2006) rather than by particular government departments, as previously. While it very much built on the central principles and mechanisms laid out in the 1999 guidance, it was updated to take account of the public inquiry report into the death of Victoria Climbié (Laming 2003), the major changes being introduced by the *Every Child Matters: Change for Children* programme (DfES 2003a) and the Children Act 2004, where the aim was to shift policy and practice in the direction of prevention, while at the same time strengthening protection (Parton 2006b).

The changes introduced under the *Every Child Matters: Change for Children* programme were the most ambitious and radical since the reorganisation of local authority social services in the early 1970s and were far more wide-ranging than anything previously attempted in the history of children's services in England (Frost and Parton 2009; Garrett 2009). In aiming to ensure that 'every child' achieved their potential, and in trying to integrate universal, targeted and specialist services, there were considerable implications for everyone who worked with children and young people, including early years professionals.

A key element of the government's strategy was to strengthen the framework for single and multi-agency safeguarding practice. Under section 11 of the Children Act 2004 a new statutory duty was placed on certain agencies (including the police, prisons and health bodies) to make arrangements to ensure that they had regard to the need to safeguard and promote the welfare of children. In addition, as from April 2006, local authorities were required to replace Area Child Protection Committees (ACPCs) with statutory Local Safeguarding Children Boards (LSCBs). The core membership of LSCBs was set out in the Children Act 2004 and was to include senior managers from different services, including the local authority health bodies, the police, any secure training centre or prison in the area and other organisations as deemed appropriate.

The guidance (HM Government 2006) was framed in terms of supporting *all* children and families in terms of the *Every Child Matters* five outcomes of being healthy, enjoying and achieving, making a positive contribution, achieving economic wellbeing and, particularly, staying safe, which were seen as 'key to children and young people's well-being' (para. 1.1).

The guidance was presented as part of 'an integrated approach' so that effective measures to safeguard children were seen as those which also promoted their welfare, and should not be seen in isolation from the wider range of support and services to meet the needs of all children and families.

The Early Years Foundation Stage and the growth of children's centres and Sure Start centres were key components of the idea of locating safeguarding in the wider policy agenda on tackling social exclusion.

While protecting children from maltreatment was seen as important in order to prevent the impairment of health and development, on its own it was not seen as sufficient to ensure that children were growing up in circumstances that ensured the provision of safe and effective care and that could bring about the five outcomes for all children. The guidance was centrally concerned with trying to ensure that all agencies and professionals fulfilled their responsibilities in relation to both prevention *and* child protection, as well as safeguarding *and* promoting the welfare of *all* children, and where professionals and managers were held accountable for their actions.

If we simply compare the page length of the 1999 *Working Together* (DH *et al.* 1999) with that of the 2006 version (HM Government 2006), we see that there is an increase from 119 pages to 231 pages; the number of pages on managing individual cases increased from 15 pages to 56 pages; the number of pages on (serious) case reviews increased from 4 to 15 pages; the number of footnotes increased from 12 to 43; and the number of references increased from 50 to 78. For the first time, references in the form of internet links and web addresses were included, accounting for 69 of the 78 references. The 'Assessment Framework' (DH *et al.* 2000b) continued to be fully incorporated into the 2006 guidance.

Working Together in the post-'Baby Peter' era

However, the period after November 2008 was one of considerable turmoil and had the potential to undermine the aims of the *Every Child Matters: Change for Children* programme and the other attempts by the New Labour government to refocus and reform child protection over the previous ten years.

On 11 November 2008 two men were convicted of causing or allowing the death of 17-month-old 'Baby Peter' Connelly, one of these men being Peter's stepfather. The baby's mother had already pleaded guilty to the charge. During the trial the court heard that Baby Peter was used as a 'punchbag' and that his mother had deceived and manipulated professionals with lies, and on one occasion had smeared him with chocolate to hide his bruises. There had been over 60 contacts with the family from a variety of health and social care professionals and he was pronounced dead just 48 hours after a hospital doctor failed to identify that he had a broken spine. He was the subject of a child protection plan with Haringey local authority in London – the local authority that had been at the centre of failures to protect Victoria Climbié back in 2000.

The media response was immediate and very critical of the services, particularly the local authority, Haringey (in north London). The largest-selling tabloid newspaper, the *Sun*, ran a campaign aimed at getting the professionals involved in the case sacked from their jobs under the banner of

'Beautiful Baby P: Campaign for Justice' (*Sun*, 15 November 2008). Two weeks later the newspaper delivered a petition to the prime minister containing 1.5 million signatures, claiming that it was the largest and most successful campaign of its sort ever. In addition, a large number of Facebook groups, comprising over 1.6 million members, were set up in memory of Baby Peter and seeking justice for his killers. This weight of expressed opinion put strong pressure on the government minister, Ed Balls, to be seen to be acting authoritatively in order to take control of the situation. He responded by:

- ordering the Office for Standards in Education, Children's Services and Skills (Ofsted), the Healthcare Commission and the Police Inspectorate to carry out an urgent Joint Area Review (JAR) on safeguarding in Haringey;
- ordering the preparation of a new and independent Serious Case Review following the publication of the original one on 12 November 2008, which he deemed to be inadequate and insufficiently critical;
- establishing a Social Work Task Force to identify any barriers that social workers faced in doing their jobs effectively and to make recommendations for improvements and the long-term reform of social work and to report in late 2009 (Social Work Task Force 2009).

In addition, the Secretary of State asked Lord Laming to prepare an urgent independent report on 'the progress being made across the country [England] to implement effective arrangements for safeguarding children'. The report was published the following March. In the introduction to the report, Lord Laming said:

> The Government deserves credit for the legislation and guidance that has been put in place to safeguard children and promote the welfare of children over the last five years. *Every Child Matters* clearly has the support of professionals, across all of the services, who work with children and young people. The interagency guidance *Working Together to Safeguard Children* provides a sound framework for professionals to protect children and promote their welfare…. However, whilst the improvements in the services for children and families, in general, are welcome it is clear that the need to protect children and young people from significant harm and neglect is ever more challenging. There now needs to be a step change in the arrangements to protect children from harm. It is essential that action is now taken so that as far as humanly possible children at risk of harm are properly protected.
>
> (Laming 2009: 3–4; original emphasis)

The message was clear: while Lord Laming was supportive, in general, of the recent changes, more needed to be done to strengthen child protection. The government accepted all of Lord Laming's 58 recommendations, 17 of which were to be responded to by a revision of *Working Together* (HM Government 2009). In addition, there were to be a further six changes that related to the statutory guidance in chapter 8 on Serious Case Reviews, together with the government's commitment to appoint lay members to LSCBs.

Further growth in guidance

Following a public consultation, the revised *Working Together* was published on 17 March 2010 (HM Government 2010a). While the guidance had the same title as both the 1999 and 2006 documents and followed a similar chapter structure and layout, the revisions very much reflected the changing policy and organisational climate of the period after November 2008.

The guidance explicitly attempted to respond to the recommendations made in the Laming Report (Laming 2009) and the 'Government Action Plan' (HM Government 2009); however, the document was much more than this. In attempting to reflect and respond to the changes evident since the last *Working Together*, published in April 2006, it became apparent how rapidly the field had been changing in other ways. As a result, both the length and complexity of the document grew considerably. Concerns about the increased length and complexity of the document were clearly an issue and were commented on by numerous respondents to the consultation (HM Government 2010b). These concerns were something that government planned to respond to in due course by producing a navigable web-based version, producing a short practitioner guide and identifying ways in which the statutory requirements were not obscured by non-statutory guidance.

The expansion and growing complexity of the document were reflected not just in the increased page length, from 231 to 390 pages, but in the huge increase in the number of references (from 78 to 200), internet links (from 69 to 124) and footnotes (from 43 to 273) in just a four-year period. In addition, while the chapter on 'managing individual cases' had only increased by one page, to 57 pages, that on 'serious case reviews' had increased in length by eight pages to 23 pages.

Chapter 6 of the document, which outlined and provided references and links to ten other statutory 'Supplementary Guidance' documents on 'safeguarding and promoting the welfare of children', provided further evidence of the rate of change since 2006, only in part as a result of responding to the fallout from the death of 'Baby Peter' and the Laming Report (2009). Ten other pieces of supplementary guidance were referred to in relation to:

1. sexually exploited children (DCSF 2009a), 96 pages;
2. children affected by gang activity (HM Government 2010c), 52 pages;
3. fabricated or induced illness (FII) (HM Government 2008a), 88 pages;
4. investigating complex (organised or multiple) abuse (DH 2002b), 94 pages;
5. the Female Genital Mutilation Act 2003;

6. forced marriage and honour-based violence (HM Government 2008b), 26 pages;
7. allegations of abuse made against a person who works with children (appendix 5), 10 pages;
8. abuse of disabled children (DCSF 2009a), 84 pages;
9. child abuse linked to belief in 'spirit possession' (HM Government 2007a), 23 pages;
10. child victims of trafficking (HM Government 2007b), 55 pages.

What this demonstrated was that after the publication of the 2006 *Working Together* (HM Government 2006), seven additional pieces of supplementary guidance had been published, in effect adding a further 424 pages to the existing guidance. There had been a huge expansion in the amount of government guidance published since 2006.

Additionally, in the 'non-statutory practice guidance' section there was an updated chapter 11 entitled 'Safeguarding and promoting the welfare of children *who may be particularly vulnerable*' (HM Government 2010a: 292; emphasis added). Here there is additional guidance in relation to:

- children living away from home;
- abuse by children and young people;
- children whose behaviour indicates a lack of parental control;
- race and racism;
- violent extremism;
- domestic violence;
- child abuse and information communication technology (ICT);
- children with families whose whereabouts are unknown;
- children who go missing;
- children who go missing from education;
- children of families living in temporary accommodation;
- migrant children;
- unaccompanied asylum-seeking children (UASC).

Since coming to power in 2010 the Coalition government has continued the trend of revising and updating the *Working Together* guidance – this time, however, by seeking to greatly reduce the size and complexity of the guidance. A formal consultation was launched in 2012, and the new guidance, published in March 2013 (HM Government 2013), is 97 pages cover to cover. This guidance, which came into effect on 15 April 2013, is limited to five chapters and replaces not only the previous working document but also *Framework for the Assessment of Children in Need and Their Families* (DH *et al.* 2000b) and the statutory guidance on making arrangements to safeguard and promote the welfare of children under section 11 of the Children Act 2004. The five chapters cover:

1. assessing need and providing help;
2. organisational responsibilities;
3. Local Safeguarding Children Boards;
4. learning and improvement framework;
5. child death reviews.

The 2013 version of *Working Together* does not include any distinction between statutory and non-statutory guidance and instead asserts the duties, responsibilities and requirements of professionals and organisations to act under the guidance and powers of the Secretary of State. Supplementary guidance for safeguarding in particular situations remains in force.

Key points: the historical context

The development of central government child protection policy and guidance can be divided into key periods of reform:

- The period 1974–1991 was primarily concerned with establishing systems to encourage professionals to work together for the purposes of identifying child abuse and improving child protection.
- The mid-1990s to 2006 was concerned with broadening the objects of concern towards safeguarding and promoting the welfare of children.
- Between 2006 and 2010 the focus was on ensuring that child protection lay at the heart of the expanded focus of concerns, and a key benchmark for judging the effectiveness of the systems and the performance of managers and practitioners was provided.
- From 2010 the concern has been to refocus attention away from safeguarding back onto child protection.
- Conservative/Liberal Democrat government efforts have also been concerned to reduce bureaucracy and regulation.

Economic and political contexts for child protection, 2010 and beyond

The important developments of the period from the early 1990s to late 2008 involved a widening of the debate of what constituted risk to children, with a concomitant concern that professionals emphasise 'safeguarding' rather than 'child protection'. Since late 2008, however, significantly following the death of 'Baby P' (Peter Connolly), the focus has returned to child protection (Parton 2011). A change in government in May 2010 has seen no change in this emphasis; indeed, the Conservative/Liberal Democrat government has approached this aim with some resolve. So while wider childcare policy embraces child protection, the latter is not framed in terms of broader approaches to risk for children; it is developed as a focused, narrower forensic concern for child safety. In this context, although the government is introducing policies that emphasise early intervention, child protection policy and procedure are not dependent on these.

In practice this means that child protection is focused on those children at risk of significant harm or the likelihood of significant harm as enshrined in the Children Act 1989 rather than on broader conceptions of risk. The shift is significant since 'whereas, previously, policy and practice had been framed in terms of "safeguarding and promoting the welfare of the child" ... child protection [has], again, moved centre stage' (Parton 2011: 867). This is not to say that 'promoting the welfare of the child' is not important; it is. However, focus and definition have shifted so that child protection is a specific task with social work given lead responsibility, whereas the promotion of welfare has broader scope that includes the possibilities offered by early intervention with obvious implications for early years professionals.

The shift in emphasis has also been accompanied by a desire to reduce bureaucracy and regulation. Whereas the priorities of the previous New Labour government included a desire to tackle social exclusion through tighter ties between employment and social provision, including significant social investment, the priority of the Conservative/Liberal Democrat government is to strip away bureaucracy and give professionals the space for professional judgement.

Soon after it came to power it became clear that the government wished to decentralise power, to reduce the role of the central state and its reliance upon top-down systems of performance management of services and professionals, and to try to improve individual civil liberties. Much of this was articulated through the prime minister David Cameron's ideas about 'the Big Society' and its emphasis on the importance of communities, mutualisation and the voluntary sector (Ellison 2011). However, from the outset the government made it clear that its overriding political priority was the reduction in public finance debt, and immediately set about reducing public expenditure, with local authorities having cuts of around 28 per cent over the course of the parliament (Parton 2012).

Consequently, while the government places working families at the heart of childcare policy, not all children are considered a priority in welfare spending in the way they were under the previous administration (Stewart 2011). The flagship New Labour *Every Child Matters: Change for Children* programme has been withdrawn, along with the Children's Workforce Development Council, with increased targeting of both children's benefits and services, including Sure Start children's centres (HM Treasury 2010). Consequently, an analysis of changes to tax and benefit entitlements by the Institute for Fiscal Studies illustrates that households with children will be more out of pocket than those without children across all income levels (Brewer 2010).

Significantly, many services relevant to child protection are also being squeezed. In 2011/2012 a Directors of Children's Services survey (Higgs 2011) estimated 13 per cent average cuts to children's services. This involves average cuts of 44 per cent to early years and children's centres. Confirming the perilous situation for children's centres, an analysis by 4Children (2011) predicted that over 250 children's centres faced closure. It is feared that early years is to take a disproportionate cut in the overall reductions to the education budget (Chowdry and Sibieta 2011), and there are reports of increasing unmet need (Action for Children 2011) – a situation that is not helped by a concurrent shrinkage in voluntary and community-sector provision (Gill *et al*. 2011).

The economic imperative is therefore shaping the numerous reviews of childcare services instigated since May 2010. The most significant of these for early years services are:

- The Field Review (2010), which argues for the primacy of early years services and intervention in enhancing life chances for children, including the need for targeted, quality services that enable secure and safe attachment between carer and child, loving and responsive relationships and clear behavioural boundaries.
- The Allen Reviews (2011a, b). The first of these, published in January 2011, focuses on the needs of 0- to 3-year-olds and in particular argues that good parenting has a greater impact on a child's development than any other social factor. The review recognises the work of 19 'top programmes'. The second review, published in July 2011, deals with resourcing, specifically how early intervention services could be paid for within existing budgets and by attracting funding from other sources.
- The Tickell Review (2011) considers the Early Years Foundation Stage (EYFS) (DCSF 2008b), recommending that the standards be made more manageable for parents, carers and practitioners; there are now 17 early learning goals as opposed to 69 previously. As such, the review seeks to set out the conditions for effective partnership between parents, carers and practitioners in realising the early development needs of children.

A joint Department for Education and Department of Health (in part in recognition of Michael Marmot's work on health inequalities) policy document, *Supporting Families in the Foundation Years* (2011), sets out the government's policy for early years and early intervention. The need for affordable, targeted and effective services is recognised, as is a system for delivery of services that places more responsibility at the local level, with less bureaucratic and regulatory burden placed on practitioners in doing their jobs.

Key points: the contemporary context

Child protection is a social construction, and policy and procedure are therefore influenced by prevailing social, political and cultural attitudes of the day. From late 2008, following the death of Baby P (Peter Connolly), government has sought to:

- refocus away from safeguarding to child protection as a central concern with risk defined in terms of actual or likely significant harm;
- emphasise child protection, therefore, as a specific, forensic activity;
- develop targeted services, including early intervention as a broader policy concern in meeting developmental needs;
- decrease the bureaucratic and regulatory burden on practitioners;
- achieve change within tight budgetary demands.

Reflection activity
Consider the current government policy for early years and early intervention. How has this had influence in your setting?

The Munro Review of Child Protection

Just as reviews have informed government policy on early years and consideration of early intervention, so has another important review influenced child protection policy. When the Conservative/Liberal Democrat Coalition government came to power, one of its first acts was to establish an independent 'Review of Child Protection' to be chaired by Professor Eileen Munro to provide a final report in April 2011. In his letter to Professor Munro announcing the establishment of the review, Michael Gove, the Secretary of State, said:

> I firmly believe we need to reform frontline ... practice. I want to strengthen the profession so ... workers are in a better position to make well-informed judgments, based on up to date evidence, in the best interests of children, *free from unnecessary bureaucracy and regulation.*
>
> (Gove 2010: 1; emphasis added)

Concern about the growth of bureaucracy and regulation in children's work was not new (Howe 1992) and was something that Eileen Munro had drawn attention to on numerous occasions (see, for example, Munro 2004). These were also issues that had been commented on by Lord Laming in his Inquiry Report into the death of Victoria Climbié in 2003:

> Judging by the material put before the Inquiry, the problem is less about the ability of staff to read and understand guidelines, and more about the

huge and dense nature of material provided for them. Therefore, the challenge is to provide busy staff in each of the agencies with something of real practical help and manageable length. The test is of ensuring the material actually helps staff do their job.

(Laming 2003: para. 1.61, p. 12)

Lord Laming was convinced that to prevent 'such terrible events' happening in the future, 'the answer lies in doing relatively straightforward things well. Adhering to this principle will have a significant impact on the lives of vulnerable children' (para. 1.66).

At the core of the child protection system in England is government guidance which provides the framework for policy and practice and which local authorities and other social care, health and criminal justice agencies are required to implement in their local areas. This guidance has been revised over a nearly 40-year period, with a version published on 17 March 2010 just prior to the new government coming to power (HM Government 2010a). Up to this point what becomes evident, however, is that at each stage of revision the guidance had become longer, more detailed and more complex, including the revision following Lord Laming's Inquiry Report into the death of Victoria Climbié (HM Government 2006). This is, therefore, a particular challenge for anyone wishing to reform the child protection system in order to free it 'from unnecessary bureaucracy and regulation' – a point demonstrated in the significant delays in bringing forward the new, slimmer guidance promised by the Coalition government review in 2012.

These changes in guidance result from a variety of social, media and political influences which are discussed in detail elsewhere (see, for example, Parton 1985, 1991, 2006a; Frost and Parton 2009; and Chapter 3 of this book) and are not the focus of attention here. The purpose of this part of the chapter has been much more modest. It has aimed to describe and outline the growth and development of government guidance on child protection in England since 1974. However, in the process we are provided with important insights into the changing nature and aims of child protection policy and practice during the period, particularly in terms of its priorities, focus and organisation. What will become apparent is not only that the guidance had grown enormously and become more detailed between 1974 and 2010 but that also the object of concern had broadened from 'non-accidental injury' to 'child abuse' to 'safeguarding and promoting the welfare of children'. These developments are summarised in Table 2.1.

TABLE 2.1 The changing structure, contents and focus of government child protection guidance in England since 1974

Document	Number of pages	Number of footnotes	Reading lists, references and internet sites	Other directly related documents	Other
1974 *Non-accidental Injury to Children LASSL (74)(13)* (DHSS Circular)	7	1	The footnote included 4 references, 3 of which were previous DHSS circulars	None	
1988 *Working Together: A Guide to Arrangements for Inter-agency Cooperation for the Protection of Children from Abuse* (DHSS and the Welsh Office)	72 (made up of 48 pages of Guidance and 9 Appendices of 24 pages)	None	11	None	Part 5, 'Working Together in Individual Cases', was 13 pages long. For the first time, in Part 9, a system of senior management 'case reviews' in cases of child death or serious harm where child abuse was confirmed or suspected (4 pages long) was introduced.
1991 *Working Together under the Children Act 1989: A Guide to Arrangements for Inter-agency Cooperation for the Protection of Children from Abuse* (Home Office, Department of Health, Department of Education and Science, the Welsh Office)	126 (made up of 60 pages of Guidance and 9 Appendices of 66 pages)	None	39, of which 35 were HMSO or a government department	None	Part 5, 'Working Together in Individual Cases', was 15 pages long. Section on 'Case Reviews' (now Part 8) 4 pages long.

continued

TABLE 2.1 *Continued*

Document	Number of pages	Number of footnotes	Reading lists, references and internet sites	Other directly related documents	Other
1999 *Working Together to Safeguard Children: A Guide to Inter-agency Working to Safeguard and Promote the Welfare of Children* (Department of Health, Home Office and Department for Education and Employment)	119 (made up of 102 pages of Guidance and 6 Appendices of 17 pages)	12	A 'reading list' (Appendix 6) of 50 references, of which 31 were HMSO/Stationery Office or government departments. There were no internet links or web addresses.	Published at the same time as Department of Health, Department of Education and Employment, and the Home Office (2000) *Framework for the Assessment of Children in Need and their Families.* Also issued under section 7 of the Local Authority Social Services Act 1970 and was incorporated into *Working Together to Safeguard Children*	The *Assessment Framework* was 109 pages long; including 7 Appendices of 20 pages; had a Bibliography of 140 references of which 83 were HMSO/Stationery Office or government departments. There were no internet links or web addresses.
2006 *Working Together to Safeguard Children: A Guide to Inter-agency Working to Safeguard and Promote the Welfare of Children* (HM Government)	231 pages long, including 155 pages of Statutory Guidance, 30 pages of Non-statutory Guidance, and 6 Appendices of 28 pages	43	78 references and internet links, including 69 internet links or web addresses, of which 60 were gov.uk	*Assessment Framework* (2000) as in *Working Together* (1999) above, primarily through the Integrated Children System (ICS)	

2010 *Working Together to Safeguard Children: A Guide to Inter-Agency Working to Safeguard and Promote the Welfare of Children* (HM Government)	399 pages, which included Executive Summary 15 pages; Statutory Guidance 228 pages; Non-statutory Guidance 51 pages; 6 Appendices of 34 pages	273	200 references and internet links, including 124 with internet links/web addresses, of which 78 are gov.uk	*Assessment Framework* (2000) as in *Working Together* (1999) and (2006) above. Chapter 6, Supplementary Guidance on Safeguarding and Promoting the Welfare of Children, makes direct links to other supplementary statutory guidance:

1. Sexually exploited children (2009), 96 pages
2. Children affected by gang activity (2010), 52 pages
3. Fabricated or induced illness (FII) (2008), 88 pages
4. Investigating complex (organised or multiple) abuse (2002)
5. Female genital mutilation, LA circular 2004
6. Forced marriage and honour-based violence (2009), 26 pages
7. Allegations of abuse made against a person who works with children, plus Appendix 5, 10 pages
8. Abuse of disabled children (2009), 84 pages
9. Child abuse linked to belief in 'spirit possession' (2007), 23 pages
10. Child victims of trafficking (2007), 55 pages

continued

TABLE 2.1 *Continued*

Document	Number of pages	Number of footnotes	Reading lists, references and internet sites	Other directly related documents	Other
2013 *Working Together to Safeguard Children: A Guide to Inter-agency Working to Safeguard and Promote the Welfare of Children* (HM Government)	97 pages cover to cover. There are 5 chapters: • Assessing need and providing help • Organisational responsibilities • Local Safeguarding Children Boards • Learning and improvement framework • Child death reviews.	None	No reference list. There are links to external sources on the electronic version of the document: • Department for Education guidance, for example on child exploitation (16) • Other government departments and agencies guidance (19) • Guidance from external organisations (5) • Additional guidance on assessing need (3) • Guidance in support of the Learning and Improvement framework (3)	The guidance states that it replaces the previous 2010 version and the Framework for the Assessment of Children in Need and their Families (2000). However, the latter is still listed as one of the 16 additional Department for Education-related documents.	

Conclusions

This chapter has provided some insight into the economic and political context for contemporary child protection practice. Since 1974, child protection has been defined by different periods of concern. Later periods have been particularly underlined by the considerable growth in the media, political and public profile of Serious Case Reviews since November 2008. Case Reviews, and subsequently Serious Case Reviews, which had originally been intended to try to avert and pre-empt the considerable media attention previously given to public inquiries in the 1980s, now seemed to be having the opposite effect.

Throughout the New Labour era, in the spirit of wanting to provide a wide-ranging preventive early intervention and integrated range of services for children, young people and families that prioritised safeguarding, an increasing number of children and young people could be seen to be falling under the child protection net – a net that has been tightened and regulated in increasingly rigorous ways and through which practitioners, managers and politicians were held accountable for what they did and the decisions they made (Parton 2006a, b). The scope of the Munro Review in 2011 shows that we have come a long way since the circulation of the early guidance on 'non-accidental injury to children', which established the modern child protection system in 1974, with redress in the government's policy of reducing the amount of regulation and bureaucracy faced by practitioners.

This chapter demonstrates that a historical analysis of official guidance since 1974 provides important insights into the changing nature of child protection policy and practice, particularly in terms of its priorities, focus and organisation. Such documents also act to constitute what is meant by child protection in light of its previous incarnation, safeguarding and promoting the welfare of children.

What is perhaps most striking is how the guidance had grown in size and complexity. Far from the emphasis being placed on an approach that tried to ensure that agencies and professionals did 'the relatively straightforward things well' (Laming 2003: para. 1.66), the opposite seems to have been the case. At each point of revision, until the Munro Review, the guidance had grown, and in recent years the growth has been dramatic.

It is a significant challenge for the government to reverse this trend, and clearly there is more to reducing 'unnecessary bureaucracy and regulation' in child protection practice than trying to reduce the size and complexity of child protection guidance. However, what is clear is that the changes in child protection procedures since 1974 have played an important role in transforming the nature of practice and the organisational culture in which the work takes place, with the growth in bureaucracy, regulation and procedures having been a central feature.

Whatever the policy context, whatever the term used, the protection of children from harm is a concern for all childcare professionals. Social workers may be moved to the centre of current child protection practice but the Children Act 1989 places a general duty on local authorities to safeguard and promote the welfare of all children living in their area. Hence, it is not just the local authority's responsibility to safeguard; section 11 of the Children Act 2004, section 175 of the Education Act 2002 and section 40 of the Childcare Act 2006 place duties on organisations and individuals, including those in early years, to ensure that their functions are discharged with regard to the need to safeguard and promote the welfare of children. In the next chapter we shall look more closely at legal duties and responsibilities placed on early years practitioners and settings by legislation. The chapter begins, however, with further insight into the social and cultural milieu that affects child protection, highlighting again how examples of severe abuse and child deaths have impacted upon the development of legislation.

Further reading

Frost, N. and Parton, N. (2009) *Understanding Children's Social Care: Politics, Policy and Practice*. London: Sage.

This book provides a comprehensive overview and critical analysis of children's social care in England following the introduction of *Every Child Matters* and the 2007 Children's Plan. It offers a critique of the period prior to changes in policy and legislation following the election of the Conservative/Liberal Democrat Coalition in 2010.

Parton, N. (2012) 'The Munro Review of child protection: an appraisal', *Children and Society*, 26: 150–162.

In this article, Professor Nigel Parton provides important insight into the main findings and recommendations of the review and locates it in its immediate policy and practice contexts. The paper also begins to identify some of its possible gaps and challenges, and argues that the success of the review is likely to depend on cultural, political and economic factors well beyond its influence and outlines what these are.

3

The social, legal and practice context for protecting and safeguarding children

James Reid

In the previous chapter we provided a brief history of central government guidance and in this chapter I develop germane themes in the development of child protection legislation. We begin by learning further from the history of a small number of child tragedies that help to illustrate child protection as a social construction. The importance of trans-national conventions is then highlighted. Discussion consequently moves to brief consideration of examples of abusive practices by early years practitioners before consideration is given to the prevalence of child abuse for young children. The subsequent duties and responsibilities placed on early years practitioners by legislation and the conditions necessary for effective practice with parents and carers are covered.

By the end of this chapter you will:

- further appreciate the social, cultural, political and moral milieu that affects child protection legislation, policy and practice;
- understand how various duties and responsibilities are enshrined in international conventions and national law;
- recognise the conditions necessary for effective practice with parents and carers;
- recognise the need for a critical approach to safeguarding practice.

A brief history of child protection: a social construction

In the previous chapter we were reminded that concepts of child protection are a social construction – that is, our understanding, knowledge, definitions and practice in the child protection arena are determined by a range of social, cultural and personal influences. Chapter 2 of this text looked in depth at the development of policy and guidance since the mid-1970s at a time when awareness of child abuse was heightened by Henry Kempe and colleagues regarding the prevalence of 'battered baby syndrome' (1962). Significant in this period was the voice of women and feminisms in raising concern about violence and the broader misuse of power. What is clear is that both emerging research and significant voices influence child protection legislation, policy and practice. Indeed, Parton and Reid argue that one of the more significant voices in determining currently what constitutes a protection matter for a child is the media.

As was stated in Chapter 2, history has a lot to tell us about the current state of child protection, and that history is replete with examples of change based upon social, cultural or moral developments. One of the first instances of recognition of child abuse occurred in New York in 1874 when 10-year-old Mary-Ellen McCormack was discovered in a neglected state with severe physical injuries inflicted by her adoptive mother. There was no protection available to her at the time since physical punishment of children was permissible. The mantra of the day, 'spare the rod and spoil the child', meant that physical punishment was not only acceptable but encouraged as an appropriate and necessary approach to child care. Undoubtedly this has resonances with the ongoing debates in England about physical chastisement of children by parents. There was no legal basis for the authorities to intervene in family life to protect Mary-Ellen from the severe physical abuse she was experiencing – that is, until the American Society for the Prevention of Cruelty to Animals persuaded a judge to classify Mary-Ellen as an animal to allow it to remove her from her adoptive mother's care.

Mary-Ellen's experience was reported as a moral outrage by the media (see Howard Markel's 2009 article in the *New York Times*) and was instrumental in the development of the New York Society for the Prevention of Cruelty to Children, the model for the National Society for the Prevention of Cruelty to Children (NSPCC) in the United Kingdom. It is worth noting that she lived to the age of 92 and had many children and grandchildren. Subsequently, philanthropic interest in the maltreatment of children led to new laws, changes to existing laws and therefore further protection for children. By the end of the 1880s the United Kingdom had its first law enabling the state to intervene in family life.

The influence of children's deaths

The right of the state to intervene in private family matters, and in particular in the right of parents to bring up their children as they see fit, has always been fraught. On many occasions the untimely and tragic death of children has led to legislative change. In the post-war period the death of Dennis O'Neill saw the introduction of Children's Committees, a forerunner of Area Child Protection Committees (ACPCs). However, the latter did not come into being until the 1974 inquiry into the death of Maria Colwell criticised local agencies for their lack of co-ordination. This theme has continued in the more recent inquiries undertaken by Lord Laming (2003, 2009) into the deaths of Victoria Climbié and Baby Peter, which recommended that ACPCs be replaced by Local Safeguarding Children Boards (LSCBs).

Since the 1970s a growing corpus of research allied to increasing vocal concern about the rights of children and women and damning child death inquiry reports saw an escalation in coverage of child abuse as a concern in the media. At the same time as knowledge was developing of 'children at risk', a second narrative of 'children as risk' – young tearaways, feral, destructive and out of control – had acquired momentum, in part as a reaction to the prevailing economic conditions and the explosion of the punk culture. This dichotomy of children as at risk or risky was similar to the many other conflicts facing children and young people, including the rights of parents versus the rights of the child, the role of the state versus the role of the family, and the welfare of the child versus the rights of the child. Increasingly the lexicon of moral panic was entering the debates surrounding children and risk (Parton *et al.* 1997).

Changing understanding of the family

Just as new research, rights movements and moral panics were shaping approaches to childcare policy and practice, so were changes in understanding of family structures and relationships. Increasing divorce rates, decreasing marriage rates, societal ease with sexual partnerships not based in marriage, and children living in more diverse family situations meant that the focus moved from children growing up within the nucleus of a family to kinship networks and partnerships (Beck and Beck-Gernsheim 2002; Smart and Neale 1999). The New Labour government, rather than pursuing traditional policies to strengthen and maintain marriage and the family, focused instead on enhancing children's life chances and wellbeing, and on secure and stable attachments. According to Parton, the family was deconstructed and disaggregated so that policy

> subtly but significantly shifted from a focus on the family to one that was concerned directly with childhood vulnerability and well-being and upholding parental responsibility. Childhood was moved to the centre of policy priorities, seen as lying at the fulcrum of attempts to tackle social exclusion and the investment in a positive, creative and wealth-creating future, and many of the challenges posed by the social and economic changes related to globalisation.
>
> (2011: 857)

While the New Labour government considered the nature of partnership between individuals an essentially private matter, the issue of parenting was of considerable interest to the state, particularly in relation to the welfare of children, including the right to protection. Safeguarding the welfare of the child was in vogue, with child protection integrated into a predominantly child-centred rather than family-focused framework. The most significant manifestation of this was the *Every Child Matters: Change for Children* (DfES 2003a) programme.

Unsurprisingly, the current government, particularly the Conservative part of the Coalition, has a rather different view about the definition and provision of welfare and 'moral' questions such as the nature and status of the family. The difference in ideology is immediately apparent: the prime minister attacked the previous administration for failing to tackle poverty and a range of social ills, arguing that too much emphasis placed on 'state action' rather than 'social action' (Cameron 2009). The approach known as 'the Big Society' is one that seeks empowerment of the third sector, local interests and parents. As Page (2010: 154) suggests, 'the government's role in fixing the broken society will involve an expansion of its *enabling* as opposed to its *provider* function' (original emphasis). Two years into the government's term of office, 'the Big Society' has had a somewhat muted impact. What has exercised the government, however, is the economic conditions of a prolonged recession. In part, moves to create a context for child protection work that involves more autonomy, less bureaucracy and less regulation stems from a desire to move responsibility from the centre and to manage costs.

The death of Baby Peter in 2007 and the ensuing media outrage also remain pivotal in current child protection policy. Not only has the focus shifted ideologically from broader safeguarding and welfare concerns to a more focused child protection policy, it has also shifted politically, since no government can risk moral outrage or media indignation by appearing weak on child abuse or poor professional practice. Nor can the government be implicated in maintaining structures and systems that contribute to ineffective child protection practice. So, while the government seeks less regulation, the powers of the regulator, the Office for Standards in Education, Children's Services and Skills (Ofsted), alongside that of the Secretary of State, have been enhanced. Moving practitioners and not systems to the centre of child protection practice enables the government to establish a buffer between it and any future child tragedy. However, it has not just been national tragedies or political expediency that has had an impact on legislation and policy.

Trans-national conventions on the rights of the child

The United Nations Convention on the Rights of the Child

Moral indignation at the behaviour of children and the contrary vociferous debates about children as morally vulnerable and at risk from abuse was, in a manner of speaking, brought to a head with the ratification of the United

Nations Convention on the Rights of the Child (UNCRC) in 1989. The Convention came at a time of increasing international concern of harm through armed conflict, slavery, trafficking, prostitution, lack of health care and education, and the abuse of disabled children.

The Convention, in article 3, established the primacy of the best interests of the child and tackled the issue of when the state could intervene in family life. As a signatory, the UK government had a responsibility to ensure that national law conformed to the requirements enshrined in the articles of the Convention. In relation to child protection several articles apply, including article 6 (Right to Life), article 19 (Protection from Violence), article 34 (Sexual Exploitation of Children), article 35 (Prevention of Abduction, Sale and Trafficking), article 36 (Protection from Other Forms of Exploitation) and article 37(A) (Prohibition of Torture, Inhuman or Degrading Treatment). The UNCRC is not binding in UK law. However, the government met many of its responsibilities in relation to the Convention through the enactment of the Children Act 1989.

The European Convention for the Protection of Human Rights and Fundamental Freedoms

A further trans-national convention has significant influence in child protection legislation, policy and practice. The European Convention for the Protection of Human Rights and Fundamental Freedoms (ECHR) was first agreed by the Council of Europe in 1950 in the wake of the Second World War. However, it was not until the enactment of the Human Rights Act 1998 (HRA), which took effect in 2000, that the requirements of the ECHR were incorporated into UK law. The ECHR and HRA are applicable to all citizens without discrimination (ECHR article 14) and affect children in a number of important ways. First, all relevant UK legislation has to take into consideration children's rights. Second, children have the right to legal redress. Like the UNCRC, the ECHR is structured through a number of articles, including article 2 (Right to Life), article 3 (Prohibition of Torture), article 4 (Prohibition of Slavery and Forced Labour) and article 8 (Right to Respect for Private and Family Life).

While the UNCRC lays out the independent rights of children, it also recognises that the best interests of the child are usually served by supporting the child's family. The ECHR sustained the ongoing tension between children's rights to protection (article 3) and the rights of a family to be free from state interference (article 8). The balance was struck in section 1(1) of the Children Act 1989 and the introduction of the paramountcy principle – specifically, that the welfare of the child is paramount. The nuance here is important. Although both the UNCRC and ECHR are specifically framed in terms of rights, in UK child protection law it is the child's welfare and not their rights that are paramount. This leads to some conflict in legislation so that on some occasions the welfare of children has paramountcy over the rights of parents whereas in other respects, such as education, parental views have prominence.

In addition to commitments to child protection, the UNCRC required the government to address child poverty and the ECHR, social exclusion. Given this context and the commitment to globalisation, the New Labour government invested in both universal family support and child protection. Through the *Every Child Matters: Change for Children* programme, it developed integrated structures, for example at national level by bringing together responsibility for children and families under the Department for Education and Skills, and at local level it established Children's Trusts and measures for tracking and information exchange, specifically ContactPoint and the Integrated Children's System (Henricson and Bainham 2005).

Rights, globalisation and the economic imperative

As a Coalition, the post-2010 government is committed to the maintenance of rights without discrimination. However, elements within the Conservative Party in particular have expressed reservations about the scope and impact of the HRA, with some calling for it to be repealed. It is likely that fractures will continue to appear within both the Coalition and the Conservative Party itself, the latter in terms of the social and financial cost of enforcing the duties enshrined in the Act. Of course, some of this discomfort with the HRA stems from its links to the ECHR and concomitant judgments of the European Court of Human Rights. Notwithstanding this, the ideological opposition for many Conservatives stems from a desire for globalisation, tax cuts, reduced central government control and, consequently, reduced public spending. According to Evans (2008), the range of ideological positions espoused by a significant number of Conservative MPs in the run-up to the 2010 general election included a desire for a Thatcherite agenda. In this regard there is pressure for policy based not on the rights agenda but on the globalising agenda of neo-liberals and bodies such as the Organisation for Economic Co-operation and Development (OECD).

Whether the UNCRC, the ECHR or the OECD, what is obvious is that forces external to the United Kingdom have influence in determining legislation and policy. The economic imperative demands the removal of unnecessary bureaucracy and regulation. In the light of this and the government's need to set aside systems that inhibit good child protection practice, it is unsurprising that in 2010 Michael Gove cancelled the ContactPoint initiative. Soon afterwards, the government moved away from New Labour's top-down performance management culture and the growth of ICT bureaucratic demands manifest in the Integrated Children's System (Parton 2011).

The prevailing political, social, cultural and moral mores of the day are significant in defining safeguarding and child protection. Both national and international experiences of the maltreatment of children help to determine legislation, policy and guidance. Safeguarding and child protection legal and moral obligations are enshrined in trans-national conventions and the United Kingdom meets these obligations particularly through UK primary legislation. The main features of the child protection and safeguarding framework in the UK are:

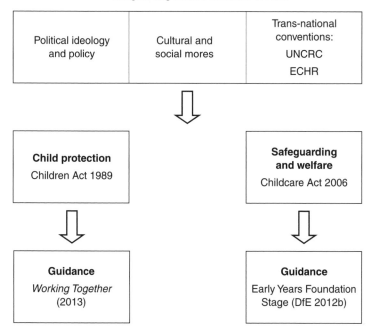

FIGURE 3.1 Reflective task: the main features of the UK framework.

Professional failings in early years child protection

Child abuse inquiry reports have consistently criticised agencies, individually and collectively, for failing to protect children. The Laming Report (2003) into the death of Victoria Climbié was the basis for the introduction of Local Safeguarding Children's Boards. Enhanced local authority accountability and 150 local programmes focused on early intervention, safeguarding and welfare, shared responsibility, information sharing and integrated services were promoted through the auspices of the *Every Child Matters: Change for Children* programme. The legal basis for these developments was the Children Act 2004, which amended aspects of the Children Act 1989 to strengthen safeguarding practice. The consequences of the death of Victoria and Baby Peter have largely focused on inter-agency co-operation and systemic failings, as discussed in Chapter 10 of this text.

Of course, the latter are not the only determinants of legislation and guidance; culture within an individual setting where poor and abusive practices have occurred has also played a role, as the case of Vanessa George demonstrates.

Vanessa George had worked at a nursery in Plymouth since 2006. She was arrested in 2009, after sexually explicit photographs involving young children, taken in the toilet area of the nursery, were discovered on the computer of Colin Blanchard in the north of England. George, Blanchard and a second female, Angela Allen from the Nottingham area, were convicted in October 2009. George admitted seven sexual assaults and six counts of distributing and making indecent pictures of children. Blanchard pleaded guilty to 17 counts of child pornography and two sexual assaults on children. Allen pleaded guilty to four child sex assaults and one count of distributing an indecent image. The three had not met in person but used the internet and mobile technologies to keep in touch and distribute the images.

The Plymouth Safeguarding Children Board Serious Case Review (SCR) (2010) into the circumstances of abuse at the nursery identified fragmentation in key parts of the safeguarding system, including with Ofsted and the Early Years Service, thus highlighting again the dangers of systemic failure. However, the SCR was also keen to highlight George's role within the nursery team, as this extract (p. 15) identifies:

> [George] has been described by staff as both *'horrible'* and more often *'the life and soul of the party'*. The predominant view is of a popular member of staff both with parents and other members of the staff team. The [nursery] individual management review comments that:
>
> *'Although she was not senior in her position, other factors such as her age, personality and length of service could have created an illusion of position of power and encouraged a sense of trust ... It is also the case that [George] is of the ability to behave in a highly manipulative manner and hence gain high levels of trust in others'*
>
> It is quite clear that [George] had gained a position of trust with the manager, who allowed her to babysit for her foster children. Some staff referred to [George] being one of a clique. Her position of power within the staff group was such that although staff became increasingly concerned about her crude language, discussion of extra-marital relationships and showing indecent images of adults on her phone, they were unable to challenge her.
>
> Another reason for lack of challenge within the staff group proposed by the nursery individual management review author is that colleagues experienced feelings of guilt and discomfort at having been exposed to this increasingly inappropriate material. By even being shown sexualised pictures it is possible that staff believed they had 'allowed' it to happen and consequently did not know how to raise this with others. By drawing others partially into her activities, [George] made challenge even less likely and may have interpreted the behaviour as implicit support.

George received an indeterminate sentence, with the stipulation that she be held in custody until she is no longer considered a danger to the public. Her minimum jail term is seven years. The organisational culture within the nursery was one therefore of blurred boundaries, fear, the abuse of trust, the misuse of power and a lack of good governance and accountability. The lessons are clear: not only should the early years practitioner be aware of the broad social, cultural and moral conditions for practice and how these drive policy, legislation and guidance, but they also need to consider the local conditions and how these impact upon guidance and practice.

Prevalence of child abuse

The case of Vanessa George brings into sharp focus the possibility of child abuse in an early years setting and the dynamic, changing nature of abuse, given her use of mobile and other communication technologies (see Chapter 8). Of course, George, Victoria Climbié and Baby Peter are some of the small number of cases that come to media attention; beyond these there are many, many more that do not make the headlines. An NSPCC report (Cuthbert *et al.* 2011: 5) into the prevalence of child abuse of children up to the age of 1 reminds us that 'the emotional abuse, neglect or physical harm of babies is particularly shocking both because babies are totally dependent on others and because of the relative prevalence of such maltreatment'. Indeed, the report goes on to suggest that '45 per cent of serious case reviews in England relate to babies under the age of 1 year' and 'in England and Wales, babies are eight times more likely to be killed than older children'. While it is always important to take a critical approach to statistics, it is probable that there is under-reporting of child abuse in very young children since they are dependent on intimate care and cannot necessarily communicate about the abuse or remove themselves from abusive situations. As with disabled children, babies are extremely vulnerable to any misuse of power. The NSPCC report (ibid.) estimates for the first time the numbers of babies living in vulnerable and complex family situations:

In the UK, an estimated

- 19,500 babies under 1 year old are living with a parent who has used Class A drugs in the last year
- 39,000 babies under 1 year old live in households affected by domestic violence in the last year
- 93,500 babies under 1 year old live with a parent who is a problem drinker
- 144,000 babies under 1 year old live with a parent who has a common mental health problem.

(ibid.: 31)

The NSPCC website (www.nspcc.org.uk) is a useful source for up-to-date research on all aspects of abuse, including prevalence. For example, the following Department for Education findings in 2012 are cited:

- In England, 4,850 children aged under one year and 880 unborn children were the subject of a child protection plan on 31 March 2012.
- 11% (4,850) of all the children subject of a child protection plan (42,850 children in total) were aged under one year (or 13% (5,730) including unborn children).
- Of the 4,850 children aged under one year and unborn children who were the subject of a child protection plan on 31 March 2012 in England:
- 2,890 were subject to a child protection plan for an initial category of neglect
- 890 for physical abuse
- 220 for sexual abuse
- 1,180 for emotional abuse
- 570 for multiple categories of abuse or for classificatory categories not recommended by 'Working together' ([DH *et al.*] 1999).

> (www.nspcc.org.uk/Inform/resourcesforprofessionals/
> children_under_one_statistics_wda79305.html)

One final statistic is worth mentioning as it reminds us how particularly vulnerable very young children are. According to Smith *et al.* (2011), infants aged under 1 year are eight times more at risk of being killed at the hands of another person than any other age group in England and Wales, with one baby on average killed almost every two weeks in the United Kingdom. The statistics will change over time, as will approaches to protection and safeguarding. What will remain constant is that children are harmed in a variety of ways and childcare professionals are charged with the responsibility of ensuring that children are protected from harm and their welfare safeguarded. Chapters 4 and 5 will consider in greater depth a number of categories of abuse.

Definitions of abuse

Just as the Vanessa George case and the statistical evidence demonstrate the centrality of safeguarding for early years practitioners, so do (as we read in Chapter 2) the definitions used by government, underlining the complexity of the issue. *Working Together to Safeguard Children* (HM Government 2010a: 37–39) set out to provide insight into the different categories of abuse and advised that

> [a]buse and neglect are forms of maltreatment of a child. Somebody may abuse or neglect children by inflicting harm, or by failing to act to prevent harm. Children may be abused in a family or in an institutional or community setting, by those known to them or, more rarely, by a stranger.... They may be abused by an adult or adults, or another child or children.
>
> (ibid.: 37–39)

The 2013 version of this document removes many of these definitions, paring down the 2010 guidance to nine items in 'Glossary A' and reference to the safeguarding and welfare of children as:

- protecting children from maltreatment;
- preventing impairment of children's health or development;
- ensuring that children are growing up in circumstances consistent with the provision of safe and effective care; and
- taking action to enable all children to have the best outcomes.

(HM Government 2013: 7)

In reducing the number of definitions of abuse, the government is clearly putting the onus back on practitioners to make judgements based on their knowledge and expertise, with clear implications for early years professionals in the bullet points above. Yet practice is only possible under a legal framework and, as we will now see, the language used in statute can sometimes be unclear.

Overarching legislation

Whereas it is the Children Act 1989 and the Children Act 2004 that provide the framework in particular for safeguarding and child protection practice, it is the Childcare Act 2006 that provides much of the basis for early years provision and practice. As was stated in the previous chapter, section 11 of the Children Act 2004 and section 40 of the Childcare Act 2006 place duties on organisations and individuals, including those in early years, to ensure that their functions are discharged with regard to the need to safeguard and promote the welfare of children. However, legislation itself is not sufficient to frame practice; the relevant guidance must also be taken into consideration. The requirements for child protection are detailed in *Working Together to Safeguard Children* (HM Government 2013) and the requirements for safeguarding and the protection of welfare in the *Statutory Framework for the Early Years Foundation Stage* (DfE 2012b). This latter framework is mandatory for all early years providers, maintained schools, non-maintained schools, independent schools and all providers on the Early Years Register. It is presented in three sections; section 3 details the safeguarding and welfare requirements for the sector, and these are given legal force by Regulations made under section 39(1)(b) of the Childcare Act 2006. The framework will be discussed further in Chapter 6.

As already highlighted, legislation alone is insufficient to frame practice and this can be seen in the duties enshrined in two of the most relevant sections of the Children Act 1989, section 17 and 47. Section 17(1)(a) of the Act imposes a duty 'to safeguard and promote the welfare of children within their area who are in need' and section 17(10) goes on to elaborate that a child shall be taken to be in need if:

(a) he is unlikely to achieve or maintain, or to have the opportunity of achieving or maintaining, a reasonable standard of health or development without the provision for him of services by a local authority under this Part;

(b) his health or development is likely to be significantly impaired, or further impaired, without the provision for him of such services; or

(c) he is disabled,

and 'family', in relation to such a child, includes any person who has parental responsibility for the child and any other person with whom he has been living.

(11) For the purposes of this Part, a child is disabled if he is blind, deaf or dumb or suffers from mental disorder of any kind or is substantially and permanently handicapped by illness, injury or congenital deformity or such other disability as may be prescribed; and in this Part –

- 'development' means physical, intellectual, emotional, social or behavioural development; and
- 'health' means physical or mental health.

Several questions immediately arise. What is 'a reasonable standard of health or development', or a significant impairment? Similar queries arise in relation to section 47 of the Act, which places a duty on any local authority, the police or other persons authorised by the Secretary of State to make inquiries where there is 'reasonable cause to suspect that a child is suffering, or is likely to suffer, significant harm' (s. 47(1)(b)). Consequently, what is reasonable cause, how do you predict the future and what is significant and what is harm?

Reflective task: John

John is 4 years old and the youngest of three siblings, all aged under 9. They live with their mother on a local estate and are socially isolated. The mother has difficulty in managing the children's behaviour and in managing their daily care. When she is cooking or dealing with the older children, John is confined to a buggy in front of the television. His speech and mobility are not what you would expect for a 4-year-old and he has difficulty in mixing with other children. He is loved dearly by his mother.

Think about the following:

- Are his health and development being impaired?
- Is the impairment significant and, if so, what evidence and judgements are you using to come to this decision?
- Is he suffering harm?
- Is the harm significant and, if so, what evidence and judgements are you using to come to this decision?

What is harm?

It is of course difficult to make judgements based upon little information, but in such instances some of our assumptions and prejudices come to the fore when what is required is a more forensic approach based upon knowledge, evidence and research. Under section 31(9) of the Children Act 1989 as amended by the Adoption and Children Act 2002:

> '[H]arm' means ill-treatment or the impairment of health or development, including, for example, impairment suffered from seeing or hearing the ill-treatment of another; 'development' means physical, intellectual, emotional, social or behavioural development 'health' means physical or mental health; and 'ill-treatment' includes sexual abuse and forms of ill-treatment which are not physical.

The concept of harm is a difficult one to deal with, particularly since cultural, social and personal mores come into play. The change made to the definition of harm by the 2002 Act includes the reference to 'impairment suffered from seeing or hearing the ill-treatment of another', meaning domestic violence, once again underpinning the point that the development of child abuse is a culturally defined phenomenon. What is regarded as reasonable is different within and between communities and societies. In a country where a large proportion of the child population is afflicted by malnutrition, a parent's inability to provide sufficient food to their child would not be categorised as neglect on the parent's part. Is this any different for a child growing up in poverty in the United Kingdom? In more affluent countries there have been changes in the recognition of the potentially abusive nature of some behaviours that were previously accepted as reasonable. In Scotland it is no longer acceptable to 'smack' your child; in England, 'reasonable chastisement' is permissible. A 1995 survey by Creighton and Russell of the childhood experiences of a national UK sample of adults aged 18–45 found that some 35 per cent said they had been hit with an implement. Only 7 per cent felt that it was acceptable to do that to a child now. 'Within any society there is continual evolution of the parental behaviours that are deemed unacceptable towards children' (Hobart and Frankel 2005: 25).

How we as individuals define child abuse depends on our beliefs about acceptable and unacceptable behaviours, where we were born, how we were raised, our customs and beliefs, and how we view 'children' and family life. We must take this into consideration when making judgements about harm or impairment, particularly in a context where the government has moved to place the responsibility for safeguarding and protection squarely on the shoulders of professionals and where professional guidance has been pared down to a minimum.

The context of harm

This is not to say that further guidance is not available; it is. Indeed, it is still possible to look at the definitions in the 2010 version of *Working Together* for some help when making decisions, and, most importantly, there is guidance available on the website of the Local Safeguarding Children Board. Yet guidance is simply that: a guide, albeit a statutory guide. There are no absolute criteria, for example, on which to rely when making decisions about what is or what is not significant harm. A child who never experiences physical punishment but who is slapped once may experience the incident as abusive and harmful whereas a child who is frequently slapped may not. Under section 31(10) of the Children Act 1989, 'Where the question of whether harm suffered by a child is significant turns on the child's health and development, his health or development shall be compared with that which could reasonably be expected of a similar child.' It is necessary therefore to consider the social context, the severity of the slap, the level of physical harm, the duration and frequency, premeditation, and the presence of threat. It is possible for a single incident to constitute significant harm, for example a violent assault, use of a weapon or implement, or poisoning. More frequently, significant harm is a combination of factors, such as physical and psychological harm, that adversely impact upon health and development. In every circumstance it is necessary to consider the harm or potential harm from the child's perspective alongside the family's strengths and supports that indicate capacity for change and improvement.

Guidance and where to find it

The foremost government guidance to protecting children is *Working Together to Safeguard Children* (HM Government 2013). This sets out how all organisations and professionals should work together to promote children's welfare and protect them from abuse and neglect. The *Statutory Framework for the Early Years Foundation Stage* (DfE 2012b) sits alongside *Working Together* to further detail the policies and practices that are necessary within a setting to ensure a safe environment. This is only some of the guidance available. Some deals with children and young people in specific circumstances, for example abuse linked to faith or belief (including spirit possession), while other guidance considers safer recruitment, disclosure and barring practices. Details of all the relevant guidance can be found on the Department for Education website and, of particular help, the Local Safeguarding Children Board website, both of which can be found by using an internet search engine.

Understanding key government documents and agendas is an important underpinning for safeguarding practice, as are children's rights and the concept of childhood. The guidance cannot be ignored but we should remember that it is implemented in a context of cultural, societal and personal mores. The personal element in child protection and safeguarding is important since it is not merely a matter of cognitive ability; it also involves feelings and skills.

Effective and critical practice with children, families and carers

The Department for Education (2012a) promotes 'evidence based practice' as the basis of skills and knowledge needed by people whose work brings them into regular contact with children, young people and families. It brings together the need for knowledge of the most up-to-date research, particularly of social learning theory, attachment theory, parenting styles and human ecology, with practitioner skills as the basis for practice. What is not sufficiently emphasised is the need for criticality and a questioning approach by the practitioner both to practice and to the knowledge that supports that practice. While attachment theory, for example, is extremely important, the practitioner should also bear in mind other possibilities such as theories of loss. When one is thinking about parenting styles in a safeguarding context, is what is being assessed the parent's approach to parenting or the parent's capacity to parent? These are very different things but potentially either could be assessed using existing tools. Indeed, an assessment of each with the same child and family could lead to very different outcomes. It is the role of the critical practitioner to constantly question their approach, to consider the cultural (organisational and wider), societal and personal mores that mould practice. Consequently, the practitioner must also decide whether they have the necessary skills for effective practice with children and their families and carers.

These necessary skills are wide-ranging and include aspects of direct practice with children but also with the important adults in a child's life. The minimum requirement involves skills in understanding what is meant by child protection and safeguarding, and the many ways in which children can be harmed. This necessarily requires keeping up to date with developments in the field, for example through the use of information and communication technologies and the internet. Understanding also involves recognising the key role of parents and carers in safeguarding and promoting a child's and, as stated above, that parenting styles and parenting capacity are very different. Involving parents and carers immediately throws up the need for clear and effective communication skills and personal skills. It takes confidence to discuss difficult issues with parents and carers, particularly if challenge enters the interaction. In this regard, all practitioners need to be aware of the boundaries of personal competence and responsibility, take steps to involve others if necessary, and therefore know where to get advice and support.

Empowerment in child protection and safeguarding

However, having the relevant skills is meaningless if these are used uncritically and in a manner that seeks to disempower rather than empower children and their parents and carers. This can be seen in approaches to assessment adopted by practitioners. Three different models of assessment were identified by Smale and Tuson (1993 – cited in Milner and O'Byrne 2002: 29–31):

1. *The questioning model*: here the … worker holds the expertise and follows a format of questions, listening to and processing answers. This process reflects the … worker's agenda.
2. *The procedural model*: the … worker fulfils agency function by gathering information to see whether the subject fits the criteria for services. Little judgement is required, and it is likely that checklists will be used.
3. *The exchange model*: all people are viewed as experts on their own problems, with an emphasis on exchanging information. The … workers follow or track what other people are saying rather than interpreting what they think is meant, seek to identify internal resources and potential, and consider how best to help service users mobilize their internal and external resources in order to reach goals defined by them on their terms.

Of these models of assessment, practice should lend itself to the 'exchange model', but only if the practitioner has sufficient time to exercise their skills and work at the individual child's pace. Where the practitioner does not work at the child's pace and does not adequately take account of prejudice, values and ethics, or where it is assumed that the practitioner holds a 'monopoly of knowledge' (Calder 2003: 43), partnership and empowerment will be affected and the assessment will lean towards the questioning and procedural models.

The model chosen by the practitioner is also likely to be influenced by perceptions of risk and need, and how the setting approaches each of these concepts. While policy since the 1990s has sought to 'refocus' intervention with children and their families away from risk to need for many, the predominant system used to provide support remained focused on protection, with assessment of risk as the major outcome. Part of the reason for this is historical and structural in that the Children Act 1989 went some way to defining risk through the concept of 'significant harm' but did little to provide guidance and structure to the assessment of need.

The dichotomy remains prevalent. Many of the services, such as Sure Start, developed to tackle social exclusion have safeguarding and need as their primary focus, whereas statutory services such as social work are required to focus on child protection and on risk. Nonetheless, it is very easy to get sidetracked by the dichotomy of risk versus need debate and there is a possibility that the discourse will fail to recognise practice, particularly assessment practice, as a means of empowerment, of working in partnership and of enhancing understanding about children and their families. To focus solely upon the concepts of risk and need is to focus upon the objective and outcome of the work. Such an approach ignores the variety and richness of the human condition and relationships, and it is these that are crucial to an ecological model and exchange model of assessment (Dalgleish 2003).

Inclusive and critical practice

For safeguarding practice to be meaningful, it must be seen as an inclusive process. Practitioners will have explicit understanding of the context of both the family and themselves. Holland reminds us that it behoves the practitioner to develop their practice in recognition of the constraints of the prevailing frameworks and policy and practice contexts, further arguing that the core principles of assessment practice include:

- Consulting family members (including children) about the assessment aims, methods of assessment and how to evaluate the assessment work.
- Working with an openness to others' perspectives, especially professionals from other disciplines and family members.
- Working within a stance of consulting and listening, rather than measuring from an expert distance.
- Maintaining the safety and welfare of the child as top priorities (whilst being aware that these are not always easily definable).
- Ensuring access to the assessment process through careful attention to aspects such as assessment methods, language choice, gender, cultural norms and literacy and articulacy levels.
- Being constantly critical and reflexive about dominant explanations for a particular family situation and aiming not for the correct conclusion, but the one that is most useful and least likely to be wrong.

(2004: 157–158)

Reflective task: partnerships with parents and carers

Millar and Corby (2006) discuss the circumstances in which parents and carers feel genuine partnership and empowerment, including:

- when honesty and trust have been developed;
- through open and clear communication;
- through genuine involvement in the process;

- when empathy and genuine concern are evident;
- when practice is accountable – enabling the service user to challenge what is said and written.

Consider your own practice and that in your setting. What evidence can you provide of the above generally and, more specifically, in relation to safeguarding practice?

If you have little experience of safeguarding practice, how would you ensure the conditions above are met?

Suspected abuse

If you are worried a child is being abused, you should discuss your concerns with the person in your setting who has lead responsibility for safeguarding. You can also seek advice from the police or children's social care. It is preferable that you identify yourself and give details. You can also ring the National Society for the Prevention of Cruelty to Children (NSPCC) helpline. Knowing how damaging abuse is to children, it is up to the adults around them to take responsibility for stopping it.

If a child tells you about abuse:

- Stay calm and be reassuring.
- Find a quiet place to talk.
- Believe in what you are being told.
- Listen, but do not press for information.
- Say that you are glad that the child told you.
- Say that you will do your best to help and support the child.
- Seek the help of the safeguarding lead practitioner. Other colleagues can also offer help but be sensitive about the information and work within guidance and procedure for the setting.
- Acknowledge that the child may have angry, sad or even guilty feelings about what happened, but stress that the abuse was not the child's fault.
- Acknowledge that you will probably need help in dealing with your own feelings.
- Record as soon as you can what has been said, by the child and you, and what actions you have taken.

Conclusion

Social views about standards of child care change over time. Historically, societies have initially been concerned about protecting children from serious physical injury and neglect. Increasingly, awareness and condemnation of the sexual abuse of children have grown, followed by growing concerns regarding emotional abuse. As societial views of what constitutes 'good child-rearing practices' continue to evolve, views of what is acceptable and unacceptable practice will need also to evolve. Safeguarding practice therefore is more than a cerebral task and the practitioner should be aware of those working practices, experiences, values and mores that impact upon decision making. However, it is essential that practice outcomes are based upon critical use of research, with attention being paid to the presence and use of predominant ideas. The existence and use of frameworks does not guarantee good practice, nor does the completion of a particular form always constitute an assessment. It is crucial that the practitioner consider and analyse the information gathered in the light of relevant literature and research. Good practice depends on the practitioner's skill in analysis.

The need to work inclusively with parents and carers is also acknowledged and accepted by the professional community. Inclusive practice is a main tenet of policy and procedure, and is engrained within the laws, regulations and requirements of the childcare profession. When safeguarding practice is holistic, it can be a platform for partnership and consequently will leave many parents and carers feeling more involved in the decision making affecting their and their children's lives. This can only be of benefit to the child.

Further reading

Batty, D. (2005) 'Timeline: a history of child protection'. *Guardian*, 18 May. Online, available at: www.guardian.co.uk/society/2005/may/18/childrensservices2 (accessed 8 August 2012).

David Batty's article provides a helpful timeline of the history of UK legislation from the late 1880s until 2005, a period that covers the death of Victoria Climbié and the subsequent introduction of the Children Act 2004.

Cuthbert, C., Rayns, G. and Stanley, K. (2011) *All Babies Count: Prevention and Protection for Vulnerable Babies*, London: NSPCC.

This NSPCC report includes new analysis into the number of babies aged under 1 year who are affected by parental substance misuse, mental illness and domestic abuse, which are all important risk factors for abuse and neglect.

4

Neglect in the early years

Neil Ventress

Neglect is a form of significant harm as defined in the Children Act 1989, and it is the most common of the four reasons why children are made the subject of a multi-agency child protection plan. While traditionally associated with the dirty child – perhaps with ill-fitting clothes, perhaps a little smelly, perhaps with a poor health and dental care record – physical neglect is only one part of the range of experiences to which the neglected child is exposed. The term 'neglect' is used to describe a wide range of adult behaviours and childhood experiences. Neglect can have a major impact on all areas of the child's development, and that impact can continue throughout childhood and even throughout adulthood. Sometimes, by the time a child has been removed from a neglectful situation, irreversible damage has already been done. Neglect can poison childhood and permanently damage life chances; at its worst, children die from neglect.

Neglect sometimes starts before birth, so this chapter will consider neglect from pregnancy until the end of the early years. By the end of this chapter you will:

■ understand the range of experiences that constitute neglect in the early years;
■ understand the impact of neglect on the developing child in their early years;
■ know and be able to carry out the legal and procedural requirements that apply when neglect is identified.

Definitions of neglect and the law

Just what is neglect? This is not an easy question to answer, in part because neglect is difficult to define and there are different definitions for different purposes. Nonetheless, neglecting a child is a criminal offence under the Children and Young Persons Act 1933, as follows:

Section 1(1)

If any person who has attained the age of sixteen years and has the custody, charge or care of any child or young person under that age, wilfully assaults, ill-treats, neglects, abandons, or exposes him, or causes or procures him to be assaulted, ill-treated, neglected, abandoned, or exposed, in a manner likely to cause him unnecessary suffering or injury to health ... that person shall be guilty of a misdemeanour...

Section 1(2) For the purposes of this section –

(a) a parent or other person legally liable to maintain a child or young person shall be deemed to have neglected him in a manner likely to cause injury to his health if he has failed to provide adequate food, clothing, medical aid or lodging for him or ... has failed to take steps to procure it to be provided under the Acts relating to the relief of the poor.

However, for a prosecution to be successful it has to be proved (beyond reasonable doubt) that the neglect was 'wilful', i.e. deliberate. It is not always easy to do so (which may explain why relatively few people are convicted of the offence of child neglect), particularly since much neglect is related to apathy, indifference or ignorance, or is a consequence of the caregiver's own experience of neglect.

Allowing a child to be neglected can also be a breach of article 3 of the Human Rights Act 1998, which states that as human beings we have the right to be protected from torture and inhuman or degrading treatment. In 2001 the European Court found in *Z and Others* v. *United Kingdom (Application 29392/95)* that the neglect experienced by the four children in the case crossed the threshold of inhuman or degrading treatment, and as the local authority had been aware of the neglect and had failed to respond appropriately, it was therefore in breach of article 3. The Court awarded the children significant compensation.

In relation to safeguarding children, the definition used in England (the Welsh definition is slightly different) is set out in the 2013 version of *Working Together to Safeguard Children*:

Neglect is the persistent failure to meet a child's basic physical and/or psychological needs, likely to result in the serious impairment of the child's health or development. Neglect may occur during pregnancy as a result of maternal substance abuse. Once a child is born, neglect may involve a parent or carer failing to:

■ provide adequate food, clothing and shelter (including exclusion from home or abandonment);

■ protect a child from physical and emotional harm or danger;

- ensure adequate supervision (including the use of inadequate care-givers); or
- ensure access to appropriate medical care or treatment.

It may also include neglect of, or unresponsiveness to, a child's basic emotional needs.

(HM Government 2013: 86)

This definition has its limitations; for example, we may differ in our opinions about persistence or seriousness, we may not all agree on what are the child's basic needs, and we might argue that there are many other forms of neglect during pregnancy beyond maternal substance misuse. Furthermore, the definition makes no mention of the child's educational needs; learning about the world is a crucial developmental task in the early years.

Horwath has collated a 'working definition' of neglect, based on an overview of a range of definitions of neglect from the United Kingdom and internationally. Practitioners might find this helpful because it reminds us that neglect involves judgement, and this judgement can and should take account of a wide range of factors such as poverty and the level of support available, as well as the unique circumstances of each individual child.

Child neglect is a failure on the part of either the male and/or female caregiver, or pregnant mother, to complete the parenting tasks required to ensure that the developmental needs of the child are met. This should take into account the age, gender, culture, religious beliefs and particular needs and circumstances of the individual child. This failure may be associated with parenting issues. It has occurred despite reasonable resources being available to enable the carer/s to complete the parenting tasks satisfactorily. Whilst neglect is likely to be ongoing, one-off incidents and episodic neglect can affect the health and development of a child.

(Horwath 2007: 38)

The line between poor care and neglect is difficult, though not impossible, to draw. There are likely to be times in every family when the care that a child receives is less than optimal and we must take care to ensure that we do not step in too early and label as neglectful the kind of parenting mistakes common to many families. Neglect needs to be seen within the context of the child, taking account of their age and developmental progress. From a pragmatic perspective, issues of definition should not trouble any early years practitioner who is worried that a child is being neglected; the priority should always be to ensure that action is taken to keep the child safe.

How many children are neglected?

It is difficult to be specific about how many children are neglected, not only because of the difficulties in defining neglect but also because so much neglect takes place within the confines of the family and is never identified by professionals. Unlike physical abuse, neglect is rarely a single event; rather, it is a process, and there may not be a precipitating crisis (such as a young child being left unattended, or a serious accidental injury) that brings the child to the attention of the safeguarding agencies. In this case the child may be left for years to endure abusive care without any professional intervention.

More than four out of ten children who are made the subject of a protection plan fall within the neglect category (Brooks *et al.* 2012: 25) and, alarmingly, Brandon *et al.* (2012: 46) report that in their analysis of 139 serious case reviews, carried out when a child dies or is seriously injured, neglect was a feature (though not necessarily the prime feature) in some 60 per cent of the cases. When Radford *et al.* asked over 4,000 children and young people (and over 2,000 parents) about childhood experiences, some 9.9 per cent of respondents reported experiencing some form of neglect (2011: 14). This is consistent with an earlier study (Cawson *et al.* 2000) with a broadly similar methodology, and paints a worrying picture of childhood experiences that are often never addressed. Of course, accepting that one in ten children may be experiencing neglect does not help the early years practitioner to identify *which* children should be the subject of our concerns. In fact, practitioners generally (not simply those who work within early years settings) are not always confident in recognising neglect. What Radford *et al.*'s figures rather startlingly indicate is that while children who are formally recognised as experiencing neglect are numbered in their thousands, children who actually experience neglect number hundreds of thousands, or even millions.

Different types of neglect

Neglect takes many forms, and every child's experience of neglect will be unique. However, Horwath (2007) offers a very useful framework for understanding neglect as a failure to provide the care that a child needs, as follow~

Different types of neglect

- *Physical neglect*: failure to provide a warm and h~ which the child can safely learn about the world
- *Emotional neglect*: failure to provide a se~ warmth; failure to react positively to the ch~
- *Nutritional neglect*: failure to provide suffici~ developmental needs or, conversely, providin~ hood obesity.

58

- *Medical neglect*: failure to present the child for routine screenings or failure to access treatment for medical or health needs.
- *Educational neglect*: failure to provide a secure environment from which the child can interact with their world; lack of encouragement or stimulation; indifference towards the child's achievements.
- *Supervisory neglect*: failure to ensure that the child is protected from accidents or other adversities.

(Source: Adapted from Horwath, 2007.)

Although these different types of neglect are expressed in terms of the caregiver's omissions – a failure to meet the child's needs – they are all measurable in terms of outcomes for the child.

It is important to remember that children rarely suffer only one form of neglect and that the distinctions between different forms can be complex, as boundaries are unclear and different forms interlink. For example, a toddler living in squalid housing conditions may be regarded as suffering physical neglect, but there is a strong likelihood of this child having a poor diet, not being presented for routine medical screenings, being poorly supervised, and not being stimulated to explore and learn about the world. We use the blanket term 'neglect' to describe each and all of these adversities. It is important to remember that being neglected gives no protection whatsoever from other forms of abuse, which may be occurring simultaneously with neglect. Abuse often occurs in combination, and even in the early years the neglected child may also be the victim of physical or sexual abuse and will inevitably be damaged emotionally by their experiences of neglect. The neglected child may also experience other adversities; we know, for example, that there are correlations between parental drug and alcohol abuse and a range of social problems such as deprivation associated with poverty, physical health problems, mental ill health, housing issues, domestic violence and criminal and antisocial behaviour.

Worryingly, Cleaver *et al*. (2011: 42) cite research suggesting that 'parental abuse of drugs or alcohol, or both, is found in more than half of parents who neglect their children'. As if this were not enough, the neglected child may also experience social isolation, stigmatisation and bullying. Neglect can be intentional and malicious, or it may be the result of a caregiver's ignorance or illness. While the latter may provoke more of our sympathy, it is the severity and duration of the child's experience, not the caregiver's intent, that should determine whether or when we should take action.

e web of neglect

bies are born with very limited resources for self-protection, and despite
r amazing ability to interact with and learn from their new environments

and experiences they are totally dependent on others, not just for their survival but also for the stimuli that will guide their development. Caregivers who are apathetic or indifferent and do not provide that stimulation will compromise the child's development. As development is incremental, with the child building on and extending that which has already been achieved, a delay at one stage can be magnified into a more significant delay later. Furthermore, children's development cannot be compartmentalised: delay in one area of functioning can have a major impact on other areas. For example, neglect can have a profound effect on language development, and we know that speech and language development is fundamental to optimal learning. Similarly with social development: Smith *et al.* cite research which suggests that 'children who experience irritable and ineffective discipline at home, and poor parental monitoring of their activities, together with a lack of parental warmth, are particularly likely to become aggressive in peer groups and at school' (2003: 161), which can obviously lead to compromised social development. Chapter 7, 'Safeguarding children's health and wellbeing' goes into these issues more broadly.

Although there are circumstances in which a child who has previously been receiving adequate care suddenly starts to be neglected, such as the sudden onset of parental physical or mental health problems, or a major change in the family's composition or circumstances, there is a strong likelihood that the child in the early years who is being neglected has already had a lifetime of neglect, or indeed that the neglect may have started even before the child was born.

Pre-natal neglect

Children can experience physical, emotional, nutritional and medical neglect for months before they are born; any one of these can have a significant and sometimes lifelong impact. Exposing an unborn child to illicit substances may actually be regarded as a form of physical abuse, but there is also an argument that failing to protect the unborn child from the impact of a damaging illicit substance is neglectful. Although a mother who smokes during her pregnancy may not always be labelled as neglectful, we know that

> smoking during pregnancy reduces babies' lung function. Babies born to heavy smokers are more likely than those born to non-smoking mothers to suffer a higher risk of spontaneous abortion, premature delivery, stillbirth, sudden infant death syndrome and the possibility of low birth weight with its consequent negative effects.
>
> (Cleaver *et al.* 2011: 100)

Of course, many smokers give birth to perfectly healthy babies. Researchers have now identified a wide range of damaging consequences related to maternal drug abuse, from low birth weight and prematurity (sometimes associated with health complications in adult life) to addiction (sometimes referred to as neo-natal abstinence syndrome) and increased risk of cot death. Like smoking, the consequences of drug misuse are not inevitable; they are affected by the nature of the particular substance used, its amount, duration of use, and the route by which it is delivered, as well as the stage of the pregnancy. The foetus is most susceptible to structural damage during weeks 4–12 of gestation; drugs taken later generally affect growth or cause neo-natal addiction (ibid.: 103).

Alcohol consumption during pregnancy, especially binge drinking, can cause miscarriage and, for a small proportion of babies, foetal alcohol syndrome disorder (FASD), or its slightly less severe manifestation, foetal alcohol effect, typical symptoms of which include poor feeding, tremors, irritability, occasional seizures and increased risk of sudden death syndrome (Cleaver *et al.* 2011: 106). Longer-term impacts of FASD can include facial and other physical abnormalities, growth deficiencies, and damage to the brain and central nervous system, leading to both psychological and behavioural problems. The British government advice at present is to avoid drinking alcohol during the first three months of pregnancy, and then to consume no more than one or two units not more than twice per week.

Some drug users lead chaotic lives; Bate (2005) points out that many drug users live in poor housing, sometimes in unstable and violent relationships, and are sometimes involved in criminal activity. Perhaps unsurprisingly, some of these mothers are likely to fear negative consequences and avoid contact with the services that can help both them and the child, and thus may miss opportunities for both routine screenings and specialist advice.

Even for the unborn child, emotional health is arguably as important as physical health. We know that foetal exposure to trauma can affect the development of the central nervous system, leading to a predisposition to impulsivity and possibly even violence (Hughes and Owen 2009: 67). Over the past couple of decades it has become clear that bonding or attachment is not something which suddenly starts at birth; attachment generally develops during the pregnancy. This process can for some mothers (and fathers) be enhanced by ante-natal care, including ultrasound examination, which opens up a 'window' through which the unborn child can be seen, its heartbeat observed and its sex identified. Research by Dykes and Stjernqvist in 2001 concluded that this made the child more real to the parents and reported that a number of mothers said they felt closer to their child as a result. This is important, because there is powerful evidence that the nature of pre-natal attachment influences post-natal attachment (Laxton-Kane and Slade 2002). Practitioners will need no reminder of how Bowlby's work from 1969 onwards demonstrated the importance of attachment in infancy to the child's development.

Neglect always has consequences; the difficult-to-settle baby or the anxious and impulsive toddler (even if clean and well dressed) may already be displaying the evidence of the neglect they suffered before they were born.

Key points: the complexity of neglect

- Neglecting a child is a criminal offence if it can be shown to be intentional, but much neglect stems from apathy, indifference or ignorance.
- The definition of neglect in Working Together to Safeguard Children (2013) has some limitations, but it is unlikely that any definition could capture everything that we regard as neglect.
- Neglect is usually expressed as a failure on the part of caregivers to meet a child's needs, but it is important to remember that neglect always has measurable outcomes for children, and these outcomes are always negative.
- Safeguarding agencies come into contact with only a small proportion of the children who experience neglect.
- Children can suffer from different kinds of neglect, either simultaneously or sequentially.
- Children who are neglected are not protected from other forms of abuse.
- Neglect can affect every area of a child's development.
- Neglect can start before birth and its impact can be lifelong.

Physical neglect is often associated with children presenting in dirty or ill-fitting clothes or with dirty skin, sometimes accompanied by a distinct smell. While it is true that dirty babies and toddlers will still grow, from the age of between 2 and 6 months the immunoglobulin antibodies that protected the neonate from infections decrease, and the child's innate immune system develops. As this process is not instantaneous, there is a period (from around 6 months to 2 years) when the child is particularly susceptible to infections, and a lack of hygiene can compound this problem. This can result in what seems to be a perpetual cycle of sore throats, ear infections, runny noses or skin complaints. Even children who are very well cared for will acquire infections from time to time, of course, but some neglected children seem to have little respite from these problems. Conversely, not all children who are physically neglected will show signs of illness or infection; some children seem to maintain robust good health in spite of their poor physical care, seemingly developing resistance to the perils of physical neglect.

Unclean children often come from cluttered and unclean households; while the immobile baby may not be damaged by clutter, the mobile child needs space to explore the world, to fall over without hurting themselves, and to use their strengthening leg and arm muscles to interact with their environment. For some neglected children the lack of opportunity to explore the world is compounded by their being confined to a buggy or chair. While for the neglectful caregiver this might resolve the problem of their child having no clear space to play, for the child this hampers their physical, cognitive and social development and frustrates their desire to learn about the world.

With appropriate toilet training, children are typically dry and clean during the day at around the age of 2; until this point (which itself is unlikely to be a spontaneous process but is more likely to be the result of encouragement and praise) the apathetic caregiver who leaves the child in a soiled nappy is responsible for discomfort and, at worst, painful nappy rash. Staying dry overnight is often achieved during the early years, but many children may not fully overcome night-time wetting until well beyond this period. Again, the child smelling of urine as a result of a lack of physical care may be uncomfortable and even in the early years setting may stand out as being different, occasionally even finding themselves targeted by other children.

Night-time wetting can be exacerbated by a lack of clean and appropriate bedding, or even the lack of a clean and appropriate bed. Pre-school children typically need around 11 hours of sleep each night (Rudolph 2009: 41), so a clean, welcoming sleeping place is important. Lack of sleep can obviously make children tired during the day, but can also manifest itself in hyperactivity and attention difficulties, and because lack of sleep can cause an imbalance in hormone levels there can be a direct impact on growth and development as well as energy levels. The routine of quiet time–bath–story–lights out is largely unfamiliar to the physically neglected child.

By the age of about 2½, most children will have developed a full set of 'baby teeth', which they will keep until they are replaced by 'adult teeth' anywhere from five to ten years later. Being encouraged to take proper care of these teeth will not only enable the early years child acquire the positive oral care habits which will be helpful for them throughout adulthood, but will also prevent tooth decay. The Scottish Intercollegiate Guidelines Network (SIGN) (2005) views tooth decay as a failure to manage the child's teeth-cleaning habits and their diet, and argues that all tooth decay can be prevented. The consequences of tooth decay for the early years child can be difficulties in speech and language development, difficulty in eating, and extreme pain. SIGN's research suggests that there is a correlation between deprivation and poor oral health, with poorer children having three times the level of tooth decay compared with children in more affluent households, though it is more likely to be parental ignorance or indifference rather than poverty that is responsible for poor dental hygiene. Depending on the severity of the child's experience, this lack of caregiver intervention may cross the threshold and become neglect.

Caregivers who lack the motivation and organisation to provide their child with clean and safe physical care or to meet their child's physical needs will often be living a chaotic life in chaotic circumstances. The child who is frequently brought late to the early years setting, or is brought or collected by a wide range of adults, or whose attendance is sporadic, or who seems tired or hungry or inappropriately dressed, is almost certain to be experiencing unpredictability and unreliability in all aspects of their care to the level that we would regard as neglect.

Emotional neglect

The child who endures severe physical neglect could never be described as 'dirty but happy'; there is evidence that physical neglect and emotional neglect often coexist. The same inability to manage, or indifference towards, physical conditions can also be expressed as lack of interest in, lack of time for, lack of attention to, or lack of positive regard for the child's emotional wellbeing.

Children in their early years need to feel secure for them to be able to explore their environment. To achieve a healthy attachment, the child needs to have experienced their needs being met and therefore to feel that they are valued, thus leading to a positive self-image and an appropriately confident approach to the world. The child who is emotionally secure will feel confident to explore and learn about their world, safe in the knowledge that their caregiver(s) will protect them. Daniel *et al.* report that in their early years, secure children not only will feel free to explore but will play more harmoniously with their peers, cope better with frustration and develop empathy towards others (2010: 149).

As separation anxiety diminishes, typically between the ages of 2 and 3 years, the securely attached child will approach the early years setting with confidence and trust, and by the age of 4 may even need prompting to wave goodbye to their departing caregiver. They will be able to regulate their own emotions with much more self-control, and they will start to use language rather than behaviour to express these emotions. They will feel confident, in control and loved. Contrast this with the child who has endured emotional distance or apathy, who will be more likely to have a poor self-image, to feel unimportant and isolated and to feel unable to make sense of their own feelings and those of others. Stevenson (2007) reports a study by Egeland *et al.* comparing neglected pre-schoolers with peers who had endured other forms of abuse. Those children whose parents were emotionally unavailable to them displayed a range of worrying behaviours, including unusual sexual behaviours, wetting or soiling, excessive appetite, repetitive movements such as rocking, and self-punishing behaviours. These children had low self-esteem and were the most impulsive and unpredictable children in their group (ibid.: 74). The long-term consequences for these children if their emotional neglect is unresolved are likely to include poor academic performance, difficulty in making and sustaining relationships, and difficulty in understanding and following rules and expectations of others. Ultimately, some of them will face consequential lifelong disadvantage and social exclusion.

Medical neglect

Parents and caregivers have choices about the level of state intervention in their child's health, and a parent who makes an informed judgement not to have their child vaccinated or makes a decision to treat an accidental injury that they feel does not need professional medical attention may not always accord with what we might see as optimal care, but is unlikely to constitute neglect. On the other hand, avoidance of health oversight or treatment because of parental apathy or lack of interest quite clearly falls within any definition of neglect. Many neglected children do have additional health needs and are perhaps in greater need of health oversight than the general population, but in the chaos, confusion or apathy that characterises their family life, missed appointments are a routine feature. Similarly, ongoing health needs can be ignored. The Association of Optometrists (www.aop.org. uk/media-centre/campaigns/childrens-eye-health/practitioners) suggests that one in five school-aged children has an untreated vision problem, and there is nothing to suggest that this figure would be different in the early years population. Vision problems such as lazy eye and squint are frequently very amenable to treatment when identified early, but this may rely on a child's wearing spectacles, or a patch. Failure to follow professional advice in these circumstances can result in permanent damage to the child's eyesight and would almost certainly be regarded as neglectful.

Nutritional neglect

The pattern of rapid growth in infancy changes as children enter their third year. When babies are born, the brain is about 25 per cent of its adult size, and doubles in size in the first year. By the age of 3 the brain will reach about 90 per cent of its adult size. A child in their third year will typically grow about 8 or 9 centimetres and gain over 2 kilograms in weight; as well as requiring warmth, sleep and stimulation, optimal growth depends on an appropriate supply of food and drink. Children in the early years typically will need between 1,400 and 2,000 calories per day, and should be given an appropriate balance of different types of food; for example, brain growth needs fat, although in general children need the amount of fat in their diet to be regulated. Similarly, while sugar can help cognitive functioning, too much sugar can lead to tooth decay and obesity. While children are often very good at regulating the quantity of food that they eat, in the early years some children can be quite selective in their food preferences. This can be quite a challenge for even the well-intentioned caregiver. For families living in poverty, finding the right food for their children can be even more challenging. However, some children eat what they can find. A diet of poorly balanced convenience foods or, even worse, crisps, biscuits and fizzy drinks can sometimes be all that the uninterested caregiver makes available. Children who are hungry will make little attempt to restrict their diet to one that is healthy, and the result of inadequate or inappropriate food intake can be either slow growth on the one hand or obesity on the other.

Some children who appear at first sight to be malnourished are quite healthy and developing normally. Food intake is not, of course, the only determinant of our body size and shape, and sometimes the child who appears to be painfully thin is simply a child who is predestined to be smaller and thinner than their peers. The opposite extreme, of course, is childhood obesity (discussed more fully in Chapter 7); one in five children are now overweight or obese by the age of 3 (HM Government 2010b: 9) and although at present there is still scope for debate about the exact level of damage done in childhood, we can observe some of the difficulties faced by very overweight or obese children in their early years, and the limitations that their weight creates for them. We also know that eating habits and food preferences acquired in childhood are difficult to change, and we know that if the overweight child goes on to become an overweight adult then they face an increased risk of heart disease, circulation problems, diabetes and joint problems. This is an area demanding sensitivity, not least because many overweight children have overweight parents, and furthermore there are many other factors besides neglect that can contribute to this problem. However, one can argue that where childhood obesity is the result of parental apathy to the problem then it surely constitutes neglect.

Educational neglect

Optimal development does not simply occur spontaneously. The amazing period of extremely rapid development that starts before children are born and continues until about the age of 3 will then slow down slightly, but we now can fairly safely assert that child development is not something that 'just happens' but is the result of both genetic factors and the child's interaction with their environment and the significant people in it.

When we are born, our relatively well-developed brain does not need to be stimulated in order to control our basic physical functioning, such as breathing, heart rate, sucking, and controlling body temperature. However, some parts of the brain (the hippocampus, limbic system and cortex) are experience-dependent and will develop optimally only when stimulated. Our visual cortex, for example, develops as we see the world around us, and our auditory cortex responds to sound; if unstimulated, they will not develop fully. Synapses, the neural connections between the hundreds of billions of neurons in our brain which store and transmit information, are similarly developed by stimulation, and a pruning process takes place to remove those synapses that are not stimulated. Those parts that are stimulated are reinforced, and the Solihull NHS PCT (2004) cites research suggesting that the number of neural connections can vary by as much as 25 per cent as a result of this stimulation. Put simply, our brain grows and develops, at least in part, according to how it is used. Stimulating neural connections is not beyond the capacity of most parents. In the main it simply involves interacting with the child and providing them with materials and experiences that will maintain interest and encourage exploration. However, in the same way as an uninterested parent leaving a child fastened in a buggy for much of the day will ultimately affect the child's acquisition of mobility skills, so a child who is unstimulated by neglectful caregivers will similarly be disadvantaged in terms of their cognitive skills. Cognitive development will occur, but at a slower pace.

The area that perhaps demonstrates the importance of stimulation most clearly is speech and language development; there is a clear correlation between the level of stimulation and the pace of language acquisition and the development of speech. In order to make the range of sounds we use in spoken language, children need to have developed sophisticated muscle control, changing the shape of the mouth and placing the tongue in the appropriate relationship to the teeth, and this requires both physiological and cognitive development. Crucially, though, this is stimulated by exposure to language. Normal language development occurs amazingly fast. By the age of 2, children will typically use at least 50 words, and will understand many more, although constructions are simplistic and conversations are sometimes incomprehensible! Contrast this with the well-stimulated child only three years later, who will use adult sentence constructions, have a wide vocabulary, and will have learned to use language in context by adjusting style and delivery to suit the circumstances.

Hart and Risley (1995) conducted longitudinal research in the United States measuring the frequency, at different points in childhood, with which adults talked to their children. They concluded that children who lack interaction with their parents, who are ignored or who are understimulated are considerably disadvantaged. They argue that the quantity of talk and interactions between parents and child correlates directly with the child's subsequent IQ and vocabulary size, and they believe that this is the single most important variable, being more important than the level of parents' education or socioeconomic status. They concluded that children's academic successes at age 9 and 10 are attributable to the amount of talk they hear between birth and the age of 3.

Even more worryingly, Hart and Risley's findings suggest that children whose language development has been impaired by lack of interaction are unlikely to be able to catch up, stating that after the first four years, closing the huge gap between children who have had optimal exposure to language and those who have not is virtually impossible. As language is the principal vehicle for learning, children whose language development is impaired by neglect are likely to face a lifelong negative impact. Daniel *et al*. encapsulate the point perfectly when they affirm that '[e]xperiences of neglectful caregiving can profoundly affect language development' (2010: 162).

Of course, the importance of stimulation is not confined to speech and language development. Helping the child to achieve the 'next steps' will be a concept familiar to most early years practitioners; one of the ways in which children learn is by being encouraged to try something that is just beyond their capabilities, going into the area that Vygotsky (1978) called the zone of proximal development. Smith *et al.* describe this as 'the distance between the child's actual developmental level and his or her potential level of development under the guidance of more expert adults or in collaboration with more competent peers' (2003: 497). Typically, parents and caregivers take advantage of every opportunity to help their child to extend their accomplishments, and the ensuing celebrations by both the child and the caregiver can be a source of mutual joy. The neglected child who is left to their own devices may still learn, but that process will be diminished, lacking the celebration of achievement and, at its worst, confirming to the child that they are isolated and unvalued.

Supervisory neglect

Young children who are not appropriately supervised will soon come to harm; they lack the skills to make risk assessments, and they are often adventurous and like to try new experiences. They also like to copy grown-ups, and if allowed will enthusiastically experiment with adult paraphernalia such as sharp knives, cigarette lighters, matches, stiletto-heel shoes or whisky! For the mobile child the family home is an adventure playground, but unfortunately this means that even the carefully supervised child faces a high level of risk. While obviously accidents are generally preventable, it would be unrealistic to suggest that they will not happen, and most parents will at some point recognise that their child has harmed themselves because the adult was distracted or briefly absent. The Royal Society for the Prevention of Accidents (RoSPA) points out that those most at risk of an accident in the home are aged 4 or less, with boys being at greater risk than girls. It also points out that 'children from poorer backgrounds are five times more likely to die as a result of an accident than children from better off families' (RoSPA: online).

According to RoSPA, some 43,000 UK children aged between 0 and 4 have accidents in the kitchen each year. Around 500 children under 5 are admitted to hospital after incidents of scalding with hot bathwater, with further large numbers being treated in Accident and Emergency departments. One or two children die every year after being entangled in the cords of window blinds – with many more near misses. These occur in children between 16 months and 36 months old, with the majority happening at about 23 months. Other common accidents involving children in their early years include falls (from buildings, from furniture and down the stairs), scalds from hot drinks (young children have sensitive skin, and a hot drink can still scald a child 15 minutes after it was made) and poisoning (in 2008–2009 over 4,000 pre-school children were admitted to hospital following ingestion of medicines, household products or cosmetics). On average about one young child per year will die from suffocation as a result of putting a nappy sack over their mouth and nose or from choking after putting a nappy sack in their mouth (RoSPA 2012: online).

These truly awful figures probably only represent the tip of the iceberg and the vast majority of these accidents will be, at least in part, the result of a lack of appropriate supervision. Not every instance will involve neglect, but where the lack of supervision is the result of indifferent care, or where the child suffers repeated injuries, we may well consider that the threshold of neglect has been crossed.

Supervisory neglect may take the form of leaving a child unattended or in the care of an inappropriate carer. In an ideal world a child in the early years should not be left alone at any point, but there are times when it is almost unavoidable; most parents will confess that they have left a child alone in a room while they used the toilet, took an important telephone call or put the kettle on. However, in the main they will have done this after making a judgement that the child is likely to be safe, so this is unlikely to constitute supervisory neglect. On the other hand, the parent who leaves a child in their early years unattended to visit friends, to go the local pub or to go to work is certainly guilty of supervisory neglect.

Supervisory neglect can occur when the caregivers remain in the same building as the child, or even when they are in the same room. The child who is locked into their bedroom while the caregiver meets their own needs is likely to meet our threshold of supervisory neglect, as is the child who is left with a caregiver who is incapable of meeting the child's needs because of the influence of alcohol or drugs. Similarly, the early years child who is left unsupervised in the bath, or in any other situation where the caregiver's expectations are beyond the developmental capabilities of the child, would fall within this category. Supervisory neglect can also occur when the child is left outside unsupervised; the interested and concerned parent will always monitor their child's safety and wellbeing even during the times that they are not directly interacting with them.

Thresholds of supervisory neglect are not always straightforward. The parent who collects their tired child from an early years setting and who risks briefly leaving them asleep in the car while they go to the kiosk to pay for their petrol may not be neglecting their child, but the parent who leaves the child asleep in the car in the supermarket car park while they go shopping most certainly is. The child left playing in the garden, securely contained, with safe toys and play equipment and immediate access to a nearby adult may not cross our threshold, but the young child whose explorations have led them out on to the pavement of a busy road when the caregiver is incapacitated (e.g. by substance misuse) almost certainly will. The early years child who confounds their caregiver by appearing to be transfixed by the DVD that they are watching, or fast asleep, and then, as soon as they are left alone for a few seconds, manages for the first time in their life to open the front door may not be neglected, but if the caregiver does not notice their absence for 15 minutes then there is a clear cause for concern.

The emotional distress to children of realising that they are alone should never be underestimated. Many well-intentioned parents or carers who have unintentionally left a child alone will recall the distraught child with whom they were reunited, and in fact a child who takes in their stride the fact that there is no caregiver present should cause a high level of concern.

Finally, supervisory neglect may become apparent to staff in an early years setting who notice that the child is being dropped off or collected by a wide range of carers, by carers who have not previously been identified to the setting as responsible adults who are appropriate to take care of the child, by older siblings who are themselves children, or by carers who appear to be under the influence of alcohol or other substances. It is to be expected that settings will have clearly established procedures to address all these issues, some of which may actually constitute a criminal offence; they also clearly fall within our definition of neglect.

Key points: the harm done by neglect

- Neglect is not just about a grubby child or an untidy house. Children can be clean and well dressed but still endure a variety of different forms of neglect.
- Children who are neglected are not 'dirty but happy'. Neglect can be uncomfortable, and even painful, as well as emotionally distressing. There are no positive aspects to the experience of neglect.
- Children who are not securely attached to their caregivers will not feel confident in exploring and learning about the world. Neglected children can suffer delays in all aspects of their development.
- Childhood accidents are always preventable, but equally it would be ridiculous to suggest that all children who have accidents are neglected. Children's accidents resulting from the apathy or indifference of their caregivers may well fall within the definition of neglect.
- While much neglect is chronic and long-lasting, single episodes of neglect should not be ignored; young children are poor at assessing risk and can die or be seriously injured if left unsupervised even for a short time.
- Children's development does not occur spontaneously. Encouragement, support and praise are key to enabling a child to attain their 'next steps'. These should not be beyond the capacity of most parents of children in their early years.

Confronting neglect?

It is expected that sub-optimal care will be challenged by early years practitioners long before it reaches the stage of neglect. However, this is not always possible and cannot be guaranteed to be successful. In spite of the perceived lack of clarity about particular thresholds for neglect and the absence of a trigger event (such as that which might lead to safeguarding action in cases of, for example, physical abuse), practitioners in an early years setting are ideally placed to recognise first-hand the impact of neglect.

In the main, safeguarding systems are quite efficient in their response to incidents and episodes (such as a bruise or a fracture where the cause is non-accidental) but can seem less so in relation to a process, where the impact is cumulative, such as neglect. This might make some practitioners less willing to report their concerns for a child, perhaps because they feel that that they may be overreacting, or perhaps because they are afraid that they will not be taken seriously, or perhaps for one of many other reasons.

The role of the supervisor or the child protection lead professional can be extremely useful when there are concerns about possible neglect: to help practitioners to talk through their concerns, agree what should happen next and agree a written account of their discussion and its outcomes. Perhaps practitioners might even be helped to see that the lack of a specific definition of neglect is not necessarily unhelpful. When there are concerns for a child then the Children Act 1989 requires judgements to be made: is this child suffering or likely to suffer harm, and is that harm significant? As we read in Chapter 3, there is some guidance under sections 31(9) and (10) of the Children Act 1989 as amended by the Adoption and Children Act 2002. These are worth repeating here:

> Where the question of whether harm suffered by a child is significant turns on the child's health and development, his health shall be compared with that which could reasonably be expected of a similar child.

- '[H]arm' means ill-treatment of health or development (including, for example, impairment suffered from seeing or hearing the ill-treatment of another);
- 'development' means physical, intellectual, emotional, social or behavioural development;
- 'health' means physical or mental health; and
- ill-treatment includes sexual abuse and forms of ill-treatment which are not physical.

There are few professionals who have the same in-depth knowledge of the individual child as the early years practitioner, and therefore there are few professionals better placed to make such a judgement.

Addressing neglect

Every setting has specific procedures to follow if they have concerns for a child. Typically, the Local Safeguarding Children Board (LSCB) will have online procedures (where these exist, practitioners should refer to them rather than paper copies unless they are certain that the printed version is absolutely up to date), to which every professional who works with children should have access. Professionals who are unclear about how to access these (internal or LSCB) procedures need to resolve this issue, even where the setting gives the responsibility for making a referral to specific staff members. Local Safeguarding Children Boards will also provide training, usually on a multiagency basis, which sets out the locally agreed criteria for referral to children's services and the particular guidance which should be followed.

Routinely, all concerns that a practitioner feels meet the threshold for intervention by safeguarding agencies (usually the police or, more likely, Children's Social Care) should be discussed with the child's caregivers, and their agreement to a referral being made should be sought. However, it is the child's interests, not the caregivers' wishes, that should be regarded as paramount, and the appropriate action should never be delayed or compromised by the need to involve parents or caregivers. Additionally, discussion should not take place with the caregivers if there is reason to suspect that this will cause further difficulties for the child (or anyone else), but in the main honesty and openness are essential, not least in protecting the relationship between the caregivers and the early years setting. The fear that passing on concerns will damage the working relationship that settings have with caregivers is largely groundless. Of course caregivers may be angry or distressed, at least for a while, when challenged about the care of their child, but the tension is usually resolved quite quickly by keeping parents and caregivers informed and involved in the process and by reinforcing the point that all settings are driven by the best interests of the children for whom they provide care.

Conclusion

While rarely fatal, neglect in the early years can be extremely damaging and can ultimately affect every aspect of a child's functioning. This damage may be long-lasting, and indeed may be lifelong. Neglect can never be excused by poverty or ignorance, and although it may be explained by the caregivers' own experiences or circumstances, these should never be used to justify the harm done to children by their experience of neglect. Neglect may be deliberate or unintentional; the child's experience is unlikely to be significantly different.

Neglect is usually a process, often starting before the child is born and sometimes continuing throughout childhood or until the safeguarding agencies intervene, although one-off incidents of lack of supervision can leave a child exposed to significant danger. Acknowledging that fatalities are thankfully rare, we must still remember that a small number of children do die every year as a result of neglect, and many thousands suffer preventable injuries or other serious harm.

Early years practitioners are ideally placed to recognise and respond to poor care, sometimes well before it reaches the point of neglect, and it is acknowledged that this preventive work is happening every day in numerous early years settings. However, to judge by the stories of children and young people themselves it seems that for the vast majority of neglected children their neglect is either not identified or does not receive an adequate response when identified, and they are left to endure neglect, sometimes for many years.

Great care must be taken to avoid imposing inappropriate standards on families that for one reason or another may never be able to attain the desired standards of home conditions, achieve optimal levels of stimulation or impose order and routine on their disorganised lifestyle. Caregivers have choices about how they bring up their children, and sometimes we must accept that the choices made by others would not be those that we ourselves would make. However, when those choices result in actual or likely significant harm, or where choices are not made because of apathy or indifference, we need to intervene. The vulnerability of children in their early years and the long-term damage caused by neglect demand that we take action.

Further reading

Daniel, B., Taylor, J. and Scott, J. (2010) 'Recognition of neglect and early response: overview of a systematic review of the literature', *Child and Family Social Work*, 15 (2): 248–257.

This article provides an overview of a systematic review of the literature on child neglect. There is a discussion of evidence that professionals can identify signs of neglect but are not always clear about how best to respond.

Ward, H., Brown, R. and Westlake, D. (2012) *Safeguarding Babies and Very Young Children from Abuse and Neglect*, London: Jessica Kingsley.

This book relates the findings of DCSF-funded research into children who were identified at risk of harm in the Early Years Foundation Stage. The authors explore the safeguarding process and whether interventions by professionals work. They also consider the impact practitioners have on children's life pathways.

5

Socialisation and consequential abuse

Neil Ventress

Introduction

How do we become the unique person that we are? How do our experiences, positive and negative, influence how our lives will unfold? Scientific advances are helping to clarify the intricacies of the nature/nurture debate, to clarify the degree to which we are a product of our genes or a product of our environment. We can now say with some confidence that we are shaped by neither nature nor nurture alone; we have certain biological predispositions that we inherit from our parents which underpin who we are and what we will become, but which (in the main) cannot be taken in isolation as the sole determinants of our development. Environmental factors also play a large part: the knowledge, skills, abilities and behaviours of our parents, the family in which we are raised, the people with whom we come into contact and the neighbourhood and culture that we live in all help to shape our ultimate selves.

This chapter looks at how children in their early years are socialised – how they learn to fit into their world – before going on to consider the impacts of 'consequential abuse'; this is the term coined to describe the actions of adults which are not in themselves intentionally damaging to children but which can still result in children suffering significant harm. After considering the impact of parental learning disability it considers the 'toxic trio' of parental mental illness, parental substance misuse and domestic violence. Ultimately the chapter considers the building of resilience and the part that early years practitioners can play in moderating some of the negative impacts on children.

By the end of this chapter you will:

■ recognise that children's development is a complex blend of inherited factors and their experiences;

■ understand the term 'consequential abuse' and how it relates to parental mental illness, parental substance misuse and domestic violence;

- understand the potential impacts for the early years child of living in a household where one or both parents have a learning disability;
- be aware of how to respond when there are concerns that a child is being maltreated, including when the child is suffering consequential abuse.

Gender and socialisation

Perhaps a good place to start this exploration would be with a basic characteristic – our sex. The biological explanation for our sex is simple; that we are born that way. A human body cell normally contains 46 chromosomes (the structures that carry the genes which will determine our gender as well as characteristics that we will inherit from our biological parents), arranged in 23 pairs. If one specific pair has two X chromosomes, a specific set of hormonal actions will be triggered which will mean that the cell, and subsequently the person, becomes female, and if the pair is one X and one Y chromosome then a different set of hormonal actions is triggered and the cell will become male. Thus we become boys or girls, and men or women. In the main we develop an identity associated with that sex which we keep throughout our life – although of course for a minority of people this is not the case. The environmental explanation for who we are is equally simple: we are the product of our experiences. On its own this is obviously flawed; put bluntly, a boy brought up as a girl will still be a boy.

This is, however, a narrow and polarised framework of masculinity and femininity, which in some ways mirrors the heredity/environment (nature/nurture) polarisation. In fact there are both biological and environmental factors underpinning who we are, and it is the complex interactions of these, moderated and influenced by a whole range of factors, that ultimately determine the person we are to be (Perkins 2006). And let us not forget that boys do not always have to be boyish and girls do not always have to be girly. If we see masculinity and femininity as a continuum, accepting that as human beings we are rarely at one end or the other and that it is perfectly normal and acceptable to be located on different parts of the continuum at different times, then perhaps we will more accurately reflect our contemporary reality.

In neonates there are very few differences, apart from the obvious (though usually hidden) physical characteristics associated with gender. As a result, many of us find it difficult to distinguish male and female babies without some tell-tale hint – perhaps the colour of the clothing, which typically reinforces gender stereotypes. Infants (up to the age of 2) start to show some slight differences; Smith *et al.* report that girls may be more responsive to people, and boys may be more distressed by stressful situations that they cannot control, and also that girls seem to talk earlier (2003: 186). By the age of 2, many children will be able to determine whether they are a boy or a girl, but some will be confused or still not know; by the age of 3 most children will be aware of their own and another person's gender.

Smith *et al.* (ibid.) report a fascinating study from 1978 where pre-school children were shown a male doll and a female doll and asked about the type of activities each would undertake. Both boys and girls, even at the ages of 2½ and 3½, reported that girls play with dolls, like to help their mother, like to cook dinner and clean house, talk a lot, never hit, and say, 'I need some help', whereas boys like to help father and say, 'I can hit you'. There does not appear to be a new, purely biological phenomenon at work in infancy, so it seems reasonable to assume that environmental factors are exerting their influence. One way of explaining this is via social learning theory.

Social learning theory (Smith *et al.* 2003: 190–194; McLeod 2011: online) suggests that children observe models (i.e. other people, other children) and encode (process) their behaviours. This behaviour is then imitated, and reinforcement or punishment will determine whether or not this behaviour is repeated. This is not simply an issue of copying other people, not least because we know that the majority of young children are likely to have more contact with female caregivers than males, yet boys do not take on a more female gender-role identity. This is a selective process, involving cognition. Simply put, social cognitive theory suggests that children in the main imitate models of the same gender as themselves, learning for themselves that this is how they should behave.

Biology and experience, then, both play a part. What we can probably say with some certainty is that whereas biological characteristics are difficult – though not impossible – to change, our experiences will determine how we build on our biology to become who we are. Children see how other people behave, they process and remember this behaviour, and then imitate it in what they think are the appropriate circumstances. The response of other people (praising, rewarding, correcting, admonishing, or whatever) will then play a big part in whether or not that behaviour is repeated. Because adults tend to have fairly constant views on gender-appropriate behaviour and gender roles, behaviour that conforms to these views is more likely to be reinforced than conflicting behaviour, so the process of socialisation, of learning to behave in a way acceptable to others, continues.

Social learning theory and social cognitive theory are not limited to understanding gender identity, but may help us to understand other aspects of how children grow and develop. These theories also remind us of the importance of modelling appropriate behaviour in the early years setting; children will develop the sophisticated filtering system that helps them to discriminate between behaviours that they should imitate and behaviours that they should abandon, but this process takes time. While this development is taking place, imitation may be rather more indiscriminate, and careless practitioners can easily find themselves the subject of inappropriate imitation! The remainder of this chapter focuses on how living with adversity, particularly parental learning difficulties, mental illness, substance misuse and domestic violence, affects the child in their early years. Our model of development – that is, that development is shaped by the interplay of genetic and environmental factors – is expanded to consider the moderating and influencing factors that can affect the development process and what the result might be in terms of outcomes for the child.

Key points: becoming who we are

■ Although our biological sex is generally fixed, neither biological nor environmental explanations alone can account for how we take on gender roles.

■ Gender differences emerge during the first and second year, although some 2-year-olds will still be uncertain in distinguishing boys from girls.

■ By their third year, children are beginning to differentiate between male and female activities and so perpetuate what we regard as gender-stereotypical behaviours.

■ Social learning theory explains this in terms of children observing and imitating their models, who may be adults or children, by filtering these observations through their own expectations about what it is that boys and girls do.

Consequential abuse

Simply by its definition, much child abuse, as defined in previous government guidance, is deliberate; it would difficult to argue that acts of physical, sexual or emotional abuse are accidental (HM Government 2013: 85). Neglect can perhaps be different, in that the 'intention to neglect' is sometimes more difficult to establish; neglect – while not accidental – is often the result of apathy or ignorance, or the result of the caregiver's own experiences. Somewhat paradoxically, there is a convincing argument that when neglect is deliberate it can actually become something else – a different form of abuse. Irrespective of the beatings she suffered, Victoria Climbié (Laming 2003) was neglected, being deprived of appropriate care in horrendous circumstances. Khyra Ishaq (Birmingham Safeguarding Children Board 2010) was deliberately starved, ultimately to the point of death. For both these children we might argue that the neglect that they experienced was so extreme it became physically abusive. In many ways this discussion is academic; it is probable that neither of these children would be troubled by the definition that we give to their suffering. This point reminds us, though, that labels are rarely adequate to describe the confounding nature of children's experiences of maltreatment and abuse.

Consequential abuse refers to the experiences of children who face adversities that may not be deliberately targeted at them, but where significant harm, or its likelihood, is very real. This harm results from:

- the behaviour of adults who are deliberately causing harm to other people but in which harm caused to children is a collateral issue;
- the behaviour of adults who are preoccupied with meeting their own needs and so the needs of their children are secondary and are unmet;
- the behaviour of adults who by reason of their own illness are prevented from providing their children with the care that they need;
- the behaviour of adults who are prevented by their own characteristics from providing their children with the care that they need.

Table 5.1 shows the association between these sources of significant harm and the typical caregiver in each case. It also proposes a continuum of both intent and perceived responsibility for consequential abuse. For example, caregivers with learning disabilities may deliberately perpetrate abuse against their children, but it is more likely that the children of learning-disabled parents who suffer significant harm will do so as a result of reduced parenting capacity, often compounded by a lack of supportive resources. In this situation there is low (or even no) intent for children to be harmed, and therefore although as adults the caregivers must be held responsible for the care of their children, nonetheless we would be overly harsh if we treated a learning-disabled parent with no intent to damage their child in the same way as someone who deliberately set about harming their child. At the other end of the continuum it is more difficult to be quite so tolerant of those who perpetrate domestic violence; domestic violence is unacceptable by any standard, and while we might still seek to understand its causes, there are few circumstances in which we might give the perpetrator significant sympathy. We must also take great care not to 'blame the victim' in cases of domestic violence; victims are usually prevented from providing optimal care for their children by perpetrators, and it is the perpetrators who should carry the responsibility for this failure in every case.

Consequential abuse is not a less serious form of child maltreatment; as we shall see, the consequences for children are just as serious as those arising from any other form of abuse. It is simply a way of categorising children's experiences, usually of emotional maltreatment or neglect, and (probably to a significantly lesser extent) physical or sexual abuse, which accepts that in some cases there is less direct culpability. Using this categorisation is not to suggest that children's experiences of unintended maltreatment are any less tolerable or any less damaging than where perpetration is deliberate.

Many people who perpetrate domestic violence are problematic users of alcohol or drugs; some 80 per cent of intimate partner violence cases are alcohol related (Cleaver *et al.* 2011: 56). Many victims of domestic violence, unsurprisingly, experience mental health problems, or use alcohol or drugs to help them to cope. Some people with mental health problems are also concurrent problematic substance misusers. Children can and do endure different forms of abuse both simultaneously and sequentially; consequential abuse is no

TABLE 5.1 Associations with consequential abuse

Issues underpinning consequential abuse:	The behaviour of adults who are deliberately causing harm to other adults but in which harm caused to children is a collateral issue	The behaviour of adults who are preoccupied with meeting their own needs and so the needs of their children are secondary and are unmet	The behaviour of adults who by reason of their own illness are prevented from providing their children with the care that they need	The behaviour of adults who are prevented by their own characteristics from providing their children with the care that they need
Typically associated with:	Caregivers who perpetrate domestic abuse	Caregivers who have problematic substance abuse issues	Caregivers who have mental health problems	Caregivers who have learning disabilities

High ← Intent and perceived level of responsibility → Low

different and can be present in any combination. While different forms of consequential abuse are, for clarity, written about in later parts of this chapter as though they are discrete and stand-alone, the existence of one should never be interpreted as precluding the existence of others.

The toxic trio

Parental mental health problems, substance misuse and domestic violence have collectively become known by the chilling epithet 'the toxic trio' because they feature so commonly in families where child abuse takes place. The number of children in the United Kingdom who are affected by these issues is frighteningly high, and the consequences for these children can be significant in both the short and the long term. A small number of children suffer the ultimate impact; in their study of serious case reviews (carried out when children are seriously abused or killed), Brandon and colleagues found that from 129 cases studied, some 86 per cent of the children lived in an environment where one or more of these factors was present, and for 30 children (22 per cent) all three factors coexisted (2012: 39). They point out that in only 20 of the 139 cases was there no evidence of at least one of these issues. While child fatalities are relatively rare, the number of children adversely affected is significant; many of these children will be those in contact with practitioners in the early years.

The existence of parental mental illness, parental substance misuse and domestic violence, singly or in combination, is not automatically predictive of poorer outcomes for children, but there are many ways in which these factors can have both short- and long-term impacts. These impacts are cumulative; the greater the number and severity of the adversity, the more likely it is that the child will suffer harm – the more the child's experience is likely to be *toxic*.

Families where there are issues of parental mental illness, parental substance misuse and domestic violence are often disorganised and are sometimes chaotic. Sometimes daily patterns of activity are sacrificed to the need for sleep or are disrupted because of the impact of drugs, so mealtimes can be inconsistent, bedtime routines absent and getting a baby or young child to an early years setting simply too much of a challenge. A mother who is trying to conceal her injuries, or whose self-esteem has been crushed, may not feel able to socialise, visit extended family members or take her toddler to the local playground. Similarly, routine screening appointments may be missed. The presence of groups of unpredictable adults involved in substance misuse, or dealers who are threatening or violent, or even police raids, can be extremely frightening for young children.

Caregivers who are preoccupied with their own needs may not be physically or emotionally available for their children. This can lead to a lack of stimulation, which may crucially affect language development, for example, or simply can result in caregivers being generally less attentive to their child. Thus, changing a nappy or preparing a feed might be delayed, or unsupervised toddlers might be exposed to the dangers of drug paraphernalia such as syringes, or even hazardous substances such as methadone, a tiny amount of which can be fatal (Alotaibi *et al.* 2012).

Non-availability of caregivers can cause physiological disturbance for the young child (Ward *et al.* 2012; Howe 2011). For example, when an infant has a need for comfort, or food, or warmth, or whatever, the main alert system in order to have that need met is to cry. If the need is met, and homeostasis (the state of equilibrium) is re-established, then not only will the child stop crying but they will receive a range of powerful messages such as that they are important, that their needs will be met in future, that they are worthy and deserving, and that they can rely on the caregiver. Endorphins, those hormones that generate feelings of well-being and pleasure, are released, and the baby settles until their next need is felt. Attachment theorists refer to this process as the arousal–relaxation cycle.

If the baby's need is not met, however, the baby's sense of helplessness will activate a stress response, one of the features of which is that the adrenal gland produces more cortisol, the purpose of which is to generate extra energy and to divert the body's resources into 'survival mode'. When this happens, any non-crucial activity, such as the desire to learn about the world, is involuntarily suspended. Frequent unrelieved stress will flood the brain with cortisol and, as Ward and colleagues point out, will eventually lower the baby's threshold for arousal (2012: 19). This can lead to the baby's nervous system becoming hypersensitive, and thus aroused by even low doses of stress. Ward and colleagues explain that this overreactive response to stress can start even in the pre-natal period, citing research which suggests that it can develop in unborn babies whose mothers are abusing alcohol (ibid.: 19). In the longer term, prolonged exposure to cortisol can damage cells in the hippocampus, the part of the brain that manages memory and learning, with possible implications for cognitive development. Thus, there are biological and experiential factors coming together to result in physiological changes to the structure of the brain, having a direct impact on the child's development.

Key points: the toxic trio

- Parental mental illness, parental substance misuse and domestic violence are known to affect millions of children in the United Kingdom.
- These factors can be found singly or in combination. Researchers studying families where children die or are seriously injured found that at least one of these factors was present in 80 per cent of cases.
- Parental mental illness, parental substance misuse and domestic violence can lead to physical and emotional unavailability, both of which can have significant consequences for the child in their early years.
- Stress, even before birth, can trigger physiological responses that can cause permanent damage to the way the brain works.

Parental mental illness

Falkov *et al.* (1998) emphasise the point that parental mental illness does not inevitably affect outcomes for children; estimates vary, but it is suggested that between one-third and two-thirds of children in this situation suffer few negative consequences. Cooklin makes the point forcefully: 'The majority of parents with mental illness do not abuse their children (and the majority of those who abuse children are not mentally ill)' (2004: online). However, we know that some children are adversely affected by parental mental illness (particularly in the longer term) and we need to acknowledge that a small number of children will suffer very serious consequences; Brandon and colleagues noted that in their study of serious case reviews mentioned above, the mental ill health of one or both parents was identified in nearly 60 per cent of the families (2012: 36).

Practitioners working with children in their early years will be familiar with the concept of the 'baby blues', which are extremely common, affecting over half of mothers but tending to last only a few days. Post-natal depression affects somewhere between 8 per cent and 15 per cent of mothers (Halliwell *et al.* 2007: 11), and is more serious in that it can be longer-lasting and is sometimes resistant to treatment. The Royal College of Psychiatrists (2013a: online) reminds us that it is very rare for women with post-natal depression to deliberately harm their babies. Puerperal psychosis is at the extreme end of this spectrum and is classified as a severe mental illness, although fortunately it affects only about one or two mothers in every thousand (Halliwell *et al.* 2007: 18). Mixed anxiety and depression is common in the general UK population; the Mental Health Foundation estimates that some 9 per cent of us meet the criteria for this diagnosis at any one time. Other common mental health problems include anxiety, seasonal affective disorder (SAD), obsessive compulsive disorder (OCD), phobias and post-traumatic stress disorder, and some 2–3 per cent of women will experience an eating disorder in any year (ibid.: 9–16). Practitioners therefore will be sure to come into contact with people in this category.

Severe mental illness includes psychotic conditions such as schizophrenia and bipolar disorder. The first onset of these illnesses tends to occur quite young, typically in early adulthood, and around one in every 200 adults experience a 'probable psychotic disorder' in the course of a year. The fact that it comes in early adulthood means that there is more potential for these people to be parents of children in their early years. Even these severe mental illnesses are often responsive to treatment, and only 10–15 per cent of people who suffer from schizophrenia will experience severe long-term difficulties (Halliwell *et al.* 2007: 17–18).

Stanley and Cox (2009) suggest that there are some 450,000 parents who have mental health problems, and the Royal College of Psychiatrists (2013b: online) suggests that 68 per cent of women and 57 per cent of men with a mental illness are parents. The differential impacts on children of the mental ill health of the mother and the mental ill health of the father do not appear to be well studied at the moment and are unclear; most research seems to focus on mothers – but for children, of course, this is only half the picture.

Between a third and two-thirds of children whose parents have mental health problems will subsequently develop problems, either in childhood or in adult life. Children of depressed parents have a 50 per cent risk of developing depression themselves before the age of 20 (Diggins 2011: 8), and recent guidance to professionals on responding to safeguarding concerns states that '[o]verall children with mothers who have mental ill health are five times more likely to have mental health problems themselves' (HM Government 2010a: 266). This brings us back to the heredity/environment debate: mental illness is not simply inherited, and once again we are seeing the complex interaction of biological and environmental factors. Many parents who experience mental ill health live in areas of high deprivation and experience multiple disadvantages. Living with any combination of chronic unemployment and poverty, poor housing, social isolation, poor diet, limited resources devoted to leisure or self-advancement, racism, or being the victim of crime would pose a challenge for the most stable of parents. It could possibly be these factors, which are, of course, experienced by children as well as parents, that contribute to or compound the mental health problems of children.

Signs of mental illness in children will rarely be observed in the early years setting. However, Cleaver et al. report that depressed parents can be 'irritable and angry with children, and depressed mothers are less likely to be emotionally available and affectionate' (2011: 69). Research that focused on babies who had mothers suffering from depression found they had 'higher rates of insecure attachment … and showed more emotional and behavioural disturbances than infants of well mothers' (ibid.: 113). The previous chapter outlined some of the issues that can arise as a result of attachment difficulties. Phobias can also be a source of concern for children in the early years; for example, the mother who is agoraphobic is unlikely to be comfortable bringing her child to the setting, and phobic behaviour in relation to any aspect of the child's care can be puzzling for practitioners and children alike.

Although most people with a mental illness are treated within the community, practitioners may occasionally find themselves caring for a child whose parent faces hospital admissions because of their condition. As with any other parent who is admitted to hospital, this will require sensitive handling; young children are puzzled and sometimes very anxious about parental absences, especially if they are unplanned. Hospitals can be frightening places for young children, and young children sometimes associate hospital admission with death, making it even more important that they receive explanations appropriate to their understanding, and continued reassurance.

Practitioners can take some comfort from the fact that as the seriousness of the significant harm to children of parents with mental health problems increases, the number of children affected decreases, and are reminded that '[t]he majority of parents with a history of mental ill health present no risk to their children' (HM Government 2010a: 267).

Parental substance misuse

Munro reports that more than 210,000 adults in the United Kingdom are under treatment for drug dependency, and at any one time about a third of these are parents. She adds that some 2.6 million children live with hazardous drinkers, and 705,000 children live with a dependent drinker (2011b: 27). A significant proportion of these children will be in their early years. Cleaver *et al.* (2011) report that some 3,500 babies are born each year to parents who are problematic users of heroin. Parental substance misuse is a significant problem for children, and because of their increased vulnerability, younger children are at significant risk of poor outcomes when those providing their care are involved in problematic substance misuse.

As was discussed in Chapter 4, babies can be affected by parental substance misuse before they are born. Low birth weight and prematurity are associated with most forms of substance abuse (including the smoking of tobacco), although there are specific problems associated with specific substances. Alcohol misuse during pregnancy can lead to foetal alcohol spectrum disorders or damage to the central nervous system, as well as increased risk of sudden infant death. Ingesting opiates such as heroin can lead to neo-natal abstinence syndrome, a particularly unpleasant experience for young babies, the long-term effects of which have yet to be confirmed. Ali and colleagues (2012) have reviewed international data concerning sudden infant death syndrome (SIDS) and they suggest that '[i]nfants born to opiate-abusing mothers have been shown to be five to ten times more likely to be at risk of SIDS than the general population'. Thus, consequential abuse can be not merely serious but fatal.

Once children are born, they enter a period when they are perhaps at their most vulnerable. Cleaver *et al.* (2011: 79) report research suggesting that the newborns of drug-dependent parents are known to be especially at risk of being neglected, and mothers who are focused on their own needs (at a 'tipping-point' time of major stress and major change) are inevitably going to be less responsive to their baby. This lack of responsiveness can manifest itself in a number of ways, ranging from simple inattentiveness to the baby's needs to, at the other extreme, giving drugs or alcohol to the baby to encourage him or her to sleep. In a small number of cases, parents have attempted to soothe their child with methadone, with fatal consequences (Morris 2010: online).

As children become mobile, they obviously need a high level of supervision. Caregivers who are problematic substance misusers may be difficult to rouse when their child wakes, may be preoccupied or may be in a state of intoxification sufficient for them not to recognise or respond to the child's needs. In these circumstances, children can be left to fend for themselves, or may be left in a cot or buggy so that they do not disturb their caregivers or disrupt their activities. Children may be left unattended while caregivers go out to seek drugs, or flee a violent dealer, or they may be left with carers who are intoxicated or otherwise unable to respond to the child's needs. Inevitably, accidents will happen, although there is a likelihood that caregivers, recognising that their actions were at least in part responsible for any injuries the child suffers, will be reluctant to seek medical attention in case their circumstances are brought to light. Communication with children may be inconsistent and based on the parent's physical and mental state rather than the needs of the child. It is not difficult to see the negative developmental consequences in such a scenario. Emotionally, the children of problematic substance misusers are potentially more likely to suffer difficulties associated with attachment. The bonding process can be damaged by substance misuse; Cleaver and colleagues cite research in this area from 2003 by Kroll and Taylor, who they say question the ability of parents to make attachments to their children when 'the principal attachment is to a substance' (2011: 54).

While much of this behaviour may not be observable within the early years setting, missed attendances, late arrivals, children arriving without having had food, children experiencing low levels of physical care – any of these can indicate problematic substance misuse. Additionally, resources that should benefit the child are sometimes obviously diverted, to be spent on a costly drug or alcohol habit, and the condition of the child's clothing or other personal possessions can reflect this.

As they grow older and become more able to communicate, children as young as 3 or 4 years may well be confident in describing drug paraphernalia and its uses, may describe the state in which they have observed their caregivers, and may be puzzled or frightened by their caregivers' unpredictability and inconsistency. They may reveal how they sometimes take on inappropriate levels of independence, for example making tea for a drowsy parent, or helping themselves to food when there is no sober adult to provide it, although sometimes children are put under great pressure not to reveal parental substance misuse. In some families the young child's knowledge of and peripheral involvement in substance misuse, perhaps by bringing alcohol from the fridge or even rolling a joint, is regarded as cute and is a source of humour.

Finally, practitioners working with children in their early years need to be sensitive to the state of adults who collect children from their setting. Being drunk in charge of a child under the age of 7 is a criminal offence under section 2(1) of the Licensing Act 1902, and any attempt to remove a child by an intoxicated caregiver should automatically be referred to the police with some urgency, as should the caregiver who insists on driving while under the influence of alcohol or drugs.

Domestic violence

Cleaver *et al.* (2011: 44) report the horrific Home Office (2002) statistic that in England and Wales two women are killed every week by a male partner or former partner, and the ONS (2013) confirms that in 2011/2012, around three-fifths (59 per cent) of female homicide victims aged 16 or over had been killed by their partner, ex-partner or lover (88 offences). Women's Aid (2009: online) suggests that there are 13 million incidents of violence or threats of violence every year in the United Kingdom, and that on average the police will receive one call about domestic violence every minute. HM Government (2010a) warns that some 200,000 children in England live in households where there is a known risk of domestic or other violence, and it is safe to infer that many of these will be children in their early years. The Royal College of Psychiatrists (2012: online) notes that where there is domestic violence, children witness about three-quarters of the abusive inci- dents. Its report goes on to say that about half the children in such families have themselves been badly hit or beaten, and it highlights that sexual and emotional abuse are also more likely to happen in these families. In their study of serious case reviews, Brandon and colleagues found that there was evidence of domestic violence in two-thirds of cases where children were killed or seriously injured (2011: 36). It is right that we should be concerned about domestic violence.

Domestic violence (sometimes referred to as domestic abuse, to emphasise the manipulation and emotional abuse that may not traditionally be regarded as violent) is not confined to any specific social group or class; neither is it confined by gender, although there is no question that the vast majority of victims are women. Where there is domestic violence there is an increased likelihood of alcohol and/or drug abuse and mental ill health, along with many of the social adversities mentioned earlier in this chapter.

Domestic violence often starts or increases during pregnancy, and some 40–60 per cent of pregnant women exposed to domestic violence will experi- ence punches or kicks to the abdomen; apart from the obvious physical dan- gers, there is the associated issue of damage caused by maternal stress. Once the child is born, there is a risk that they will become the victim of physical abuse; there have been cases of women being assaulted when holding or feed- ing the baby. However, even in those cases where babies and young children are not hurt physically, they can experience poor care. This poor care may result from the mother having to prioritise her partner's needs and wishes at the expense of the baby, or may simply be an outcome of the psychological and emotional effects of victimhood, potentially affecting the mother's capa- city to meet her child's needs. Lack of confidence, low self-esteem, depression, feelings of degradation, isolation, sleep problems and the increased use of alcohol or even prescribed medications can hardly be regarded as the optimal backdrop to caring for a child.

Domestic violence can also undermine the attachment process, resulting in the baby's being difficult to comfort and experiencing sleep disturbance, irritability and anxiety (Cleaver *et al.* 2011: 113). These can all be signs that the baby feels unsafe and insecure, and may by their nature exacerbate the problems of parenting a baby in already difficult circumstances. As the child grows, the threat to their development is compounded. Even young children can try to step in to protect their mother from physical harm, and children can witness or even be encouraged to take part in their mother's humiliation. Mothers in one study cited by Cleaver and colleagues described being sexually assaulted in front of their children, and 10 per cent of the mothers in that particular study reported having been raped with their children present (2011: 72). One can barely imagine the harm that such experiences might cause to a young child; externalising signs may include excessive irritability, regression in relation to language development or toilet training, sleep disturbance, or the fear of being left alone. Children as young as 3 who are brought up with the experience of domestic violence are more prone than their peers to be aggressive and angry, and may by this age be displaying difficult behaviours and be harder to manage. Within the early years setting they may also act more aggressively towards other children, having been socialised into the notion that conflict can be resolved by violence and mirroring what they have seen at home.

A reminder of my earlier word of warning is merited here. When we have concerns about a child who is living in a household where there is domestic violence, we must take great care not to focus on maternal deficits and thereby blame the victim; the responsibility for domestic violence always lies with the perpetrator.

Key points: parental mental illness, parental substance misuse and domestic violence

- Most people who have mental health problems do not directly harm their children, and most people who harm children do not have mental health problems. Post-natal depression is potentially the condition most likely to affect families with children in their early years. Most mothers who experience post-natal depression do not harm their babies physically, although in more severe cases there can be an impact on attachment.
- Most mental illnesses are of short duration and most people who suffer from mental health problems recover well.
- Environmental, perhaps rather more than biological, predeterminants may influence the onset or seriousness of mental ill health.
- Having a parent go into hospital, especially on an unplanned basis, can be extremely distressing for a young child.
- Some 2.6 million children live with hazardous drinkers, and 705,000 children live with a dependent drinker. A significant proportion of these children will be in their early years.

- Research makes us question the ability of parents to make attachments to their children when 'the principal attachment is to a substance'.
- Missed attendances, late arrivals, children arriving without having had food and children experiencing low levels of physical care can all be indicative of parental substance misuse.
- Young children who can describe drug paraphernalia or adult behaviours associated with intoxification should always be treated as a cause for concern.
- Children should never be allowed to leave the setting in the care of anyone who is drunk or under the influence of drugs.
- Around 200,000 children in England live in households where there is a known risk of domestic or other violence, and many of these will be children in their early years.
- Domestic violence causes physical and emotional harm to children. Neglect can occur when carers are preoccupied or forced to prioritise their violent partner's needs.
- Young children will act out what they see and experience; aggression and anger displayed in the setting may reflect what is happening in the home.

Parental learning disability

While learning disabilities are not the main focus of this chapter, our study would be incomplete without a recognition that parents who have a learning disability are a small proportion of all parents, though they feature heavily in studies of child maltreatment. Between 40 per cent and 60 per cent of parents with a learning disability have their children taken into care as a result of court proceedings arising from concerns about their care (Cleaver et al. 2011: 35). Whilst emphasising that there is no correlation between learning disability and the deliberate abuse of children, Cleaver et al. point out that there is unfortunately an increased vulnerability to many of the factors that lie beneath much child maltreatment, such as poverty, inadequate housing, marital disharmony and violence, poor mental health, childhood abuse, substance misuse and a lack of social supports. Mothers with a learning disability are especially vulnerable to predatory men; in fact, most physical and sexual abuse of the children of learning-disabled mothers is committed by male partners who have no learning disability (Cleaver et al. 2011: 36). This, rather shockingly, suggests that there are men who will form exploitative relationships with learning-disabled mothers simply in order to create opportunities to abuse their children.

Parents with learning disabilities can face increased difficulties in providing their children with the optimal levels of stimulation to promote development. Parental illiteracy may mean that books and stories are not considered important, and parents may not be able to remember nursery rhymes or children's songs, or understand their child's need for play and stimulation. Much of the maltreatment that occurs in such situations is associated with unintended neglect; a lack of routines, or the inability to focus on more than one thing at a time (such as the distraction of a partner, or even the television) can prevent the focus being on the child's needs, leaving the child ignored or forgotten about. Even though only 15 per cent of children who are born to parents with a learning disability will be similarly affected (Cleaver *et al.* 2011: 127), these children may soon fall behind their peers, and indeed on an intellectual level may eventually overtake their parents. When these children cross the threshold of needing a protection plan, the category of concern identified at the Initial Child Protection Conference is invariably neglect.

That is not to say that people with a learning disability cannot be parents; although it is impossible to be specific, there may be large numbers of parents, with varying degrees of learning disability, who successfully bring up their children. Ward *et al.* (2012: 59) advise us that '[a]dults with learning disabilities can successfully parent children, but they will need extensive encouragement, training and long-term support to acquire the necessary skills to do so'. Sadly, Ward and colleagues go on to point out that such support may not be available, particularly on a long-term basis.

Children who are disabled

There has been little empirical research within the United Kingdom into the vulnerability of children who are disabled, although the well-known research by Sullivan and Knutson in 1994 and 1995 in the United States is often considered to apply to the United Kingdom. Their findings, covering 50,000 children in Nebraska, revealed a prevalence rate for abuse at 9 per cent, although among those children identified as disabled the rate was 31 per cent (Sullivan and Knutson 2000). This is the source of the much-cited figure that children who are disabled are 3.4 times more likely to experience abuse than non-disabled children (Stalker *et al.* 2010). Government guidance certainly recognises the increased inherent vulnerability of children who are disabled (HM Government 2010a: 202). There is no reason to suppose that the increased vulnerability of disabled children will not be applicable in the case of consequential abuse. Likewise, in the absence of any clear age or developmental point at which children who are disabled start to face increased risk of maltreatment, we must assume that this is as likely to occur in the early years as at any other time.

Bringing up a child with a disability, though certainly not without its rewards, can be taxing for any parent. Poverty among families where childhood disability exists is rife, and the likelihood of having a child with a disability is higher in areas of higher deprivation. Having a child with a disability can also bring marital stress, social isolation and problems in accessing child care and leisure opportunities, thus compounding parenting difficulties and increasing the stresses under which the family must function. It would not be in the least surprising to find increased levels of mental ill health, especially depression, in families where there is a child with a disability. The potential for domestic violence and substance misuse in these situations should also not be ignored. However, in relation to children with a disability, consequential abuse may also take other forms.

If caring for a young child is challenging, caring for a young child with a disability can be even more so. When there are brothers and sisters, the establishment of household routines that meet the needs of all the children equally can be especially difficult. Consequential abuse in such a case might involve the young child being left in their buggy longer than is comfortable because parents are preparing or serving a meal for the other children, or the child being over-medicated (or under-medicated) in order to manage their behaviour. It might involve inattention to the child's need for physiotherapy, or being too overwhelmed to keep the other (often numerous) appointments that the family of a disabled child is likely to face. Empathy with and concern for the parents of a disabled child must never blind professionals to the small proportion of cases where the disabled child's needs are not being met or where the care that they are receiving is being compromised.

Key points: parental learning disability and children who are disabled

- Much of the maltreatment that occurs when parents have a learning disability is associated with unintended neglect: a lack of routines, or the inability to focus on more than one thing at a time can leave the child ignored or forgotten about.

- Parental illiteracy may mean that books and stories are not considered important, and parents may not be able to remember nursery rhymes or children's songs, or understand their child's need for play and stimulation.

- Children of single-parent mothers who have a learning disability are particularly vulnerable to the threat from predatory men.

- Many parents with learning disabilities bring up their children in an appropriate fashion.

- Children who are disabled are more than three times more likely to experience abuse than are non-disabled children, so staff in the early years setting need to be three times more vigilant in ensuring that they are safe.

- The difficulties associated with bringing up a child with a disability can be compounded by a whole range of other social adversities.

- Empathy and concern for parents must never blind professionals to concerns about the care of a disabled child.

Improving outcomes: building resilience

Children who experience abuse, in whatever form it takes, will experience it in different ways according to their age, developmental stage, temperament and previous experiences; each child's experience of abuse is unique to that child. However, we know that there are some factors which can reduce the impact of abuse or, as Daniel and colleagues suggest, 'buffer children from the effects of adversity' (2010: 16). An early years setting will hopefully be one of these protective factors; among other things, it can offer the child a safe, stable and positive environment in which to experience the world, and can offer relationships with interested and caring adults who will encourage and support the child.

Resilience is the ability to 'bounce back' from adversity. Being resilient does not protect children, but helps them to overcome the impact of the adversities or maltreatment that they suffer. Daniel *et al.* (2010: 66) describe some of the characteristics of the resilient infant or toddler, including being affectionate, good-natured, responsive and easy to deal with. They will have experienced secure attachment, will present as self-confident and independent, and will be advanced in their communication, mobility skills and social play. They go on to describe resilient pre-schoolers as having well-developed communication and problem-solving skills and being sociable but independent (ibid.: 67). The lesson for the practitioner in the early years is simple: the more we can do to help children to enhance these areas and thus enhance their resilience, the more they are likely to overcome the difficulties associated with their experience of maltreatment.

Conclusion

It may be something of a cliché that children learn what they live, and it is probably an oversimplification. However, there is no doubt that children are shaped both by the factors that they inherit from their parents and by the environment in which they are raised. There may be biological predispositions which might mean that we are more likely to grow up in a certain way, but these will be tempered and moderated by our experiences. For example, a child may be genetically predisposed to be tall, but their height will be influenced by diet. In the same way, children's experiences of adversities such as parental mental illness, parental substance misuse and domestic violence, along with any negative experiences resulting from parental learning disability, will shape their future. Consequential abuse – abuse that is not the result of intended harm but is nevertheless a consequence of an adult's behaviour – will have consequences for children in their early years and beyond. Practitioners who work with these children are ideally placed to recognise and respond to all forms of maltreatment and to help children to develop resilience and overcome the damaging impacts of their experiences.

The response to consequential abuse should be the same as that set out in the previous chapter, and Chapter 3 provides insight into the need for inclusive and critical practice with parents and carers. Moreover, as you now progress to Part 2 of the book there is much more information on aspects of approaches that will help deal with consequential abuse. In the next chapter the themes of socialisation and development highlighted here are built upon in examining the Early Years Foundation Stage requirements and recognising the unique and social child. Health and emotional wellbeing are among the topics covered in Chapter 7, and in Chapter 9 the basis of effective communication in difficult circumstances is explored. Importantly, the final chapter reminds us of the importance of reflection and supervision and the availability of advice and guidance from the Child Protection Lead.

Further reading

Cleaver, H., Unell, I. and Aldgate, J. (2011) *Children's Needs – Parenting Capacity*, 2nd edn, London: TSO.

This second edition of *Children's Needs – Parenting Capacity* provides an update on the impact on children's welfare of parental problems such as substance misuse, domestic violence, learning disability and mental illness. Research has continued to emphasise the importance of understanding and acting on concerns about children's safety and welfare when they are living in households where these types of parental problems are present.

Ward, H., Brown, R. and Westlake, D. (2012) *Safeguarding Babies and Very Young Children*, London: Jessica Kingsley.

This book explores key issues surrounding the safeguarding process. These include how the decision whether to remove children from their families is made and the impact on children's life pathways. The findings of the study show a close link between decisions, maltreatment and children's developmental problems.

Everyday practice dilemmas and experiences

6

Safeguarding within the Early Years Foundation Stage

Julie Percival

A secure, safe and happy childhood is important in its own right.

(DfE 2012b: 2)

Children learn best when they are healthy, safe and secure, when their individual needs are met, and when they have positive relationships with the adults caring for them.

(DfE 2012b: 13)

Introduction

In deciding how we work with the very youngest in society, it is important to recognise that the Early Years Foundation Stage (EYFS) framework (DfE 2012b) places responsibilities on *all* practitioners. The care offered should be respectful of each child's unique background and being. The practice choices made by each practitioner should enable children to become resilient, confident, strong and independent. This chapter considers how practitioners can interpret the EYFS so that they can support children to learn about themselves and their world.

By the end of this chapter you should be able to:

- appreciate that safeguarding relies on each practitioner's sense of personal, professional responsibility for the holistic care of children;
- take into account theories that see children as co-constructors in learning when choosing how to implement the EYFS (across all three sections);
- identify key aspects of early years practice that contribute to safeguarding children as part of everyday practice.

When children feel our unconditional acceptance, they develop increasing self-awareness and self-confidence, manage their feelings and behaviour, and build positive relationships as they grow. Safeguarding is each practitioner's daily responsibility. Such work is complex and often unrecognised because it easily corresponds with the statements that make up the 'ages and stages' development grids such as 'Look, Listen, and Note' (DCSF 2008b) and 'Development Matters' (Early Education 2012). However, it is an obligation of each practitioner to safeguard the children in their care. Indeed, the EYFS gives practitioners space to nurture children so that the latter can recognise their emotions, communicate their needs and interests, support their peers and reject unsettling and unwanted behaviour in many circumstances.

Daily practice in early years settings is part of universal safeguarding provision (DCSF 2008c). This vital caring work can help children to feel secure and valued, feel good about themselves, relate well to others, build friendships and explore and learn confidently (DCSF 2008b). It is not, however, a defence against those who are determined to exert their power and control over babies and young children. Consequently, daily practice must begin with relationships – between children, parents or carers and practitioners – and include vigilance concerning risk factors such as poor health, poverty and poor housing, discrimination, the mental health and wellbeing of parents or carers and the quality of care given to a child by both parents or carers *and* practitioners.

Practitioners are obliged to implement the EYFS (DfE 2012b), in line with *Supporting Families in the Foundation Years* (DfE and DH 2011). The case for reduced paperwork and flexibility for practitioners (Tickell 2011) masks the need for practitioners to research effective practice, look deeply at their approaches and actively choose how to implement policy. Consequently, within the professional space that complies with the policy requirements, we must also emphasise the relationships needed to safeguard children and promote their development and learning. A brief overview of the EYFS illustrates how principles and theoretical knowledge provide a rationale for practice that moves beyond checking that the safeguarding policy is in place and dealing with issues as they arise.

The EYFS requirements

The EYFS provides a framework for practice (interpreted in Figure 6.1) that identifies principles, aspects of learning, statutory rules and regulations. It is possible to work through the requirements, have appropriate policies in place, promote training, enable the implementation of new working practices such as the Progress Check at Age Two and the Early Years Foundation Stage eProfile (EYFSeP) (DfE 2012b), and identify co-ordinators for various roles, all of which leads to achievement of a 'good' Office for Standards in Education (Ofsted) inspection judgement, thus validating the setting's suitability to care for children. And yet, performativity (Osgood 2006) may dominate practice, children's needs may go unrecognised and the essence of safeguarding children never truly becomes part of the ethos of the setting because the 'relational core of early childhood practice' is absent or goes unrecognised (Urban 2008). Challenges, dilemmas and fears about the difficult aspects of practice – the inclusion of children with differing needs, pleasing parents as purchasers or 'proxy customers' of services (Lloyd 2012: 4; Penn 2011), managing risk and child protection – go unexplored and unresolved until an issue must be dealt with.

In part, the answer lies in investing time and energy in reflection, looking at the routine reasoning used to make practice choices. Even better is to share thoughts with colleagues and set aside time to get involved in 'possibility thinking' (Cremin *et al.* 2006) with children and adults to challenge everyday assumptions about practice. If children are seen as strong and capable, then it is more likely that this view will be reflected in observations and record keeping. Practitioners are more likely to look for opportunities for children to demonstrate their growing independence in a meaningful ways. Reflection is central to organising the total environment to facilitate children in making a valued contribution to the life of the setting and to give them a sense of mastery. It is important to recognise the pattern of relationships that are

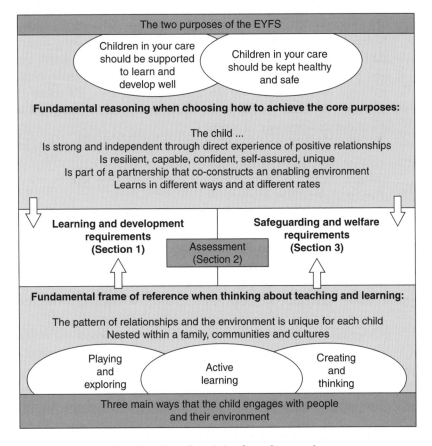

FIGURE 6.1 An overview of the Early Years Foundation Stage framework.

woven around the child. These relationships give meaning to the child's play, exploration, creativity and problem solving. Engaging with these or similar issues helps practitioners to place safeguarding children at the centre of practice within the EYFS framework.

Safeguarding in early years settings

The private, voluntary and independent (PVI) sector accounts for two-thirds of all places (Pugh 2010). Children are entrusted to practitioners so that, first and foremost, they are kept safe. In the following examples three senior practitioners talk about safeguarding and what it means for them:

> Nearly everything about our work is safeguarding because the children are entrusted to us by the parents, so we are safeguarding their child throughout the whole day, we are safeguarding them from the minute they come through the door till they're back in the responsibility of the parents.
>
> (Amrit, senior day care practitioner)

> It should be the umbrella overarching all we do. Thinking about what we do here, it goes into two columns. [In one column we have] our policies and procedures, the building layout, safety of equipment, checking that we work as a team and we share information; then it's about day-to-day hands on with the children, each practitioner and their relationships ... it's about children with a capital C.
>
> (Gail, owner manager, private daycare setting)

> Safeguarding? It's about keeping everybody safe within my care, children, staff, students, parents ...
>
> (Lynden, manager, daycare setting)

Personal responsibility and the complexity of working with young children in day care come to the fore when discussing safeguarding with experienced practitioners. They strive to comply with the EYFS and the *Working Together to Safeguard Children* guidance (HM Government 2013), which acknowledges that

> [S]afeguarding children – the action we take to promote the welfare of children and protect them from harm – is everyone's responsibility. Everyone who comes into contact with children and families has a role to play.

It defines safeguarding as:

- protecting children from maltreatment;
- preventing impairment of children's health or development;

- ensuring that children grow up in circumstances consistent with the provision of safe and effective care; and
- taking action to enable all children to have the best outcomes.

For these practitioners, safeguarding includes practical actions and procedures alongside consideration of the impact the whole day has on the child and the relationships people have with each other. This ethic of care and responsibility is founded on practitioners' beliefs about children and families and their own professional role. The fundamental beliefs that we hold about children and families (the shaded area in Figure 6.1) shapes the way we implement the three central statutory requirements.

The child as a social being

It is important to foreground theories of child development and learning in safeguarding practice. Children need professionals who are able to understand and help them (Munro 2012). We therefore need to think carefully about the theories we bring to mind when trying to understand children and to be careful that our personal, working knowledge and explanations for behaviour are reviewed and challenged. Munro (ibid.) notes that safeguarding work involves uncertainty. It is hard to be sure how and why events happen; a child's life outside the setting can never be fully understood or controlled, but that does not absolve practitioners of responsibility to reflect and be proactive in choosing how to practise. It is necessary to read and discuss new ideas with colleagues, reconsider familiar theories and use the EYFS to be specific about the evidence you have that the fundamental reasons for action and ways of looking at children are in place. While your knowledge and understanding inform the choices you make in implementing the EYFS, framework theories are rarely neutral: they reflect and shape values and beliefs. Make space for thinking about values and beliefs, and this in turn can strengthen your ability to choose how you interpret the EYFS (Morgan 2010).

Development is associated with change and growth over time, an unfolding of genetic information, influenced to some extent by environment (Smith *et al.* 2003). Learning is the provoked acquisition of knowledge and skill (Gray and MacBlain 2012). Provision for learning and development should aim to maximise opportunities for children. We need to question practice and consider the optimal conditions that nurture children. Children develop and learn from birth. Some of this learning is provoked and planned, some is incidental. Learning about relationships and the self often occurs incidentally in the course of daily life.

Sometimes it seems that our view of children and their need to develop is synonymous with their being a minor, incomplete being (Penn 2008). Considering children as contributors to their world from their birth (if not before), as Bronfenbrenner's (1979) ecological model of human development suggests, prompts practitioners to think about how they recognise and respect such contributions. Setting-based routines and activities that constantly deny children's agency – their sense that they can 'make a difference' for themselves and for others (Roberts 2010: 44) – teach and reinforce negative messages about children's capabilities as learners. This applies to formalised curriculum learning and the learning we do to become an accepted and accepting member of society. Children learn how to be safe in society and learn how to keep others safe through daily interaction. Those who matter most, make the most impact on this learning.

The child is nested within social structures such as the family, their nursery, their community (sometimes a complex web of groupings) and wider society. Each setting or site for learning is interconnected through the relationships that grow and shape the lives of those concerned. Practitioners should pay attention to 'the person's growing capacity to discover, sustain and alter [the environment's] properties' (Bronfenbrenner 1979: 9). The child is not just 'done to', as a passive subject; rather, the child, in one way or another, 'does to' those around them and influences their actions too. Practitioner plans and actions contribute to the child's learning and development, while simultaneously the child contributes to the adults' learning and development. Adult and children learn about themselves, the immediate social world and coincidentally about curriculum matters such as the seven areas of learning as outlined in the EYFS. Understanding relationships and their reciprocal nature is central to safeguarding practice.

Case study: Eliot

Consider the mutual and supportive interaction between Meg and Eliot

Meg, a childminder, is unexpectedly visited by a plumber who has recently completed some work for her. She holds Eliot (20 months, her only child that morning) on her hip and attends to the plumber at the door. The conversation does not go well. The previously undertaken work was not completed satisfactorily and Meg has to assert herself to rebook a time for the plumber to return. Voices were not raised; even so, throughout the short but tense conversation Eliot listens intently and from time to time strokes Meg's cheek and presses his arm around her. He waves 'bye' and claps his hands as the door shuts and beams at Meg as they turn back down the hall to the play room. Meg gently tickles Eliot in the tummy. 'You were looking after me!' she smiles and they giggle together.

Reflection on the learning

Eliot watched intently and concentrated deeply. The learning was powerful because the emotions were keenly felt. There was a direct need for the matter to be resolved, so all parties were highly involved. Dealing with the situation became a joint activity. Eliot was given (and experienced at first hand) a clear example of a calm, assertive way to resolve a dispute. He was held safely and so had the confidence to face a difficult situation with Meg. Eliot learned that he could offer support to another person. He realised his own agency.

Meg learned that Eliot can 'read' emotions sensitively and she gained support from knowing a fellow human being empathised with her predicament. The professional and emotional connection with Eliot, along with her under- standing of child development, enabled Meg to be open to a significant moment for them both: she was practising listening (Rinaldi 2006).

They were both rewarded for their close and mutually supportive relation- ship. There was a 'gain' both emotionally and cognitively through their social interaction (Vygotsky 1978). Meg was proud to share the learning with the par- ents at home time and her childminding network co-ordinator.

The connection to safeguarding

Everyday situations are a source of learning about our world. It is important to have the resilience we are born with reinforced throughout our lives. Resilient and confident people, who read social situations effectively, are more likely to be able to assert themselves and cope with life's challenges. This disposition will never protect a child from a determined abuser but will give the child a sense of their own power that they can use to support and nurture others. In the case study, Eliot felt a sense of risk in an essentially safe context. He dealt with his own feelings and was able to practise the mutually rewarding skills of supporting a fellow human being. Eliot is developing a positive disposition to learning about all aspects of life, and if this attention to learning in (social) context is maintained, he will be more likely to enter adulthood successfully.

Looking within the child and finding a social being

Gerhardt (2004) draws on neurological and biochemical research and her experience as a psychotherapist to assert that emotions can no longer be seen as an added complication or hindrance to researching and supporting young children. As emotions are experienced, brain activity can be mapped. The location and nature of chemical changes in the brain have been traced when emotional responses to situations have been made. For Gerhardt there is an internal ecology of biological functioning from which and with which emo- tions are produced. Aroused physiology can be evident through changes in breathing and muscle tension, blood pressure and hormones, and, over time, sleep patterns, eating and excretion. While 'findings from neuroscience that apply directly to the EYFS are still sparse' (Evangelou et al. 2009), the 'dualist model of separate cognitive and affective domains' is being challenged by research that 'suggests these processes are not separate but inextricably entwined' (Manning-Morton 2011: 23).

In settings, there can be a sense that strong emotions are the enemy to order and smooth running of the room and setting as a whole. A familiar tactic is to distract the child and hope the unwanted behaviour disappears. Tantrums and biting, for example, are often explained as developmentally normal behaviours, and a certain level of challenging behaviour is acceptable. Prolonged crying of babies, especially at times of transition, can be rationalised and remain unquestioned. Alternatively, with the correct techniques practitioners should be available to service each child's needs, manage behaviour effectively and ensure children meet the Early Learning Goals (DfE 2012b) as expected. This discourse asserts that if provision is correct, children's unsettling behaviour and powerful emotions should be rare or eliminated. Both ways of experiencing practice put a strain on practitioners, who find that their own needs are not met, possibly leading to their feeling 'angry, resentful and professionally frustrated or failing' (Manning-Morton 2011: 24).

The building of 'mental muscles' (Gerhardt 2004: 44) relies not on maturation (waiting to be older when tantrums disappear and children are more 'ready' to learn) but on the predictability of safe and responsive contact. In the earliest years, positive experiences are based on smell, touch, sounds and the physical rhythms of the person holding you. More positive experiences produce a more richly networked brain, which in turn helps a person organise their experiences, predict what could be happening and process their feelings constructively. From a psychoanalytical perspective, the co-ordination of 'care seeking' and 'care giving' enables a secure attachment relationship between child and carer (Bowlby 1969). Emotional holding or containment (Roberts 2002) seems to be not only a physical comfort but internally a way of settling emotions and biochemical reactions. Learning how to regain a sense of constructive control or emotional regulation is supported when a carer responds to what is actually happening in the moment, processing feelings through joint activity, using close observation of the baby's or young child's behaviour. The body's chemistry sustains this sense of trust, and the careful observer can see that physical signs of powerful, stressful feelings subside.

Distressed, abused, neglected babies have missed the physical and verbal holding that an experienced caregiver can offer. Children in full day care build relationships with a range of people who cannot replace their parents (Dahlberg et al. 1999). However, unconditional regard and metaphorical 'holding' (Roberts 2002) must be provided if children are to be healthy and secure. Emotions inform our thinking: we do not have space to think if, first and foremost, emotional states are not recognised in observation-taking, supported through sensitive 'reflection in action' and response, and, later, 'scrutiny, reinterpretation and development' (Paige-Smith and Craft 2008: 22; Schön 1987) of events to help plan future actions. A chronic, long-term lack of attention to emotions weakens a child's ability to thrive in all aspects of development and learning. Safeguarding children is about building their inner resources to process feelings, to have the confidence to explore, to make decisions, to sometimes manage risk.

Institutionalised practice

The term 'institutionalisation' refers to the way 'people are socialised into the rules, requirements, routines, restrictions and values of the setting' (Beresford *et al.* 2011: 156–157). Group care and daily life must always include routines and systems balanced with unique and noteworthy opportunities for care and learning. Thoughtfully negotiated, such patterns of socialisation can be a source of comfort and security for those concerned. A national research project supported by the Joseph Rowntree Foundation (Beresford *et al.* 2011) captures people's opinions of the social care services they received. For some adults, young people, their families and, indeed, some practitioners, negative, institutionalised practice is current and still impacting on their lives despite studies from the previous century and aspirations for change.

Some features of institutionalised care and learning are set out in Table 6.1 (see over).

Such practices make for uncomfortable reading. In essence, children and staff have reduced decision-making opportunities; they are dependent on practitioners or managers to establish and deliver the routine and are frequently told what and when they may do things. Some readers will be outraged by the contents of Table 6.1. Some will defend such practices as part of the 'real world' of what is practical and possible in the circumstances. Children are more than capable of benefiting from and contributing to 'a flexible web of relationships that focus on shared cultural activities not the needs of solitary individuals' (Rogoff 1990: 97). The very positive benefits of being part of a community must not be turned into a justification for doing *everything* as a group: there is no excuse for practice that works against children's sense of mastery and self-esteem. Children are not units of production. Routines that become negatively institutionalising and dehumanising are not validated by the EYFS and they do not promote children's wellbeing.

When children learn to be dependent and believe that their voice does not count, they become potentially vulnerable. This socialised vulnerability is part of a continuum of safeguarding matters, where those with certain sorts of power are able to exert inappropriate control and harm others. This ranges from small but significant aspects of daily life through to causes for concern and child abuse. Institutionalised practice harms children. Rogoff (1990) argues that the individual and the group are essential to each other, and inseparable. Institutions such as the family or, more formally, the early years setting are spaces for us to find out about ourselves and our world. When people come together to find something out, solve a problem or see some task through to the end and that outcome makes a real difference to feelings and future actions, there is a deep satisfaction for practitioners and children.

TABLE 6.1 Key points: institutionalised practice

Features of institutionalised practice	Examples of observed practice
Standardised routines	• We all have snack together at a set time, interrupting the flow and involvement in other activities; we queue to wash hands; we wait to have everyone seated; we don't start to eat or drink till everyone has something; we sing the 'please and thank you' song; we don't leave the table until everyone has finished; the adults hand out the snack, otherwise there would be mess everywhere; there is no talking across the tables – it can get really noisy; we wipe each child's face and hands before anyone can get down.
Group living – being grouped according to age	• Irrespective of friendships and interests, all matters of personal hygiene and care are carried out en masse. We all sleep at the same time, share all equipment and resources. • Praise and sanctions are given in front of everyone. • Personal matters are discussed with everyone or over the heads of children.
Much of the day is taken up with physical maintenance	• Practitioners are very busy setting out equipment, wiping down, sweeping up, cleaning toilets, doing the laundry, cleaning equipment, preparing snack to a standard procedure; the children do not take part in this.
Categorisation and segregation	• Children from each room rarely meet; they are unsure what goes on in the other rooms in the setting, they are not sure of the names of other children, staff label children using some stereotypes linked to gender and ethnicity, time out is used and those who are regularly segregated are known to all.

Consequently, it is important to look for ways to support children in your care to participate in as many of the necessary routines as possible, and for opportunities to offer choices, problem solving and risk taking. You will learn more about them and they will learn about you. They will inevitably learn things that you can record under the Areas of Learning (DfE 2012b), but the story of your learning together will be far more interesting to read and remember for you, the parents and the child. Mutually rewarding reciprocity safeguards young children.

Play

The EYFS asserts that

> [p]lay is essential for children's development, building their confidence as they learn to explore, to think about problems, and relate to others. Children learn by leading their own play, and by taking part in play which is guided by adults.
>
> (DfE 2012b: 6)

This seems to be a categorical endorsement of play across a continuum of styles: free-flow play where children can be seen to wallow in their thinking and doing (Bruce 2001); and playfully directed sessions using resources selected by practitioners to promote particular learning outcomes. Both styles of play bring their challenges. Free-flow play often seems messy, with a logic or narrative beyond the understanding of the adult observer; it may involve children being isolated, sometimes by choice and sometimes through group dynamics. It can be exhilarating to share and create new meanings, but then deeply distressing in times of discord, aggression and hurt. Through sustained shared exploration and investigation, playful yet instructive sessions can be rewarding for both adult and child (Siraj-Blatchford *et al.* 2002). But how much generosity and confidence is needed for an adult to let go of their learning objectives when children take the learning in a different direction?

Daily safeguarding practice pays attention to the pro-social and antisocial aspects of play because it is important to see how children negotiate and use their abilities to manage their own emotions and read the behaviour of those around them (Canning 2011). It is vital to observe who plays easily and spontaneously and then consider why that might be. Why is it that some children find free-flow play challenging? Theoretical models of development, experience of being together with the child and talking with the family support understanding of the child's wellbeing. To aid your understanding, listen to verbal and non-verbal communication, look for patterns in play behaviour and notice changes in themes, use of equipment and friendship patterns. Plan thoughtfully and children can feel their mind being exercised; complex concepts are explored and new understandings develop.

The role of the key person

The EYFS states that

> [e]ach child must be assigned a key person. Their role is to help ensure that every child's care is tailored to meet their individual needs ... to help the child become familiar with the setting, offer a settled relationship for the child and build a relationship with their parents.
>
> (DfE 2012b: 18)

The key person is seen as the means by which relationship-led practice can provide for children's learning and development. A key person approach can be embedded in systems and procedures to ensure all are aware of their duties. For a busy setting this must be the case, but that system must avoid becoming mechanistic. The practitioner must not simply compile 'Learning Journey' records of children's achievements (Elfer *et al.* 2003). The practitioner will need to carefully, reflectively and emotionally engage with the children and their families. It is vital to find ways to understand children and families (Munro 2012; Whalley and team 2007) and challenging to engage in such emotional labour (Manning-Morton 2006; Colley 2006). It is a further challenge to have enough detachment to be an advocate for the child when child protection issues evolve not only suddenly but over time in complex circumstances. A settled, reflective, more detailed understanding of the child is possible through the key person approach. Under this approach, practitioners are more likely to be able to contribute to multi-professional team meetings with useful and supportive information. Parents are more likely to appreciate that a practitioner has been an advocate for them and their child in the past and during difficult times will be again. Daily safeguarding practice entails:

- learning to manage uncomfortable feelings (if you can do this, you are more likely to tolerate them in the children and be able to support them to manage them);
- being emotionally available;
- being open and reflective so as to notice signals;
- regulating the child's states of being without being controlling;
- keeping on an even keel by identifying feelings and labelling them for future constructive – not destructive – use;
- providing safe risks and the freedom to explore those risks;
- reviewing routines – to check for disempowering ways of working that stop you noticing the impact of words and deeds;
- to listen to children (Rinaldi 2006) and document significant moments in learning.

Through a range of observational techniques and discussion, the key person can collaborate and steer the child's development. The discussion should take into account the child's view of their learning and their environment (Lancaster *et al.* 2010; Clark and Moss 2005) and in turn recognise that view as part of the planning process. Such practice actively plans to make children's rights a reality (United Nations 1989: articles 5 and 12 UNCRC) so that they can fully participate in the life of the setting. Practitioners who are conscious of their power are in a better position to use that power more respectfully for the benefit of all concerned.

Building relationships, however, is more complex. If we are to accept that children shape their world as well as learn from it, we must acknowledge that although adults are physically stronger and often more knowledgeable in most contexts (and therefore appear always to hold the balance of power), babies and children hold the 'trump card' in any relationship. They will refuse to give their attention to some things; or if they do co-operate, they may do so in unexpected ways with unexpected consequences. Most adults will have the understanding to adjust their behaviour and either secure the child's attention or abandon their plans. Mutual readjustment takes place. Power is redistributed and both parties learn about their relationship. This need for adjustment may be resisted or resented by practitioners, leading to a misuse of power. Misuse of power to dominate another person and exercise control is a safeguarding matter. Examples of misuse of power include:

- making children sleep or sit for extended periods of time when they do not want to or need to;
- restricting food and drink, making it conditional on desired behaviour;
- physically moving children when there is no immediate danger;
- repeated labelling of children in semi-affectionate ways that are actually undermining;
- readjusting children's pictures and models so that they look more attractive to the practitioner's eye;
- using reward systems in decontextualised ways – where children cannot remember whether they have been 'good', or are not sure what it is they need to be 'good at', or do not understand the relevance of a particular goal or activity at the centre of the reward system;
- requiring signs of affection not freely given.

Children may resist this kind of practice by quietly avoiding confrontation, sitting quietly and waiting for a time when they can move away and do other things. Young babies may become unsettled and cry for prolonged periods; other children ask questions and distract adults through appropriate and inappropriate behaviours. Sometimes children are provided with an individual plan to correct *their* behaviour. It is important for a key person to reflect on practice, from the child's perspective. As one practitioner reasoned:

I realised I was saying 'no' to quite a few of the children's requests, and when I thought about it, I was only saying it because that made it easier for me and as I was in charge I could choose. When I thought about it, I couldn't see a good reason for saying 'no' and neither could the children … it was my choice almost every time. And yet we ask them to do things and expect them to say yes to us!

Behaviour management

Supporting young children can be a source of frustration for many practitioners. How children behave 'for us' is often seen as an indicator of professional competence. Three paragraphs relating to behaviour management form part of the safeguarding and welfare requirements of the EYFS. Corporal punishment is not permitted. Any physical intervention with children must be recorded and parents and/or carers notified on the same day or as soon as reasonably practicable.

To safeguard children, behaviour management policies and procedures should not be tools for control but tools for supporting children to learn how to:

- promote the good and wellbeing of others;
- recognise that everyone deserves justice, even through difficulties;
- stay as safe as possible;
- exercise autonomy and self-control.

We need to be advocates for children in negotiations with colleagues and parents. We need to use strategies that help us teach considerately so that children are considerate in return. Unmet need and unrecognised feelings may build up and be expressed through violent means, either physically or verbally. Children need to feel able to control aspects of their lives. Promoting and recognising competence feeds self-esteem. This is particularly important for children at risk of neglect and harm, but shields all children from responding negatively to life's occasional setbacks and provides a secure platform for learning and development.

Inappropriate behaviour can be a response to believing that you do not match up to your ideal self. That ideal may have been constructed in part from your own beliefs but also from perceptions you have of how others see you and their expectations of you. A child may wonder, 'Am I a good boy?'

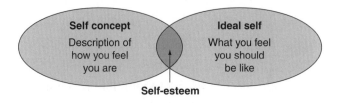

FIGURE 6.2 Sources of self-esteem (adapted from Porter, 2003).

'Can I do what I should be doing?' 'They want me to do this but am I sure I want to?' The kind of uncertainty that undermines the child on a long-term basis is not healthy.

To safeguard self-esteem, analysis of observations should start with consideration of children's intentions and aspirations. 'Interpreting the activity of people without regard to their goals renders the observation meaningless' (Rogoff 1990: 117). Practitioners need to be careful to consider possible interpretations, and deciding to plan time to talk helps develop shared understandings. When choosing possible 'next steps' in learning, consider teaching the skills and concepts that the child values and needs. Consider teaching in its widest sense, so that carefully chosen 'devices' can 'light the fire' and 'fan the flames' of children's learning (Mac Naughton and Williams 2009: x). There are so many ways to inspire children, to help them appreciate the capabilities they do have and yet may not recognise; and there are so many opportunities for children to be increasingly independent in their daily life. Give feedback carefully. Listen and look, then commentate, showing you understand, or appreciate that something has been a challenge. Note how skilful or persistent a child is being. Identify key aspects of their behaviour that are helping them to be successful. Perhaps they are concentrating, planning, checking their own progress, making adaptations as they go (Claxton 2002).

Praise should be carefully considered. It is 'risky' (Porter 2003) because children may realise they only need to think about pleasing the person offering the praise. For self-worth and self-reliance, children need to develop their own interpretation of the standards and rules. They need to develop internal guidelines that will help them be a successful member of the group long after the practitioner has left or the goals have changed. Internal guidelines about group dynamics and ways of being together, negotiated and built together, keep the group strong and mutually rewarding. Children who expect a tangible reward (such as a sticker or food) to follow their actions may feel the absence of a reward as a punishment, even when no punishment was intended. Acknowledgement and feedback that scaffolds further confidence and skills for learning should form part of provision for safeguarding and wellbeing.

Respect for a child's identity and the diversity of life experiences

'The EYFS seeks to provide ... equality of opportunity and anti-discriminatory practice, ensuring that every child is included and supported' (DfE 2012b: 2). The setting must be clear about how its staff address the following:

■ Practice should meet individual needs for all children and make reasonable adjustments for those with a disability or special educational need, ensuring they are included and valued.

- Inclusiveness practices should promote and value diversity and difference. These practices should be reviewed and monitored for their effectiveness.
- Inappropriate practice should be challenged.
- Provision should encourage children to value and respect others.

Collaboration with parents and professionals beyond the setting is also written into the document.

'The rules and habits that bind a society together' allow 'its members to find meaning in their lives' (Baldock 2010: 2). Rules and codes of conduct that seem obvious to some can be a source of ambiguity if not confusion for others. The responsibility for finding and seeking out sources of ambiguity lies with the setting, providing a service to children and families. The starting point for this work is not a series of projects on festivals and enhancements to continuous provision. Time spent with children and parents over days, weeks and months building mutual regard and a shared language should form part of every business plan for day care. This relationship building is as much a part of a practitioner's day as nappy changing, mealtimes, doing the laundry and engaging in sustained shared thinking to promote areas of learning and development.

It is helpful and interesting to learn about common practices that a group might undertake, but limiting if practitioners cannot look beyond this to learn about a person's unique identity – an identity that is constantly evolving as the ecological system of development ebbs and flows.

For Baldock, respectful practice starts with 'intercultural competence' – a kind of sensitivity and understanding that 'does not start with knowledge about the other, but a readiness to look at oneself. *If the other person is different, I am different for the other person*' (2010: 45; emphasis added). Children may spend ten hours a day, five days a week being cared for outside their home. The setting cannot be home, but neither are such children visitors. The setting belongs to them – not just the practitioners and proprietor.

Case study: Noticing Nigel

Consider the risky freedom children were offered through Gilly's carefully planned use of a Forest School area within the grounds of her setting

Noticing Nigel (a puppet, but also star of a video made by Gilly) was introduced to the 3- and 4-year-olds in a first-phase children's centre as a means of inspiring the children to 'lock onto learning' using their 'noticing muscles'. Inspired by the work of Claxton (2002), the key disposition of resilience is promoted through *noticing*: the ability to perceive nuances, patterns and details in experiences. On an expedition to the Forest School area, a teddy was discovered, stuck upside down in a tree with various clues, for example a piece of string tied to his wrist, a necklace with the letter A on it, shorts and T-shirt and a burst balloon with matching string on another tree. A morning of critical thinking ensued, with children 'noticing' aspects of Teddy's surroundings, deciding how he came to be in such a predicament, how he might be helped to safety. Noticing and discussing possibilities informed their discussion. Children gathered sticks, negotiated uneven ground and explored the unfamiliar surroundings; they managed to do this with a high level of independence and without hurting each other; and, importantly, they rescued Teddy. Once rescued, Teddy was taken to more familiar ground, down the hill, nearer the centre building where the children were more confident, so all could join in. The children had noticed and discussed the properties of the sticks and their suitability for reaching and poking Teddy. In the safety of familiar ground, children gave their ideas as to why Teddy was in the tree: to expand on these ideas, the children were encouraged to look more closely at Teddy, and the range of suggestions widened. Gilly was careful not to lead with solutions but to comment and ask open questions. Thinking time was important. Verbal and non-verbal responses we accepted. The children were so intrigued that they were able to consider other questions, such as how long Teddy had been there. There was a strong sense of satisfaction as the children walked back into the centre and this was recognised by Nigel, waiting back in the room with *'Nigel says I did good noticing'* stickers for each child. As each sticker was handed out, Gilly was able to give each child a specific description of something they had done which showed they had used their 'noticing muscles'. They in turn gave her examples of things they had noticed. There was a clear sense of achievement, of a job well done.

Reflection

Children unfamiliar with anything other than the pavement and playground felt safe to venture into the Forest School area. They were given the freedom to take risks, to touch new things, to balance and move on uneven and slippy ground, to wave sticks of different sizes about and use them purposefully to get a job done. The instructional element of 'noticing' did not rely on recall of facts allied to an area of learning, but did directly contribute to the children's 'learning power' – a disposition or capability that helps them notice things about themselves, those around them and their physical environment. The sense of mastery and control over oneself and being a support to others adds to this powerful learning experience. As the children get to know Gilly, they will grow even more confident in trying out ideas without the worry of being wrong or being labelled negatively. On this occasion they were free to comment, to risk offering solutions, to sort Teddy out and make sense of his predicament. Preparation for formal subject-domain learning took place through *playful* exploration that was facilitated by adults yet led by the children. Significant learning to support the safeguarding of the child's wellbeing and self-esteem was also part of the narrative. This too should be written up in the child's Learning Journey and/or assessment records and be celebrated by the children and their carers.

Learning journeys and more formal assessment and planning documents should reflect ongoing intercultural learning and competence. A review of your record keeping for assessment and learning could be guided by the following questions:

- Do all our records look exactly the same irrespective of children's backgrounds?
- Who are the significant people in the child's life?
- How is this network of relationships structured?
- How is the day organised in the home and the setting?
- How do these routines provide for personal needs around sleep, rest, diet, managing personal hygiene and participating in religious observance?
- What are the main rules that govern social interaction, including non-verbal communication?
- How can we communicate most effectively?
- What potential barriers do children and families face in understanding how the setting runs?
- How can you work out a way of relating to each other that enables you all to learn respectfully about the families who entrust their child to your care?

Avoiding learning and worrying about offending someone is never a reason for ignoring the wellbeing of a child (Laming 2003). Each day there is opportunity to increase the store of small understandings. Arrangements should be made for specific times where the key person, children and parents and/or carers consider the culture of the setting and the home and decide on ways of working together.

The characteristics of effective learning and teaching (DfE 2012b: 7) have been determined through a systematic review of children's development (Evangelou *et al.* 2009; Early Education 2012). The way children engage with people and the environment is nested within their unique experiences of their family and community. Planning for learning and development and safeguarding children's welfare starts with an appreciation of how particular children *play and explore* in their first environment, with the people who mean most to them. Their *creativity and critical thinking* are expressed through the culture closest to them. Their sense of who they are is confirmed through their *active participation* in the necessary routines of life, which they in turn will influence and change just through their being.

Conclusion

Practitioners continue to worry about record keeping and performativity in the face of scrutiny from those with authority such as parents, consultants and inspectors. Ofsted inspection regimes have successively held practitioners to account, placing emphasis on certain practices and outcomes, perhaps to the detriment of other ways of working.

For the team at Pen Green, a nationally recognised centre for childcare provision and research, particular attention is paid to the relationships between children, practitioners and parents (Whalley and team 2007). Key principles guide their practice. Again, rephrasing these principles can help practitioners review and evaluate their practice.

In our work together:

- Do individuals learn how to be self-directing?
- Can people exercise control over their own lives?
- Do children, parents and practitioners develop and actively build self-esteem?
- Are children and parents supported to learn through stories about learning in its widest sense – stories based on meaningful experiences?
- Is each person's identity recognised as a dynamic positive contribution to their development, rather than a barrier to learning a prescribed curriculum?
- Is constructive discontent able to move thinking and learning on?
- Do we recognise the power we have to change aspects of ourselves and our environment?
- Do we understand enough about the family to support self-fulfilment?

These principles comply with the EYFS. They appreciate that all people engaged with their services contribute to the community of practice. This expectation steers everyone's learning, whether they are discovering more about children's schemas, their emotional wellbeing or how to recognise and nurture high levels of involvement in children's learning.

Early years settings have responsibility to safeguard children in their care. The greatest resource we have to achieve this is the children themselves. We know this when we research theories of child development. Children for the most part want to be an active part of our world. They care about the significant people in their lives. They show their interest and their feelings in a multitude of ways. We know this when we watch them play and go about daily life. The more we tune into their play and listen to their routines, the more we learn. They thrive when we respect their unique identity and their ability to identify with their significant others, their family, friends and community. Their family and friends are more generous with their understanding of the child when we respect their aspirations and identity. We notice unsettled times and times of danger when we know children and families well and they trust us. The key person approach is one means of facilitating that trust.

The EYFS is a framework to remind us about basic statutory duties. How we bring those duties to life is in many ways a matter of choice. We know this because settings are unique in many, many ways. Practitioners need to value their abilities to reflect and understand how practice nurtures and *harms* children – unless we are careful, it is possible to slip into controlling and institutionalising ways. We safeguard children when we review, monitor and reflect on our impact together. When practice is relationship-led in the ways this chapter has begun to explore, rather than curriculum-domain-led, practitioners have the depth of understanding and confidence to be an advocate for the child. When situations demand it, they tune into indications of risk and notice when harm is being done. The EYFS legitimates this approach to safeguarding children.

Further reading

Roberts, R. (2010) *Wellbeing from Birth*, London: Sage.

This text provides a framework for understanding the complex relationships between affect (how we feel) and cognition (our knowledge and understanding). It is grounded in clearly presented theory and research alongside insightful snapshots of children's experiences. The concept of 'companionable learning' offers practitioners specific approaches to practice that are an excellent anchor for daily safeguarding work in early years settings.

7

Safeguarding children's health and wellbeing

Sharon Frankland

There is overwhelming evidence to suggest that all types of abuse and neglect will potentially have a long-term negative influence on a child's physical, intellectual and emotional wellbeing (Lazenbatt 2010). Accordingly, article 24 of the UN Convention on the Rights of the Child (UNCRC) states that children should have access to the 'highest attainable standard of health and to facilities for the treatment of illness and rehabilitation of health'. Additionally, there is a responsibility for states party to ensure that 'no child is deprived of his or her right of access to such health care services' (United Nations 1989). The centrality of health as a key component of safeguarding is recognised in British law within section 31(9) of the Children Act 1989, which states that 'harm' means ill-treatment or the impairment of health or development, further acknowledging that 'health' means physical or mental health. The requirement for a child to 'be healthy' was also enshrined as one of the five *Every Child Matters* outcomes (DfES 2003a), and is currently being delivered through the 'Healthy Child Programme' (DH 2009a).

In my previous role as a health visitor I was often faced with some very difficult dilemmas around whether professionals should intervene if they consider parents are not fully supporting their children to achieve what they believe to be positive health and wellbeing. The question of whether parents have the right to make their own health and lifestyle choices may pose an ethical dilemma, but as adults they have the right to make their own informed choice. It could be suggested that by adhering to the guidance set out by the Children Act 1989 to respect parental autonomy and responsibility, there may be occasions when we are inadvertently putting children at risk. When the wellbeing of the child is at risk, then the decision becomes a professional judgement, using knowledge of current policy around child protection as well as consideration of the risk of 'significant harm'.

This chapter considers what being healthy is, exploring where responsibility lies in relation to children being supported to be healthy. Discussion then moves to the possible dilemmas that may be encountered, with examples from practice used to demonstrate the importance of considering children's holistic wellbeing, particularly keeping them safe from harm. By the end of this chapter you will:

- be able to outline the differing concepts of what 'being healthy' means;
- understand the role of the practitioner in relation to supporting children to be healthy;
- be aware of some of the current issues and debates around supporting and empowering children and families to be healthy;
- identify a number of dilemmas and their consequences when children are not given the opportunity to achieve optimum health and wellbeing.

What is health?

Prior to the early 1990s, health was largely viewed using the medical model, based on the 1948 definition of health as 'a state of complete physical, mental and social well-being and not merely the absence of disease or infirmity' (WHO 1948). However, this did not take into account that health, like child abuse, is a socially constructed phenomenon, and made little acknowledgement of individual experiences of what being healthy meant (Naidoo and Wills 2009). More recently there has been a greater acceptance of the social model of health, recognising the different perceptions of what individuals believe it is to be healthy, and the many influential factors that can affect this (Dahlgren and Whitehead 2007). This includes a greater awareness of the social and environmental influences on health, which will be explored later in this chapter.

A joint report by the Department of Health and the Department for Schools and Families (2007) claimed that children in Britain today have better health than previous generations, and pledged to continue to support this improvement. This claim was disputed, however, by the findings of an Innocenti report (UNICEF 2007) that placed the United Kingdom bottom for 'subjective well-being' out of all the members of the Organisation for Economic Co-operation and Development (OECD), highlighting many negative issues around children's physical and emotional wellbeing despite the numerous policies introduced over the years focusing on improving children's health.

Social determinants of health

Since the publication of the Beveridge Report in 1942 and subsequent introduction of the welfare state in the United Kingdom, the health and wellbeing of the nation have been largely considered the responsibility of the government of the day. The introduction of the National Health Service (NHS) in 1948 gave British citizens the right to health care that was free at the point of delivery. This has resulted in a radical improvement of the health of the nation, with a reduction in infant mortality and long-term limiting illness and disability resulting from diseases such as poliomyelitis, TB and meningitis. Yet despite these significant improvements, the United Kingdom in relation to the social determinants of health is frequently referred to as 'broken Britain', portrayed by the media as having disproportionately high levels of single-parent households, and high levels of crime, drug misuse and benefit dependency (Barnes *et al.* 2006). There also remain a large number of children who, despite continued policy initiatives, are living below the poverty line. With recent welfare benefit reforms following the enactment of the Welfare Reform Act 2012 and the introduction of the 'Big Society' by the Coalition government, it appears that the locus of accountability is again shifting, devolving greater responsibility to individuals and communities, rather than perpetuating a culture of dependency (Fisher and Gruescu 2011). This shift in responsibility raises questions as to how individuals and communities will adapt and how professionals working in these communities will support and promote new ways of working.

Consideration of approaches to health adopted by previous governments and how these have changed and developed over time help our understanding of contemporary health behaviours. Throughout history the United Kingdom has experienced huge differences between the morbidity (incidence of disease) and mortality (death rate) between the richest and poorest members of society (DHSS 1980b; Acheson 1998; Marmot 2010).

Although this was generally accepted without question within pre-Second World War Britain, the Black Report (DHSS 1980b) heralded a raft of health promotion measures designed to address these differences. Acheson (1998) and latterly the Marmot Review (2010) have reaffirmed the existence of these inequalities, concluding that despite many attempts to address them, little progress has been made.

The inequalities in health highlighted by the above reports have been consistent in their findings: the poorer you are, the worse your health will be. Figures produced for mortality and morbidity show vast variances between the richest and poorest, and can be reduced to geographic location, indicating that those living in communities highlighted as being socially deprived not only have poorer life expectancy but also are disadvantaged in terms of their education, social status and their potential to gain a good job. Government statistics indicate that life expectancy at birth in the United Kingdom between 2008 and 2010 was highest in Kensington and Chelsea and lowest in Glasgow City (ONS 2011); the difference can be linked directly to the levels of poverty and unemployment within these areas. Although life expectancy in both locations had improved, the relative gap had increased from 12.5 to 13.5 years for men and from 10.1 to 11.8 years for women. These worrying statistics suggest that although generally all groups within society are living longer, the most deprived within society are falling further behind, and are not showing the same level of improvements as the least deprived.

In addition to these class- and gender-related inequalities, there are also differences related to ethnicity and culture. Some of these differences can be explained by genetic disposition; for example, the incidence of coronary heart disease and stroke is higher in those of Afro-Caribbean and Asian heritage. However, Nazroo (2003: 277) suggests that 'social and economic inequalities, underpinned by racism, are fundamental causes of ethnic inequalities in health'.

Frank Field's report (2010) into 'why poor young people become poor adults' lays some responsibility at the door of the government of the day, suggesting that it has a responsibility to safeguard and promote the health and wellbeing of these children and families in order for them to break out of trans-generational poverty and disadvantage. There are concerns that the current Coalition government has not fully taken this on board, as it appears to advocate the taking of more personal responsibility, indicating that individuals should be taking more control over their own wellbeing. Previous attempts to alleviate child poverty and to minimise its effects have been notoriously disappointing, and existing concerns around the longer-term impact include poor educational attainment, health inequalities, intergenerational unemployment and decreased overall wellbeing of individuals and families (Parekh *et al.* 2010). The number of children living in low-income households in 2008/2009 was 3.9 million after deducting housing costs, which, although that indicating some progress had been made, was still 0.6 million above the New Labour government's 2004/2005 target (www.poverty.org.uk). Current strategies employed by the government that place pressure on parents to return to work may perpetuate a culture of blame and parental failing and, according to Crossley and Shildrick (2012), may lead to an inevitable increase in child poverty.

Article 24 of the UNCRC (United Nations 1989) provides that it is 'the right of the child to the enjoyment of the highest attainable standard of health', which necessarily includes access to good-quality health care, nutritious food and the best information to help them stay healthy. The *Ottawa Charter for Health Promotion* (1986: online) states: 'To reach a state of complete physical mental and social well-being, an individual or group must be able to identify and to realize aspirations, to satisfy needs, and to change or cope with the environment.' This gives rise to the question of who is responsible for ensuring children that achieve positive health and wellbeing and, consequently, when should professionals intervene to reduce the risk of significant harm?

Key points: the social context

- There is a proven association between poverty and ill health.
- Inequalities in health persist within the United Kingdom despite a raft of policy initiatives.
- Without further intervention it is likely the pattern of trans-generational poverty and disadvantage will continue (Field 2010).

Responsibility: parents (agency) or state (structure)?

It is now generally accepted that health is a multidimensional phenomenon and has many contributing determinants. Since the advent of the welfare state, health and social welfare measures have been put in place to prevent those from poorer backgrounds from being excluded from health, education and social care services. The Field Report (2010) and the Allen Report (2011a) propose that the first five years of a child's life are the most important in terms of promoting positive wellbeing. They suggest that if the child's wellbeing is not promoted within this crucial developmental period, long-term serious problems may arise, leading to the child's failing to meet their full potential. Bronfenbrenner's (1979) theory of ecological development further supports this idea, suggesting that the influence of the environment has a profound effect on a child's long-term progress. Positive health, development and wellbeing are not only dependent on the physical environment and access to different services, but also influenced by cultural and social factors, including current policy and legislation developed and implemented by the government of the day. By far the greatest influential factor, however, is that of parents, carers and the immediate family environment of that child. The Early Years Foundation Stage (EYFS) (DfE 2012b) states that parents are the child's first and most enduring educators, not only in terms of providing them with their earliest learning experiences but also acting as role models for the future. If parents do not have the skills required to give children positive health messages, it is unsurprising that many examples of trans-generational neglect and poor levels of wellbeing continue to be seen.

So where does the responsibility of the state end and parental responsibility and informed choice start? The *Every Child Matters* framework introduced following the untimely death of Victoria Climbié (DfES 2003a) aimed not only to protect children from abuse and neglect, but also to help them to reach their full potential. In conjunction with the Children Acts of 1989 and 2004, the framework placed great emphasis on the importance of working co-operatively in partnership with parents. Even though the framework does not reflect the current government's agenda, it continues to act as a useful framework for practice. The Childcare Act 2006 and the EYFS (DfE 2012b) reflect this, reaffirming the vital role parents play in supporting children to achieve positive wellbeing. This raises two key questions:

1. What happens when there is a lack of consensus between the 'professionals' and parents and carers?
2. Who takes responsibility for deciding when and how to intervene?

It could be assumed that as most children are not in a position to make their own decisions, it should be the role of the government and public-sector employees to act as advocates in protecting and safeguarding children to ensure that parents give their children this optimum chance to achieve their full potential. However, with changing emphasis on parental empowerment and a shift in ideology and political requirements, discussed in Chapters 2 and 3, this may be open to question.

In line with the recent change in political philosophy, childcare professionals now endeavour to support and encourage individuals and communities to take more responsibility for their own health and wellbeing (Fisher and Gruescu 2011). David Cameron's notion of the 'Big Society' advocates the promotion of social capital to encourage less state dependency and, in fruition, is a challenge to professionals to adopt new ways of working. The term 'empowerment' is a frequently used expression that can be defined as 'an elusive concept incorporating many elements including self-esteem, control and decision making' (Naidoo and Wills 2009: 78). To achieve empowerment, it could be suggested that individual and community change is required by means of a multi-agency approach that foregrounds local initiatives and agencies. It is evident through previous studies and research, however, that those least able to make informed decisions are frequently those who are poorly educated, financially poor and, for many reasons, socially excluded. There are also issues to be considered around social and cultural diversity and the acknowledgement that there is no such thing as a typical family.

To further explore the concept of empowerment and working in partnership with children and families in safeguarding health, two current issues will now be explored: childhood obesity and children's emotional wellbeing. Through these examples we will look at possible ways of supporting parents more effectively in helping their children achieve the best possible outcomes.

Key points: intervention

- Tensions exist between ideas of parental responsibility and empowerment. The right to a private family life versus the need for state intervention is a perennial issue for government.
- Poverty and environmental issues need to be acknowledged and addressed when considering where responsibility to intervene lies.
- Changing policy and ideology means that practitioners face dilemmas when making decisions about when and why they should intervene.

Current issue: childhood obesity

Statistics gained from the National Child Measurement Programme (NCMP) (DH 2009c) suggest that one in four children in reception class and one in three children in year 6 are either obese or overweight, with boys having higher levels in both groups. The aim to safeguard the health of all children will be severely compromised if the trend for childhood obesity continues

(DfES 2003a), particularly since obesity has many short- and long-term con-sequences affecting all areas of physical, social, emotional, psychological and economic outcomes (DH 2009a).

In addition to individual factors such as poor diet and insufficient exercise contributing towards the incidence of obesity, there is also a strong associ-ation between obesity and poverty. Research indicates that families living in social disadvantage often have a liking for 'unhealthier' foods and an increase in sedentary lifestyles (Wardle 2005). Additionally, babies from lower socio-economic groups are less likely to be breastfed, and studies indicate that exclusive breastfeeding was found to be a protective factor against obesity in later life. However, these results were not entirely conclusive, suggesting that breastfeeding contributed towards reducing obesity but did not prevent it (Reilly *et al.* 2005).

It is not only environmental influences but also a child's physiological and psychological characteristics that will contribute to their becoming over-weight. Having obese parents was found to be a strong indicator for becom-ing obese (Wardle *et al.* 2001). This may be genetic but could also be attributed to environmental and lifestyle issues, perpetuating the idea of trans-generational disadvantage. Obese parents often adopt a relatively high-calorie diet, which is then offered to their children, but, in addition, Bandura's (1977) social learning theory assumes that dietary and eating habits will be observed, and therefore influence future behaviours. Strauss and Knight (1999) discov-ered through their study that having an obese mother was the strongest indic-ator for childhood obesity, followed by poverty and worklessness. However, it is difficult to separate nurture from nature, and what is caused by genetics and what is attributable to the environment continues to be a subject under debate.

The negative attitudes towards obesity constructed within today's society are further compounded by the tendency to treat it as a pathology or illness, which can result in individuals losing confidence in their ability to manage their own lives (Naidoo and Wills 2009). The increasing likelihood that health professionals will approach obesity as a medical problem, rather than a moral or economic one, may lead individuals to adopt a 'sick role'. Adopting this role may allow the individual to be absolved of any responsibility or blame for acquiring the condition, therefore removing the sense of responsibility and placing it with the medical profession. This can result in dependence and low-ered self-respect (Downie *et al.* 1996; Scriven 2010). Evidence presented in the *British Medical Journal* by Moynihan (2006) concurs with this and indicates that even the process of classifying children as overweight or obese could be inadvertently labelling children as 'diseased' and could cause more problems in the future, including stigmatisation, eating disorders and avoidance of physical activity.

It is well documented that children as young as 2 years of age begin to notice 'difference', and children as young as 3 or 4 can begin to show discrimination (Bee and Boyd 2007). Studies undertaken on pre-school children revealed that obese children in comparison to their non-obese peers were less popular, and more often rejected by their classmates (Rudolph 2009). This was regardless of gender, and, surprisingly, children who were themselves obese were just as likely to show these negative attitudes. The development of positive self-esteem in the early years is an important part of social and emotional development (Bee and Boyd 2007). Failure to develop confidence and self-esteem may affect future development and subsequently affect a child's ability to 'enjoy and achieve' and 'make a positive contribution' (DfES 2003a).

It is clear that if something is not done to halt the increasing trend of obesity and incidence of being overweight in the early years, the United Kingdom may see similar patterns to those found in the United States, where up to one in seven pre-school children from low-income families are overweight or obese (Centers for Disease Control and Prevention 2012). Being overweight or obese affects children's life chances and contributes to increasing morbidity and mortality, consequently putting increasing strain on the NHS, which is already struggling to cope financially with current demands. The key question stemming from this discussion is 'Should parents be viewed as being neglectful if they allow their children to become obese?' Viner *et al.* (2010) reviewed evidence around this topic in the *British Medical Journal* and made the point that although obesity has many associated risks and comorbidities, there is little to suggest that, unless the obesity is extreme, it is associated with parental neglect. Guidance around this is unclear, but they advocate that unless obesity is associated with other factors, it should not be viewed as child abuse. There is, however, great concern about the effects of obesity when associated with other problems such as dental caries, lack of immunisation and medical care, and low levels of parental warmth, which may be indicative of a more generalised level of neglect.

It must be acknowledged that the current obesity epidemic cannot be blamed solely on individuals within society, as there are many social, environmental and lifestyle factors that contribute towards children being overweight. Some of these factors can be considered as beyond the control of the individual, for example the high cost of fresh fruit and vegetables and the relatively low cost of high-fat, high-carbohydrate foods, which result in families on low incomes making unhealthier choices. Lack of green spaces, sporting facilities and concern around 'stranger danger' coupled with the increase in screen-related leisure activities and greater use of motorised transport all mean that today's children are expending far less energy than those of previous generations. Creating a culture of blame can therefore be unhelpful, and is contrary to the idea of parental choice and responsibility.

It is clear, however, that this issue is of national concern, resulting in a shifting emphasis in regard to the roles of front-line health workers such as family support workers and health visitors: they are being urged to take on a more interventional and preventive role in line with the Munro Review of child protection. This report suggests that professionals should not only react to issues around child protection, but actively work to 'put in place measures to reduce their incidence in the first place' (Munro 2011a: 16).

Obesity and the EYFS

All childcare practitioners, regardless of background, have a responsibility to support children's holistic development. The revised EYFS statutory framework implemented in September 2012 sets standards and provides guidance to support the learning, development and care of children between birth and 5 years of age under section 39 of the Childcare Act 2006. All registered settings are required to follow the safeguarding and welfare requirements, which are intended to help providers to create high-quality settings that are welcoming, safe and stimulating, in which children are able to enjoy learning and grow in confidence (DfE 2012b). The guidance includes recommendations for protecting children in accordance with the Local Safeguarding Children's Board recommendations.

The EYFS guidance states as part of its educational aspects that children must also 'be helped to understand the importance of physical activity, and to make healthy choices in relation to food' (DfE 2012b: 5). Disappointingly, the guidance within the EYFS around diet and nutrition is non-statutory, although it is recommended that the voluntary guidance be followed. These guidelines were developed following consultation with a number of agencies, and comply with current DH guidelines. Comprehensive guidelines and help with developing a nutrition policy are included.

It is clear that there is no simple answer to this worrying trend for increasing childhood obesity levels, and the evidence suggests that it is a major factor affecting a child's wellbeing. Therefore, everyone should share responsibility, including those in charge of government policy and those who deliver public services, to address the causal factors and offer appropriate interventions as necessary. The problem cannot just be left as the sole responsibility of parents and carers.

Key points: childhood obesity

- Obesity negatively affects a child's physical, social and emotional wellbeing.
- Tackling this issue from an individual perspective may not be the best way, as it may lead to a 'culture of blame'.
- Policy makers, parents and practitioners need to work co-operatively to address this worrying trend.

Current issue: emotional wellbeing

An issue perhaps less visible than obesity, but nonetheless of equal concern and of potential damage to a child's long-term wellbeing, is that of negative emotional wellbeing. The DfES guidance *Promoting Mental Health within Early Years and School Settings* defines children who are mentally healthy as those who are able to:

- develop psychologically, emotionally, intellectually and spiritually;
- initiate, develop and sustain mutually satisfying personal relationships;
- use and enjoy solitude;
- become aware of others and empathise with them;
- play and learn;
- develop a sense of right and wrong;
- resolve (face) problems and setbacks and learn from their mistakes.

(2001: 1)

In a speech in 2010, the deputy prime minister, Nick Clegg, reinforced the previous government's ambition to make Britain the best place for children to grow up, coining the phrase 'independent but supported families'. Policy was further developed to support the partnership approach between health, education, social care agencies and parents or carers to ensure that young children are able to achieve these aspirations, in order for them to grow and develop to their full potential.

There is still, however, a long way to go to achieve this in the light of UNICEF's study (2007) suggesting that children in the United Kingdom ranked 20th out of 21 for subjective wellbeing and 21st out of 21 for family and peer relationships. In addition to this, an investigation undertaken by Ofsted revealed that training for staff around children's emotional wellbeing was 'unsatisfactory in over a third of schools visited' (2005: 2), and that there was lack of equity in access to Child and Adolescent Mental Health Services (CAMHS). The numbers of children who were subject to a child protection plan under the category of emotional abuse in 2010 showed an increase from previous years. This is thought to be due to the increasing awareness of the link between domestic abuse and the emotional impact on the child (Radford *et al.* 2011). One in 14 children and young people in the United Kingdom are estimated to have experienced emotional neglect during childhood, with nearly one in four witnessing domestic abuse between adults in their homes. Research indicates that exposure to domestic abuse can result in behavioural problems, aggression, anxiety and difficulties at school (ibid.). This evidence suggests that children do not suffer merely short-term negative effects from emotional abuse; the effects can continue into adulthood, significantly affecting their relationships with others, including their own children, thus reinforcing the idea of trans-generational disadvantage (Finkelhor 2008).

According to Rees (2010), one of the major influential factors affecting a child's self-esteem and positive emotional wellbeing is the quality of the parent–child relationship. Disruption in the formation of secure attachments can be due to a range of pre- and post-natal factors such as maternal or child physical ill health, premature delivery and the quality of early neo-natal care. Poor maternal mental health, such as post-natal depression, is also known to have a significant effect on the emotional wellbeing of the infant, and this can be present in as many as 15 per cent of new mothers (Royal College of Psychiatrists 2013a: online). Research by Murray *et al.* revealed that male children in particular are vulnerable to poor attachment behaviours and may exhibit increased behavioural problems if their mother develops post-natal depression; this, they suggest, may have an 'enduring influence on child psychological adjustment' (1999: 1259).

Other factors that are known to have a negative effect on a child's emotional wellbeing are the existence of parental issues such as substance misuse, domestic abuse, poor housing and unemployment. There is no distinct line between what can be considered *good enough parenting*, a term first used by Winnicott (cited by Hoghughi and Speight 1998), and what may be considered poor enough to have a significant impact on a child's emotional wellbeing. Spencer describes this as the 'parenting and child mental health continuum', highlighting the fact that this is not an 'all or nothing phenomenon' (2003: 99) and that it is significantly influenced by social, economic and political contexts. Additionally, individual practitioners' personal experiences, professional heritage and personal values and principles will also add to the subjectivity of any situation.

The increasing pressure on mothers to return to work following childbirth may also have a negative impact on their ability to meet the emotional and attachment needs of pre-school children effectively. The amount of time spent with their children in the early years may conflict with a desire to improve household income – but at what cost to the emotional wellbeing of the child? The pressure to work may be even more evident when the child is from a single-parent household, where choice may not be an option. Following the enactment of the Education Act 2011, policy initiatives currently encourage parents to return to work, placing the emphasis on high-quality pre-school care and education to promote school readiness. With further monies being allocated to funding for 2-year-olds to access nursery places, it appears that ever-increasing amounts of time will be spent outside the care of parents and carers.

Key points: emotional wellbeing

- Research indicates low levels of subjective emotional wellbeing in United Kingdom.
- It can be difficult to assess what constitutes 'good enough parenting'.
- Concerns exist around staff training on emotional wellbeing and the availability of Child and Adolescent Mental Health Services (CAMHS).
- Increasing pressure for parents to return to work may negatively affect bonding and attachment.

The fact that many young children spend time within early years settings means that practitioners are ideally placed to identify and respond to concerns around emotional health and wellbeing. Adopting early interventional approaches to support parents and children through the Common Assessment Framework is one possible way forward. Working together with other agencies such as CAMHS and other qualified health professionals can encourage a partnership approach, giving parents and children a 'voice' in terms of finding solutions to their problems (CWDC 2009). As this is a process requiring parental consent, any further concerns or non-engagement may need to be assessed or investigated under section 17 or section 47 of the Children Act 1989 respectively, thus requiring a core assessment to be undertaken with the family. This would change the emphasis from one of support and guidance to one of investigation and would potentially disempower parents and carers. For this reason the use of the Common Assessment Framework would be preferable, as it aims to work with the family in a supportive and respectful way.

The role of Sure Start children's centres in safeguarding children

One of the key strategies employed by the previous New Labour government, and receiving continued commitment from the current Coalition government, is the Sure Start children's centres programme (Allen 2011a). Devised initially to target children and families living in the most deprived neighbourhoods, the centres have been subsequently developed to provide universal core services for every child, regardless of background or income. However, with austerity measures being imposed through recent spending reviews, it was highlighted that services needed to refocus on those who are most vulnerable, in particular children likely to fail as a result of living in deprived or disadvantaged circumstances (Osborne 2010).

A report published by Lord *et al.* (2011) outlined four groups to be targeted by children's centres:

1. children (e.g. those with additional needs, speech and language delay, challenging behaviour);
2. parents (e.g. with mental health issues, or parenting difficulties);
3. families (e.g. issues of worklessness, social isolation, poor housing);
4. goups (e.g. teenage parents, lone parents, black and minority ethnic (BME) groups, fathers).

All the children identified within the above groups could be considered as being at greater risk of abuse and neglect. By working in partnership with other agencies, a determined effort is currently being made to promote the wellbeing and safety of children, working in partnership with parents to determine their individual family needs. Adopting a targeted approach can be problematic, however, as it tends to stigmatise groups of people rather than considering each family's individual needs and responding accordingly. This concern has been highlighted in the discussion on obesity and emotional wellbeing. Many practitioners will admit that all families are susceptible to periods of increased vulnerability, and therefore whenever possible would favour early intervention approaches as opposed to targeted approaches (Allen 2011a). This cannot be achieved without the continuing commitment from the government in addressing child poverty and the provision of a skilled workforce who are able to provide this universal approach to safeguard children and prevent child abuse and neglect.

Providing a universal service in the current economic climate, however, may not be a realistic option. Research published for the Department for Education reveals that in providing Sure Start services, the financial cost to the British Government is up to £4,860 per child over the period of birth to age 4 (Melhuish *et al.* 2010). Nonetheless, initial costs may be offset in the short term by increasing likelihood of parental employment, although it may take a further 15 years to generate longer-term financial benefits in terms of raising attainment and reducing delinquency and youth offending (ibid.). It is unclear whether or not the current economic climate will focus policy on long-term gains or whether it will be necessary for finances to be diverted into other areas that offer more short-term and easily measurable effects.

It could be argued that the Sure Start approach supports the idea of community involvement and empowerment, as from its inception there has been a determined effort to ensure that service users are involved in determining the core offer of the centres. Putnam (1995) reinforces this idea by stating that the value of informal community engagement and education is paramount in developing the support structures to enable individuals to take responsibility for their wellbeing. The core offer and, more latterly, the core purpose allows each children's centre to provide tailor-made services to meet the diverse needs of each community, targeting resources to best address the individual health needs of each particular area. Services can be aimed to address issues around parenting, health and diet, and the centres can provide a community information point aimed at increasing educational and employment opportunities for adults. This approach views safeguarding and child protection as a public health concern, highlighting the need for a preventive model that empowers, educates and supports parents as regards meeting the health and wellbeing needs of their children.

> ### Key points: Sure Start
>
> ■ Sure Start children's centres provide a 'community hub' and support the concept of social capital.
>
> ■ Co-location of agencies supports integrated working and aids multi-agency communication.
>
> ■ The economic downturn and associated funding cuts and payment by results may threaten the idea of a universal service, leading to inequality of access.

Parent education classes: a possible solution?

There is an overwhelming amount of information available offering advice and guidance on how to be a good parent. Sources range from books, parenting magazines and websites to a range of professionals such as health visitors and family support workers. Despite this, in 2011 a staggering 50,552 children in the United Kingdom were subject to a child protection plan (NSPCC 2012) and 375,900 were classified as 'children in need' (DfE 2012b). Research suggests that many parents who neglect their children are from poorer backgrounds, are poorly educated and live in deprived circumstances, often experiencing mental health issues or substance misuse (Dowler and Spencer 2007).

The importance of providing good, accurate parenting information and support is now a shared responsibility, one that assumes a multi-agency approach to include health, education and social care practitioners (HM Government 2010a). The importance of the first five years of a child's life has been acknowledged by the current government in its commitment to increase the current health visiting workforce by recruiting an additional 4,200 staff. Its continued support of the children's centre programmes and the roll-out of free funded places for all 2-year-olds offer additional opportunities to further engage and involve parents.

Parenting programmes were first introduced in the 1970s in the United States as a way of training and educating parents (Smith and Pugh 1996) and soon became popular within the United Kingdom as part of the New Labour government's 'Supporting Families' agenda. Although many different models were used, most adopted an educational approach, building confidence and strengthening parent–child relationships. The programmes used theories of social learning and behaviour change methods in an attempt to ensure that long-term benefits were achieved (Bell 2005). Popular approaches include the 'Incredible Years' programme introduced by Caroline Webster-Stratton, and the Triple P model (Lindsay *et al.* 2011). David Cameron has recently suggested that the answer to some of the issues raised around poor parenting is to make parent education classes compulsory, but is this a realistic option? Occasionally, parents are required to attend such classes as part of the requirements of a child protection plan but it is questionable whether forcing parents to use this type of service is ultimately beneficial or whether they are merely going through the motions. If all parents were required to attend these classes, this would reduce stigma but would inevitably result in massive resource implications. However, using targeted approaches may be seen as being prejudicial and may result in resources being inappropriately used, missing the ones who would benefit the most.

Key points: educating parents

- Parenting classes can be a useful way of empowering and educating parents.
- However, they can be perceived as stigmatising when targeted towards those considered as being 'disadvantaged'.
- Resource implications may be problematic if parenting classes are offered to all parents at a time when there are cutbacks in services.

Educational approaches to changing behaviour are most often used, as they can be viewed as empowering people to take more control and responsibility. Covering a range of parenting topics in a group situation can also be advantageous, as it allows for peer learning and discussions, allowing individuals to create their own solutions and learn from each other (Naidoo and Wills 2005). There are criticisms to this approach, nevertheless, as there tends to be little acknowledgement of the social and environmental context, and a failure to recognise factors that may prevent people from acting upon the advice given. This can lead to 'victim blaming' and assumes the stance that professionals know best. This by some could be viewed as a return to the nanny state and, far from being empowering, can be viewed as interference and social control. The relationship between 'agency' and 'structure' is highly significant here as it highlights some of the possible conflicts between the objectives set by the government in terms of the benefits for individuals and those demanded of society as a whole (Barry and Yuill 2012). It could also be suggested that current policy fails to take into account the meta-narratives within minority groups, as it tends to adopt a uniform approach to addressing problems around health inequalities (Harrison and McDonald 2008).

Conclusion

This chapter has aimed to explore current perspectives on health and wellbeing in contemporary society, outlining the changing political and social context and how this is shaping early years practice. It is clear that although children are healthier than they were in pre-Second World War Britain, there are still many issues that are of concern, and may be affecting long-term out-comes for children. Early years practitioners and members of the children's workforce have an important role to play in working in partnership with par-ents to help children achieve their full potential. Having a sound knowledge of some of the current issues will help them to give support to parents in taking responsibility for making positive lifestyle and health choices, enabling their children to grow into healthy, confident and well-educated adults who in turn will become good parents themselves. If parents are failing to meet the health needs of children, or are engaging in behaviours that may negatively affect the health and wellbeing of children, practitioners need to be equipped with a range of preventive and interventional skills to make sure no child is put at risk of significant harm. Viewing safeguarding and protecting children as part of the public health agenda and as an integral part of the healthy child programme will ensure that children's health and wellbeing are given the pri-ority they deserve.

Further reading

Alexander, S. M., Baur, L. A., Magnusson, R. and Tobin, B. (2009) 'When does severe child-hood obesity become a child protection issue?' *Medical Journal of Australia*, 190 (3): 136–139.

This paper considers ethical concerns in decision making and some key questions, including 'Can severe childhood obesity be considered a form of neglect – in particular, medical neglect?'

Wofford, L. G. (2008) 'Systematic review of childhood obesity prevention', *Journal of Pediat-ric Nursing*, 23 (1): 5–19.

This systematic review identifies the state of the evidence related to the prevention of obesity in young children. The results indicate five areas of emphasis in the literature: prevalence of the problem; prevention as the best option; the pre-school population as the target; crucial parental involvement; and numerous guidelines.

8

Safeguarding children from online danger

Steven Burton

The potential online danger to children is as acute now as it has ever been. Although online predators, cyberbullying and 'sexting' have entered the lexicon, children have an unprecedented and often unsupervised opportunity of access to the online world. This chapter considers how technological advances in ICT, mobile communications and social networking impacts on children and the people who work with them, and how practice has to adapt in order to ensure that children are safeguarded.

By the end of this chapter you will:

- have a clear appreciation of the types of potential online danger;
- understand that when we allow younger children to use online and mobile technology, we as practitioners have a duty to safeguard them from potential online danger;
- be able to construct an appropriate online safeguarding policy for your early years setting.

Use of communications technologies in the early years

The impact that communications technologies have on the early years workforce is now beginning to emerge. While the vast majority of research conducted in the area of children's online safety has focused on the 8–18 years age group, it is evident in early years settings and primary school classrooms, and from observation of families with young children, that more and more children aged under 7 are using the internet and mobile technology. In early years settings, children have access to and use digital cameras for filming one another, and computers for playing educational games and accessing resources via the internet. Indeed, the current Early Years Foundation Stage standards suggest that children must 'recognise that a range of technology is used in places such as homes and schools. They select and use technology for particular purposes' (DfE 2012b: 9). Therefore, the use of digital and online technologies is firmly and appropriately entrenched in the educational standards for the age group.

A report by the UK communication industries regulator, Ofcom (2009, 2010), highlights that children aged 5–7 years use the internet for 4.5 hours per week (2010: 30) and that 10 per cent of the time spent on the internet by children in that age range was utilised either on social networking sites or communicating with others using other means (ibid.: 24). These findings are consistent with a second survey that shows two-thirds of children aged 5–7 years using the internet at home in 2009 (UKCCIS 2009: 11). Despite the lack of specific research into the risks faced by the early years age group, it is important that practitioners understand that the increase in the use of such technologies by children in the early years of their lives will expose some of them to the documented dangers experienced by older children, and must be mindful of the potential harm that can come from the improper or illegal use of technology around all children.

Categories of online risk

There have been many attempts to define or categorise the variety of online risk to children. Livingstone and Haddon (2009a), for instance, classify four varieties of risk – commercial, aggressive, sexual and value-based risk – and then subdivide these categories into the role of the child in the encounter, the child as recipient, the child as participant and the child as actor. Conversely, the United Kingdom Council for Child Internet Safety specifies seven categories of risk when it analyses the breadth of research available on the subject: negative peer contact, online risks in general, access content, meet/share details, sexual online conduct, other risks, and reinforcing negative attitudes or behaviours (UKCCIS 2009). The former British Educational Communications and Technology Agency (Becta 2008) introduced the 'four Cs' – Content, Contact, Commerce and Culture – which categorised specific areas of concern online. I argue that online risk or danger can be separated into four distinct areas:

1. exposure to inappropriate behaviour and content;
2. cyberbullying;
3. mutual online sexual activity;
4. stranger activity.

In support of this I propose a model of online danger (Figure 8.1) and highlight the relationship between the four identified areas, examining the nature of these potential dangers, and provide insight into how they can be overcome by professionals and parents.

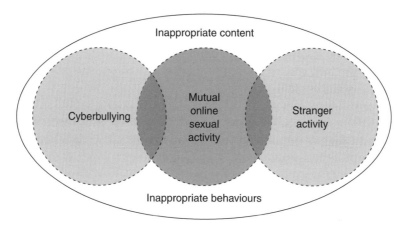

FIGURE 8.1 Model of online danger.

Exposure to inappropriate behaviour and content

While the other three categories of risk discussed in this chapter inherently have either an insidious or an intentional element to them, many fear the impact on children of accidentally stumbling across inappropriate content or behaviour online. Such areas are common in the online world and are therefore easily discoverable for the casual observer and can be happened upon completely unintentionally.

It is clear that parents and children have very different constructions of 'worry' when considering online content – according to Ofcom, 54 per cent of parents of 8- to 17-year-olds are worried about their children finding sexual content online, whereas only 13 per cent of their children have the same concerns (Ofcom 2007: 72) – but it is possible to categorise these risks into two areas: inappropriate immediate superficial content and inappropriate pervasive behavioural content.

Inappropriate immediate superficial content can be described as online content unsuitable for children which the viewer has a somewhat superficial relationship with – for instance, pornographic images on a webpage. This category contains the inappropriate elements of online content that a parent or professional would not want children in their care to access, but can be easily removed from the child's view. Other examples of this type of this immediate superficial content might include some online advertisements, overtly sexual or crude language, or images of violence.

In contrast, inappropriate pervasive behavioural content can be described as online material that contains subject matter, messages or attitudes which are likely to impact inappropriately on children and their moral, social and ethical development. This might, for instance, include online information about and support for suicide, self-harm or anorexia.

Indeed, these areas that have been well publicised in the United Kingdom in recent years (DCSF 2008a). It is evident, therefore, that the dichotomy between the two categories of content is not clear-cut, and is contingent on the nature and constructs of the viewer, the frequency of exposure and the nature of the content.

For instance, although I have highlighted pornography as an example of immediate superficial content, the nature of the pornography would perhaps have an impact on whether the content could be categorised as immediate and superficial, or pervasive and behavioural. Access in the home to more severe or graphic pornography would be likely to have a more pervasive impact on a young child, in the same way that repeated access is likely to begin to normalise pornography to the child. This in turn will influence the manner in which the child constructs their understanding of relationships, sex and adulthood.

Similarly, a pro-anorexia advertisement showing an image of an anorexic girl might be considered as immediate and superficial to some, whereas a blog giving instruction or detail extolling the virtues of being anorexic would be considered pervasive and behavioural. Thus, the constructs and reality that each individual child (or adult for that matter) brings to the content will have a direct and important impact on the classification of the content.

Key points: inappropriate behaviour and content

Inappropriate material on the web can be split into two categories:

1. inappropriate immediate superficial content;
2. inappropriate pervasive behavioural content.

As is demonstrated by the Model of Online Danger, cyberbullying, mutual online sexual activity and stranger activity can all be found within the sphere of Inappropriate Behaviour and Content.

In addition to these very specific risks, Inappropriate Behaviour and Content refers to those elements of the internet that are deemed by society or legislation not acceptable for consumption by in some cases minors and in other, more serious examples by any members of society.

Cyberbullying

Britain has been no exception to the tragic consequences that accompany chronic child depression. Already this year, 15-year old schoolgirl Megan Gillan took a fatal overdose of painkillers after bullies waged a hate campaign against her on Bebo, and, two months later, another 15-year old girl, Holly Grogan, jumped to her death after being bullied on Facebook. Beyond the tragedy of a life so cruelly cut short, the fact that these young people felt they had no alternative but to commit suicide should surely awaken us to the acute child-on-child violence made possible by cyberbullying.

(Cross *et al.* 2009: 40–41)

Cyberbullying is currently at the forefront of the public conscience. Various high-profile cases, together with campaigns to identify both bullying and cyberbullying activities as criminal offences, have created a sense of moral panic both in the United Kingdom and around the world. The Byron Review of 2008 suggested that cyberbullying 'refers to bullying behaviour that takes place through electronic means such as sending threatening text messages, posting unpleasant things about people, and circulating unpleasant pictures or videos of someone' (DCSF 2008a: 55). WiredKids (2012) provides a more contextualised definition, suggesting that cyberbullying

> is when a child, preteen or teen is tormented, threatened, harassed, humiliated, embarrassed or otherwise targeted by another child, preteen or teen using the Internet, interactive and digital technologies or mobile phones. It has to have a minor on both sides, or at least have been instigated by a minor against another minor.

I simply define cyberbullying as the use of mobile or online technology by a young person or group of people to cause intimidation, harassment or embarrassment to another young person. In this context, 'bullying is not merely "a fact of life" and nor should it ever be considered so. It ruins lives and leaves young people feeling isolated, worthless and even suicidal' (Cross *et al.* 2009: 13). Because of the very nature of the medium, cyberbullying differs from traditional face-to-face bullying in a number of key ways. First, the bully can remain anonymous. This adds to the sense of exposure and helplessness experienced by the victim, since they cannot always identify the perpetrator and therefore judge the scale of the perpetrator's influence. Indeed, according to Livingstone and Haddon (2009b), the ability to be anonymous can encourage irresponsible behaviour.

Second, the very nature of the communicated message means that often the bullying exchange can be viewed or witnessed by others, making the bullying a very public affair. For instance, a discriminatory message delivered via text or instant messaging can be sent on to and shared with the bully's allies, or friends of the victim.

Third, cyberbullying typically occurs in locations where children *should* feel safe. The pervasive nature of the medium ensures that children, and therefore the victims of cyberbullying, can be reached in their own private time at home via mobile phone technology, in their bedrooms via games consoles, or at school via classroom-based ICT facilities. The Byron Review summarised these areas succinctly when it suggested that

> [c]yberbullying can be particularly upsetting and damaging because it spreads more widely, with a greater degree of publicity; it can contain damaging visual images or hurtful words; it is available 24 hours a day; it can infiltrate the victim's privacy and the 'safe' place of home; and personal information can be manipulated, visual images altered and these then passed on to others. Moreover, it can be carried out anonymously.
>
> (DCSF 2008a: 55)

Cowie and Jennifer (2008) add a further dimension to the three factors by reminding us of the impact of bystanders in bullying episodes. Elliott suggests that when

> a child is bullied, peer pressure sometimes makes it difficult for the victim to rally support from other children ... one of the most effective ways to cut down on bullying is to work with the bystanders and those who are on the periphery of bullying groups.
>
> (2002: 4)

The impact on the victim of cyberbullying can therefore be amplified when, for instance, the 'bystanders' around a cyberbullying transaction are able either to forward abusive texts or emails to others, or to record episodes of bullying on mobile phones and circulate these images or footage to others who were not involved (Cowie and Jennifer 2008). This is exacerbated by the anonymous nature of the bystanders themselves, who will often be isolated by their distance from the incident. Thus, the impact on the victim of the bystander effect can be greater in instances of cyberbullying.

The pervasiveness of modern technology allows a myriad of communication opportunities for the user, and unfortunately this also allows bullies these same opportunities. A child with a smartphone can receive texts, photographs and phone calls through traditional telephonic means. However, added to this is the capacity to access the internet, which includes the capability to access email accounts, social media sites such as Facebook, Twitter or MySpace (which have their own internal messaging services), or forums and blogs that instantly allow posters to add content to the web. Considering that all the above can also be achieved using a typical games console, one realises that a child could easily become bombarded with communication cues, wanted or otherwise.

According to Ofcom, only 45 per cent of UK parents whose children use the internet at home use filtering or safety controls, and only a third of parents whose children use a games console to access the internet know about their access controls (Ofcom 2009). Research by the Child Exploitation and Online Protection Centre in the United Kingdom has revealed that cyberbullying most often takes place through either social networking sites or via instant messaging (CEOP 2009). Despite the fact that children should be aged

13 before they can register a profile on a social networking site, 25 per cent of UK children aged 8–12 years admit to having a profile on at least one of the Facebook, MySpace or Bebo social networks (Ofcom 2010).

Key points: cyberbullying

Cyberbullying can be defined as the use of mobile or online technology by a young person or group of young people to cause intimidation to another young person.

It can differ from traditional face-to-face bullying in three ways:

1. The bully or bullies can remain completely anonymous.
2. The bullying 'transaction' can be shared with others limitlessly through the online or mobile medium, thus intensifying its effect on the victim.
3. It can occur in locations where children *should* feel safe.

A quarter of UK children aged 8–12 years admit to having a social networking profile, despite being below the minimum age of 13 (Ofcom 2010).

Research indicates that between one-third and one-fifth of UK children have been or are being cyberbullied.

Cyberbullying sits within the arena of Inappropriate Behaviour and Content on the Model of Online Danger. It is partly mated with Mutual Online Sexual Activity, as mutually reciprocated sexual messages or content can often be used as a tool to bully and intimidate, particularly after a relationship has ended, or if sexual advances made in this way are unrequited.

Identifying the victims of cyberbullying

Alarmingly, a significant number of children appear to be affected by this particular source of online risk. Research by Cross *et al.* revealed that 30 per cent of 11- to 16-year-old children in the United Kingdom had suffered some form of cyberbullying (2009: 21), while UKCCIS suggested that one in five UK 10- and 11-year-olds had been cyberbullied in the last year (2009: 6). This is a concern when one considers that the proportion of 5- to 7-year-olds using the internet at home is increasing more quickly than the overall rate of internet uptake, with 63 per cent of children in this age range using the internet at home (Ofcom 2010: 12). Recent research in the United Kingdom has suggested that one in five primary school children have suffered from cyberbullying (Cross *et al.* 2012).

According to Cross *et al.* (2009), girls are twice as likely as boys to be the victims of persistent cyberbullying. While girls and boys are just as likely to be cyberbullies themselves, girls are more likely to send hurtful texts, voicemails and emails, and are more likely to publicise the bullying acts to peers.

The research undertaken in the United Kingdom by Cross *et al.* (ibid.) looked at a variety of different aspects of cyberbullying, including where in cyberspace children felt the online bullying was most prevalent. They identified MSN instant messenging and the Bebo social networking site as the tools most commonly used by cyberbullies. Additionally, they noted that YouTube was identified as a location for transactions of bullying to be publicised (ibid.).

Despite numerous calls from members of the public for a 'Bullying Act', cyberbullying (and, for that matter, bullying) is not named as an offence in UK law. However, successful prosecutions of offenders can be and have been brought under the Protection from Harassment Act 1997, the Malicious Communications Act 1988, section 43 of the Telecommunications Act 1984, the Communications Act 2003 or even the Public Order Act 1986. In addition to these legislative options, in 2007 the Department for Children, Schools and Families published a guidance document for educationalists entitled *Cyberbullying: Safe to Learn*, which provides practical advice and examples of procedures to follow when confronted by a cyberbullying episode in an educational context.

Mutual online sexual activity

As can be seen from the previous section on cyberbullying, much of the potential threat to the welfare of children online actually comes from other children. Although some of the areas discussed in this consequent section could and should be considered bullying, particularly where the online sexual activity is not desired on the part of the recipient, it will be considered as a distinct area of threat in its own right, owing to the vulnerability and age of the participants, irrespective of mutuality. In addition, particularly when considered as part of the Model of Online Danger (Figure 8.1), mutual online sexual activity has clear links to stranger activity, placing it centrally within the sphere of danger to children online, despite its often reciprocal nature. One of the most vigorous forms of online sexual activity is 'sexting'.

Cross *et al.* describe 'sexting' as 'sending messages or images with sexual content via mobile phones or the internet' (2009: 28). They reveal that one in three children have received a message via this route about sex, and one in four children have received a sexual image (ibid.). According to BeatBullying, 'Common "sexts" include images of young boys exposing themselves or masturbating, boys who have requested girls to remove their clothing and images of sexual acts which would be considered by most as pornographic' (2009). As in the case of cyberbullying discussed earlier in this chapter, the digital nature of the messages or images means that they can be redistributed, attached to personal websites or kept until a later date. According to the OECD:

A recent American study found that 4% of youths aged 12–17 who owned cell phones had *sent* sexually suggestive nude or nearly nude images of themselves to someone else via text messaging, 15% said they had *received* sexually suggestive nude or nearly nude images of someone they know, 8% reported *being a victim* of images transmitted over a cell phone. The likelihood of sending or receiving such content seems to increase with age: 4% of 12 year-olds reported having received such images or videos compared to 20% of 16 year-olds and 30% of 17 year-olds.

(2011: 24)

The figures appear even more disconcerting in the United Kingdom, with approximately one-third of 11- to 16-year-olds receiving unwanted messages, and one-quarter receiving unwanted messages of a sexual nature (UKCCIS 2009: 15). Although many of these transactions take place voluntarily between children who are in relationships, and are not considered to be 'unwanted', there is a great deal of evidence suggesting that these messages or images can be used at a later date (often when relationships have ended) as a means of cyberbullying, hence the partial mating of mutual online sexual activity with cyberbullying in the Model of Online Danger (see Figure 8.1). Indeed, 85 per cent of these messages or images received were sent by someone known to the child recipient (Cross *et al.* 2009: 28). To contextualise this, BBC research (2006) suggested that 30 per cent of young people have sex before the age of consent (4 per cent at younger than 14 years, 9 per cent aged 14 years, and 17 per cent aged 15 years). It can therefore be seen that a substantial number of children are engaging willingly in sexual activity, with the average first sexual experience (of any kind) being at age 14 in the case of females and age 13 in the case of males (Martellozzo 2012, citing the National Survey of Sexual Attitudes and Lifestyles, 2001).

This perhaps brings about a dilemma, in that much of this activity is clearly conducted and reciprocated by children, who take responsibility for the production and distribution of these 'sexts'. Despite this, as adults, parents and professionals we have a duty to safeguard our children in this instance, especially when one considers the obvious and actual potential links to future cyberbullying (or traditional bullying), pornography and the sphere of the child predator. The Byron Review contextualises this succinctly, stating that

this process is often more complicated for children who are still in the process of learning about the rights and wrongs of social interaction in the real world – what is appropriate or not; how others react and feel when they do or say something. Interactions online can seem somewhat unreal to children, both in terms of what they interpret (as the receiver of the message) and what they send out (the imparter of the message).

(DCSF 2008a: 56)

Despite its being an issue currently mostly associated with children over the age of 10 years, it is evident that younger children's use of online and mobile technology is becoming increasingly common. When one considers that children in the early years are developing body awareness and curiosity at a time when they are being encouraged to learn about and use online and digital technology, it is clear that some potential exists for mutual online sexual activity, even if the intention of the children in question is completely non-sexual.

Key points: sexting

Sexting is the sending of sexual messages, images or video via mobile or online technology.

As many as one in three school-aged children have received such messages via either mobile technology or the web.

Common sexts contain nudity, masturbation or sexual intercourse.

Although sexts are often sent between children who are having a relationship, they can be and have been used when such relationships end to cause humiliation and torment to the receiver.

Children often do not appreciate the potential consequences of these actions, owing to their still developing sense of social consciousness. For this reason, mutual online activity can be mated on the Model of Online Danger with both cyberbullying and stranger danger.

Stranger activity

> The grooming process consists of sex offenders socialising and grooming children over long periods of time as preparation for sexual abuse and will ensure that abuse will take place without being disclosed.
>
> (Martellozzo 2012: 38)

When members of the public think of safeguarding children, an automatic reaction is to assume that we are discussing safeguarding children from paedophiles. Indeed, it is an automatic reaction of many, when the term 'online safeguarding' is used, to immediately consider the phenomenon of paedophiles 'grooming' children in online chatrooms and arranging consequent real-world meetings. This is actually the least commonly occurring of the four areas of danger previously identified. However, it presents perhaps the most obvious and explicitly dangerous risk of all.

O'Connell (2003) suggests that there are five distinct phases to a complete grooming process:

1. the friendship-forming stage;
2. the relationship-forming stage;
3. the risk assessment stage;
4. the exclusivity stage;
5. the sexual stage.

The first stage, friendship forming, allows the child and adult to get to know one another, and for the paedophile to determine whether or not they are attracted to the child. The relationship-forming stage is a supplement to the previous stage, and allows the perpetrator to further ingratiate themselves with the child, and begin to develop the friendship. The risk assessment stage allows the perpetrator to try to determine the likelihood of their approaches being detected by others, and when they are satisfied with a positive risk assessment, they will move on to the exclusivity stage. Here, the perpetrator will build upon the relationship-forming stage and try to make the child trust the adult implicitly before entering the sexual stage, which sexualises the conversation (O'Connell 2003). The speed at which these phases are completed by the adult varies enormously, and sometimes stages are omitted. However, it is easy to see from this brief explanation how the proliferation of mobile and online communications technology has helped the perpetrator move through these stages. As Martellozzo summarises, 'they are able to contact anyone, anywhere, anytime. Furthermore, cyberspace provides the offender with an inflated sense of security' (2012: 125). The Child Exploitation and Online Protection Unit in the United Kingdom adds detail to this process, suggesting that when communicating with potential victims (children), offenders

> will often use a number of grooming techniques including building trust with the child through lying, creating different personas and then attempting to engage the child in more intimate forms of communication including compromising a child with the use of images and webcams. Child sex abusers will often use blackmail and guilt as methods of securing a meeting with the child.
>
> (CEOP 2009)

It is thought that most paedophilic activity online takes place in order to fulfil the offender's own personal needs. However, it is clear that in some cases where the groomed children are physically abused, images and video of some of these activities are shared with other paedophiles via the same mobile and online technology. According to the Internet Watch Foundation (2012: 12), the UK hotline for reporting online criminal content, 12,966 URLs (web pages) were found to contain child sexual abuse in 2011, with 74 per cent of the images showing the abuse of children appearing to be of a child aged 10 or younger.

A variety of excellent resources are available in order to help adults, parents and children understand the nature of such threats. However, research in the United States still found that 43 per cent of children aged 10–17 years interacted online with people they did not know, 26 per cent sent personal information to unknown people online, and 5 per cent (1 in 20 children) had 'talked' to unknown people online about sex (Wolak *et al.* 2008).

It is here that parents, early years practitioners and teachers can have a potentially huge impact on the safeguarding of the child online. The issue can perhaps be targeted using three distinct approaches.

First, all children should receive support and information on these dangers, and the pitfalls of communicating with strangers. To develop a mistrusting attitude in young children of adults is a point of debate beyond the remit of this chapter, and would problematise many constructions of childhood. However, to develop a questioning attitude rather than a trusting one among children who invariably will use this technology, particularly in relation to communicating with others online, can only benefit the safeguarding agenda.

Second, adults working with children should be conscious of the five-stage approach developed by O'Connell, discussed earlier in this section. If we accept that a common approach utilised by online predators is to befriend and become the confidant and closest ally of the targeted child, then adults responsible for children's safety should be particularly conscious of identifying children who may seek out or respond to an 'online best friend'. Children who play alone, are quiet or secretive, or who are experiencing personal or family-related trauma may be more receptive to an 'online friend' – and therefore could conceivably be in more potential danger than other children.

Third, more adults with responsibility for children need to familiarise themselves with the area of online safeguarding, and the patterns and approaches utilised by online predators. This in turn requires adults to develop confidence in using this technology themselves, and not view these technological advances as the domain of the young.

Key points: strangers

The impact that online strangers can have on children in the early years has received very little research.

Over a quarter of US children surveyed aged 10–17 admitted sending personal information online to people they did not know (Wolak *et al.* 2008)

One in 20 US children surveyed aged 10–17 admitted talking online about sex to people they did not know (ibid.).

Sixty-three per cent of 5- to 7-year-olds in the United Kingdom use the internet at home (Ofcom 2010).

In 2010/2011, CEOP disrupted or dismantled 132 high-risk sexual offender networks with links to the United Kingdom (CEOP 2011).

A total of 12,966 web pages containing child pornography were reported to the Internet Watch Foundation in 2011, and 74 per cent of the images showed the abuse of children who appeared to be 10 years or younger (IWF 2012).

The response of professionals

As has been highlighted in this chapter, the potential dangers of using online and mobile technology around children can be both implicit and explicit. However, the technology is also an invaluable tool for learning and an integral part of life, so it is clear that our task as professionals is not to prevent children from accessing it, but to minimise and manage the risk in doing so.

Professionals need to adopt a two-pronged approach. First, all staff working with and responsible for children in the early years must ensure that they take all reasonable steps to become as familiar as possible with online and mobile technologies. While children have a natural curiosity that enables them to experiment with and learn from playing with such technologies, adults are far more likely to resist the changes brought about by these technologies, and will often find themselves in a position of being surrounded by children who are much more comfortable with technology than they themselves are. In no other arena of safeguarding would this apathetic approach be considered appropriate. However, societal norms accept that children are more advanced and comfortable with modern technology than adults. Where professionals work with and for children, however, it has to be argued that, especially around the elements of online and mobile practice highlighted earlier in this chapter, adults must be confident and competent in their own use of technology so that they are able to interpret patterns in the children's use of technology around them.

Second, in order to emphasise the rising importance of the subject, settings and institutions should write an online safeguarding policy in addition to their existing safeguarding policy, and all staff, parents and visitors should be made aware of it. Becta stated:

> It must be recognised that e-safety is not a technological issue and is not limited to settings where children have technology. Likewise, responsibility for e-safety must not be delegated to technical colleagues or those with responsibility for ICT, but must be firmly embedded within safeguarding policies, practices and responsibilities.
>
> (2008: 2)

Some early years settings have online safeguarding policies in place, and some of these do contain most if not all of the suggestions that follow. However, it is clear that in many cases no such policy exists, or that staff are unfamiliar with the existence of such policies. It could be argued that a rigorous policy, and consequent acknowledgement and enforcement of such a policy, would have affected the opportunity for individuals such as Vanessa George, a former nursery worker who was jailed for an indeterminate period of not less than seven years (Morris 2009), to take indecent and abusive photographs of children within their care. This would remove both the power to abuse and the agency of the offender, and would in itself serve to safeguard children from such dangers.

A clear online safeguarding policy for an early years setting would contain the following:

- *A definition of ICT in your context.* Explain what ICT means to you and to the children in your care. Identify examples (not an exhaustive list) of the kinds of technology available within the setting, and also the types of technology brought into the setting, for instance mobile phones or digital cameras brought in by parents at particular times.
- *An identification of what you do with technology.* You may want to explain pedagogical principles, or give examples of how technology is used to enhance learning, linking to the current standards such as the Early Years Foundation Stage.
- *Who is responsible for technology in your setting?* Identify the practitioners responsible for both online safeguarding and online pedagogy. This would ordinarily be two different people, perhaps depending on the size of the setting. However, a practitioner responsible for technology-centred pedagogy may not be best suited to responsibility for online safeguarding. As with every other aspect of safeguarding, every practitioner has personal responsibility. This role involves external scanning for new online safeguarding threats, and being a 'more knowledgeable' single point of contact (SPOC) for the authorities should an investigation take place.
- *Online and technological security in the setting.* Highlight what technological security you have in place, for instance password protection on all computers in the setting, or an explanation of any biometric security used. Elucidate what security measures you expect staff, parents and visitors to adhere to, for instance always logging off computers after use, or ensuring that children are never left unsupervised with digital cameras.
- *The use of mobile phones and cameras.* Most early years settings have accepted that staff and visitors (including parents) must not use mobile phones in the setting. Indeed, the most recent EYFS standards in the United Kingdom state: 'The safeguarding policy and procedures must include an explanation of the action to be taken in the event of an allegation being made against a member of staff, and cover the use of mobile phones and cameras in the setting' (DfE 2012b: 13). Many settings employ an 'empty pockets' policy in terms of mobile phones. As a bare minimum, staff should not use or take mobile phones outside staff-only areas, and the only cameras to be used when photographing activities should be those bought by and kept in the setting.
- *Social networking.* Highlight your position with regard to the use by staff of social networking sites such as Facebook or Twitter. Staff must not use social media to discuss, display or refer to any aspect of their work in the setting; in particular, there must be no reference made, either implicitly or explicitly, to any child or parent with whom they are involved in a professional context. Some local authorities insist that early years staff must not become 'friends' or 'followers' of parents on social media. One would

hope, however, that the online profiles of staff would not contain matter that would be of concern to parents were they to become 'friends' online. Under no circumstances should early years staff have such social media connections to children in their setting.

- *Links to legislation to be followed*. Emphasise the legislative frameworks and Acts that will be enforced with regard to technology. The policy should include a brief statement on the Data Protection Act 1998 which explains local policy on the collection, storage and removal of personal data, and also a statement of how the setting deals with Freedom of Information Act 2000 requests.

Key points: an online safeguarding policy

An online safeguarding policy should supplement other policies such as your safeguarding policy and your ICT usage policy. The policy should:

- Define ICT in your context.
- State what you do with technology in regard to pedagogical principles. You should link this statement to current standards – that is, the Early Years Foundation Stage.
- State who is responsible for technology in your setting.
- Have regard to computer security in the setting.
- Cover the use of mobile phones and cameras in the setting.
- Set out social networking rules for staff.
- Have regard to the legislation governing your use of ICT.

Conclusion

Digital technology is a socially neutral tool: a tool for interaction rather than an inevitable weapon of abuse. As such, mobile phones and the internet can be utilised in different ways, depending on the intention and caution of the user. What is necessary is to safeguard children from the more insidious behaviour that can manifest itself via this technology whilst still allowing them to explore its capacity and harness its benefits.

(Cross *et al.* 2009: 11)

This chapter has aimed to highlight, using a simple Model of Online Danger (Figure 8.1), the potential online dangers that we as professionals must safeguard children from. The model attempts to demonstrate in a simplistic manner how cyberbullying, mutual online sexual activity and stranger activity sit within the wider sphere of inappropriate content and behaviour. It also suggests that the centrally positioned phenomenon of mutual online sexual activity, often a mutually reciprocal activity, has clear links into the perhaps more insidious areas of cyberbullying and stranger activity.

That is not to say that children should be shielded from the online world, as it can and should be a place of wonder and learning, which if used correctly can introduce new realities and new concepts, and raise expectations and aspirations in children. However, it is the responsibility of all professionals working with children to ensure that they are aware of the potential dangers and are competent in identifying, dealing with and signposting children who stumble into those dangers as they grow up 'online'.

Online safeguarding in the early years is still in its infancy in terms of research. However, it can be seen that children are using mobile and online technology at younger and younger ages, and that both children and adults can target other children online for various reasons. In order for professionals to safeguard this community effectively, practitioners must develop the same competencies and enthusiasms in technology that children seem to find so naturally. While this approach would, one hopes, prevent some of these dangers from ever taking a foothold in the early years, it is also envisaged that educating children effectively at a younger age on the potential dangers lurking within this area should in turn have a positive impact on the horrifying statistics concerning older children who are suffering from some of the phenomena described in this chapter.

Further reading

Cross, E.-J., Piggin, R., Douglas, T., Vonkaenal-Flatt, J. and O'Brien, J. (2012) *Virtual Violence II: Primary-Aged Children's Experience of Cyberbullying*, London: BeatBullying.

One of the very few pieces of work that focus on primary-aged children. Although in itself a hugely informative study, it forms part of a series of similar studies regarding the cyberbullying experiences of a variety of different age groups. They are contemporary, based on UK research, and should be considered essential reading for anyone studying or working in the field of cyberbullying.

DCSF (2008) *Safer Children in a Digital World: The Report of the Byron Review*, Nottingham: DCSF.

The seminal report to UK government on the safety of children online. Authored by Dr Tanya Byron, the report and its associated documents are a vital resource for enhancing the knowledge of readers who are new to this area. Written in a thoroughly accessible manner, the report is informative, it challenges assumptions and it also provides suggestions for solutions to a range of issues threatening the safety of children online.

Martellozzo, E. (2012) *Online Child Sexual Abuse: Grooming, Policing and Child Protection in a Multi-media World*, London: Routledge.

This book follows the experiences of the author while attached to a high-tech crime unit within the Metropolitan Police. Exploring the ways in which the police operate in relation to online criminality, and examining the activities and testimonies of online paedophiles, this book is as close to a 'page turner' as an academic textbook gets!

9

Communicating through a crisis

Steven Burton

Safeguarding episodes provide early years practitioners with perhaps the most personally challenging and distressing incidents of their careers. These episodes require precise, clear, factual information to be passed between a variety of people, including children and, where necessary, those working outside your own team. However, the very personal nature of this communication process can have a profound and often negative impact on the situation, and the relationships between the people immersed within it. In the first instance, staff working with children must have a thorough appreciation and understanding of their own abilities to communicate with the people around them.

This chapter will explore issues of personal communication during safeguarding episodes and introduce the reader to key concepts through the voices and experiences of early years practitioners and a police trainer. The early years practitioners interviewed for this chapter include settings managers, senior practitioners and room leaders, each with over ten years' experience. They are based in a variety of settings in the north of England. The police trainer has over 30 years' experience as both a front-line officer and a trainer of interpersonal communication with new police recruits.

While members of the public may well construct their own understanding of safeguarding and perpetrators, perhaps fed by tabloid sensationalism, practitioners must be conscious of far less conspicuous clues in their daily working role, as Practitioner A revealed:

> They were talking about birthdays or something and this child just said out of the blue, 'My birthday cards were up on the shelf and Daddy went mad, and knocked everything off the shelf and started saying things.' It just shows how quickly something can come out at the most random moment; it isn't necessarily when you're changing their nappy.

Hence, the unpredictable nature of such revelations dictates that staff working with children must be constantly aware of the possibility for a potential safeguarding episode to emerge. This chapter aims to elucidate to staff and students in early years the importance of both the act of communication and the theory behind communication when involved in a safeguarding episode.

By the end of this chapter you will:

- appreciate the impact that safeguarding episodes can have on the staff involved;
- understand simple theory underpinning communication and relate this to examples of communication during safeguarding episodes;
- have a framework of communication with children to utilise if you are involved in a safeguarding episode.

Being a member of staff

Safeguarding episodes occur in every setting, and every experienced member of staff has had dealings at some level with such episodes. These can have a huge impact on the practitioner and the team in the setting. As Senior Practitioner J stated, 'All the training in the world can't prepare you for when you're faced with something like this, this big issue all of a sudden. It is absolute fear the first time you're faced with it.' Senior Practitioner S, a manager from another setting, supported this, adding:

> Every situation is different and training in communication for safeguarding could well be pointless. You've just got to experience it once, and make sure you're with an experienced manager the first time it happens. No training can prepare you for the rollercoaster of emotions that you go through.

Not all interviewees agreed entirely with this, some suggesting that while training on safeguarding as an issue is plentiful, training on how to deal personally with the impact of a safeguarding issue and how to control and conduct yourself during a safeguarding episode is far less readily available. As Senior Practitioner A said, 'Let me tell you, it is terrifying to a member of staff, and remember a lot of childcare professionals are very young; you can be qualified and on your own at 18 [years of age].' Safeguarding is therefore much more than a cerebral process, but at the outset it is also important to recognise the tasks and procedures to be completed, whatever the personal impact of such an episode.

The necessity for staff to maintain appropriate records is paramount. The Early Years Foundation Stage (EYFS) confirms this, stating that

> [p]roviders must take all necessary steps to keep children safe and well. The requirements in this section explain what early years providers must do to: safeguard children; ensure the suitability of adults who have

contact with children; promote good health; manage behaviour; and maintain records, policies and procedures.

(DfE 2012b: 13)

This is not merely a managerial function, but the personal responsibility of every member of staff. In addition to the necessity for keeping records of children undertaking everyday tasks, and compiling evidence towards EYFS assessment, staff must also maintain accurate and timely records in order to safeguard themselves. As Senior Practitioner J, a setting manager with almost 15 years' experience, stated when reflecting on a safeguarding episode that she had been involved in:

> My colleague hadn't kept good records; there were no details, in fact there were no records of observations on this child at all. Thing is, you've got your little niggle, their little niggle, someone else's little niggle – it builds up a big picture. But if you didn't log it, it hasn't happened. It's as simple as that.

Senior Practitioner S confirmed, 'It can become one person's word against another; staff must, must, must safeguard themselves and get things written down when they happen.'

In addition to this, staff must be conscious of professional boundaries when dealing with parents. Practitioners must have excellent interpersonal skills, and fostering friendly, communicative positive relationships with parents can only benefit the children who are in their care. Crucially, in times of high stress and emotion, such as during a safeguarding episode, staff must be able to maintain a professional relationship with all concerned. This is not as easy as it would at first seem. Senior Practitioner S reflected on her first safeguarding incident as an inexperienced member of staff dealing with a parent when a safeguarding episode emerged:

> I didn't say much, I just wanted to give her a hug and say, look, it will be fine. We'll support you over this; we'll be there for you [sighs]. I just felt deeply sorry for her [sighs]. I didn't think I'd feel like that when faced with a possible safeguarding incident.

Senior Practitioner A also commented on an incident involving the parent of a child in her care, recalling that

> one member of staff had befriended the parent, had a really good relationship with Mum, she became defensive of Mum. She made excuses for the parents. I mean, Mum has a need, but ... you can build too strong a relationship with them, but sometimes that's *why* parents build such a good relationship with you.

These comments reflect the relational nature of early years work and demonstrate how easy it is to befriend and make relationships with parents and carers. These relationships help the practitioner and the parents or carers feel secure. It is clear that the potential impact of a potential safeguarding episode on setting staff is great, and that staff involved in such episodes have a great deal to be conscious of, beyond providing care and support to the child at the centre of the episode. However, while this is important to acknowledge, it is the welfare of the child that remains paramount.

Key points: impact on staff

Staff have a great deal to consider in terms of their own responsibilities with regard to communication when dealing with a safeguarding episode. Staff should anticipate (as far as is possible) being involved in a rollercoaster of emotions, which will affect their ability to communicate as clearly and effectively as they ordinarily would.

To attempt to alleviate the problem, staff should:

- maintain accurate and timely records of their dealings with and observations of children as per the Early Years Foundation Stage guidance;
- involve experienced staff immediately if they suspect a safeguarding episode;
- be mindful of professional relationships with parents, and how their judgements can be affected by personal relationships.

Communication theory and communicating with parents

One of the most straightforward, widely recognised and useful communication models is that of Shannon and Weaver (1949). This model can be utilised by early years staff when trying to highlight problems with communication, particularly in stressful communication situations such as those around safeguarding.

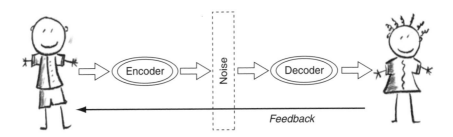

FIGURE 9.1 Adapted version of Shannon and Weaver's model of communication (1949: 34).

The Shannon and Weaver model depicts a communication episode led by the transmitter, for example an early years professional, and received by the receiver – in this illustration, the parent of a child in the setting. It could easily be reversed, with a parent or child being the transmitter and a member of the early years staff being the receiver.

Encoding and decoding

Encoding is the process of turning one's thoughts or intentions into a communication medium that can be understood by others (when they decode your message). To be expert in the encoding process, and indeed the entire communication process, early years practitioners should have an awareness of and be able to demonstrate metacommunicative competence. In this instance, this means that the practitioner should be able to deconstruct and manipulate the many communication cues that are apparent during a face-to-face conversation. For instance, Albert Mehrabian's research dealt with abstract notions of liking and disliking in interpersonal communication, and suggested that only 7 per cent of the entire message and meaning received comes from the actual words that are spoken. A further 38 per cent comes from the way in which the words are delivered, and 55 per cent comes from the facial expression and body language of the speaker (1972: 182). Therefore, it is entirely conceivable that, particularly during a stressful communication situation, a verbal message can be either perverted or contradicted by the contrary non-verbal communication cues from a person. At this point, clarity and consistency are essential. Therefore, an early years practitioner must be aware of the many aspects of communication that are identifiable in one episode, and demonstrate clear and consistent elements of communication in terms of word selection, tone and body language. This is statement is supported by Reder and Duncan, who, when examining the role of communication following the Laming Report into the death of Victoria Climbié, suggested that

> [c]ommunication involves a complex interplay between information-processing, interpersonal relating, and interagency collaboration. The need to communicate purposefully and with meaning to relevant others must be borne in mind by all practitioners at all times. Effective communication is the responsibility of both the message initiator and the receiver, and as such, it is a mindset and a skill that can be learned, rehearsed and refined.

(2003: 98)

Non-verbal communication

When taking part in such interactions, early years practitioners should be conscious of proxemics, kinesics and haptic gestures in their communication cues.

Kinesics refers to the movement of one's body and the gesturing that occurs during face-to-face communication. As with the other elements of non-verbal communication described here, the early years practitioner must be aware of the impact of stress on both their own kinesic communication and that of those around them, including parents. For instance, folded arms can indicate a person who is either uninterested or becoming defensive. This is a closed body position, or closed posture. Therefore, practitioners should be conscious of the impact of their own gestures on the parent, such as eye contact or body posturing, and be similarly conscious of those gestures reciprocated by the parent. Early years staff who find themselves involved in safeguarding episodes should be aware of these gestures in two respects:

1. They should be conscious of their own gestures if they are feeling defensive or insecure over a safeguarding incident.
2. They need to identify where a situation might be beginning to escalate out of control.

Case study: kinesics

Police officers are constantly aware of the kinesic communication occurring around them, particularly in pressurised situations. Early years professionals should be aware of the same personal characteristics when finding themselves in similarly pressurised situations, such as when dealing with parents involved in a safeguarding episode. According to Police Trainer A, an officer with over 30 years' experience:

> Stereotypically you've got the angry person, bouncing up and down, gesturing and muscles pumping – you know what they're here for, they're here for a verbal fight that they may back up with a physical attack. But equally you've got the person who is completely silent, not saying anything, they don't make eye contact, but all of a sudden they'll just glance at you and then glance away again instantly, almost as though they are sizing you up, looking for an opportunity.
>
> More often than not they'll have their head down, chin down; they're protecting themselves from the conflict that they think is coming. They'll turn side on to you, present you with their shoulder; they're making their body target smaller and taking a protective stance, which might mean they're about to launch an attack, or are about to be attacked.
>
> It might seem extreme, but you can see the same cues in people when they're getting defensive in conversation; you can often spot the person who is starting to feel uncomfortable in a conversation by being mindful of their body language.

Haptic communication is communication through touch and refers to hand-shakes, kisses on cheeks, or brushes of the arm that often accompany greetings between two adults. In a stressful safeguarding communication situation, people can be particularly conscious of their haptic cues, which can often confuse or concern the other party. For example, where two adults regularly greet each other with a handshake, this could be appropriately absent during a conversation with a parent about a safeguarding issue. However, the practitioner must be aware that this is not evidence of guilt or evasiveness on the part of the parent, but is more than likely merely a symptom of the stresses of the situation. In a similar vein, phatic communication, or small talk, is also far less likely to occur. As in the case of haptic communication cues, practitioners should not ascribe excessive meaning to this absence. In this context it should be recognised that the encoding and decoding processes are a crucial element of such communication.

Proxemics is perhaps more commonly known as personal space, and is a vital cue in non-verbal communication. Hargie suggests that proxemics refers to 'the social distances we adopt in different settings, how we mark and protect personal territory, the angles at which we orient toward one another, and the standing or seating positions we take up' (2006: 47–48). This area is routinely covered by probationary police officers in their training, and can be considered by early years practitioners when communicating with parents or guardians with regard to emotive subjects such as safeguarding. The police trainer interviewed for this chapter suggested:

> Stand back and observe and look for the signs of danger. You create reaction time; we talk about working with a six-foot arc, where you try to not let people into your personal space. You're creating what we call a 'reaction gap'. And this gap is physical but it's also mental; it can be about just taking that extra half a second to think about what you're going to say or do next, and how you're going to say or do it.

As with the other areas of non-verbal communication discussed above, early years staff should be competent in interpreting the cues displayed by others, but also demonstrate the metacommunicative competence to ensure that they do not give off similar cues, irrespective of their own feelings during the episode.

Case study: metacommunicative competence

This case study briefly reflects back on an incident where a parent had appeared to strike a child outside a daycare setting. With experience and a deeper understanding of metacommunicative competence – that is, being able to appreciate and manipulate the many communication cues that exist between two people when they communicate – this setting manager, Senior Practitioner S, is able to analyse the situation and plan for a future occurrence:

Mum was just devastated. As soon as we sat her in the office and said, 'Look, can you tell us what happened?', she just burst out into tears, and she obviously knew there and then how this was looking. I'd known this woman for a while, I was more looking at giving her a cuddle, whereas the other manager that was in there sort of sat back, there was silence, nothing was said. I feel that I was less strict because I knew her so well, but that perhaps put me in a position that I shouldn't have been in. If I was in that situation again, I think I could have been much clearer in my language, and saying the correct thing. I wasn't really sure of what lines I could cross, what I could and couldn't say. I was fidgety; I must have looked really uncomfortable because I'd never dealt with anything like this before. I should've used the policies and procedures that we have, had them on the desk or my knee, and used that language, and been calm enough to do that.

Noise

As can be seen from Shannon and Weaver's model of communication (Figure 9.2), when a message has been encoded it will pass through 'noise' before the receiver can decode the message. Noise refers to any phenomenon that might manipulate, block or pervert the message as it was originally intended.

> In modern communication theory, the term noise is now interpreted much more widely and is used to refer to various kinds of barrier to effective communication that either distort or interrupt an encoded message so that it fails to reach the receiver in its original form
>
> (Blundel and Ippolito 2008: 5)

Authors and theorists on communication have posited a variety of perspectives on noise (Shannon and Weaver 1949; Daft and Marcic 2001; Wood 2010). However, three types of noise are perhaps most worthy of exploration when dealing with stressful situations such as those alluded to in this book:

1. physical noise;
2. semantic noise;
3. psychological noise.

Physical noise refers to anything in the physical environment that can have a detrimental impact on the message. In ordinary terms, this may include some form of physical discomfort, such as being too hot or too cold, or an injury that is preventing one party from giving their full attention to the communication episode. External physical noise could come from the environment in which the episode is taking place, such as excessive competing noise from machinery or traffic, or the transmitter and receiver simply being too far

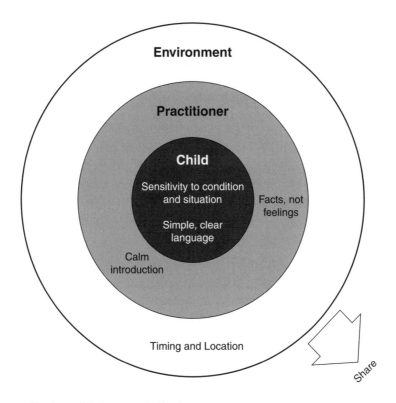

FIGURE 9.2 Simple model of communication focus.

from one another, or even too close to one another. Demonstrating how the environment around a person can have an effect on their ability to communicate effectively, Senior Practitioner J stated:

> The dad, he was the main perpetrator of the [domestic] violence, he'd always make sure he sat next to me in the [Common Assessment Framework] meetings; he'd be trying to look at my notes, and my observations. It was horrible, *absolutely* horrible. The way he made me feel, some of the stuff we were talking about, I had to be so careful and conscious of what I was saying and how I was saying it.

Semantic noise refers to a lack of mutual agreement or understanding about the meaning of a word, phrase or gesture. For instance, Senior Practitioner A, a senior member of nursery staff, revealed a typical semantic debate where an accusation had been made about a mother's physical contact with her child:

> …then she gave a statement to explain what had happened and explain the situation. Obviously she said she'd 'tapped', whereas the wording

from the member of staff was 'slapped' – then we had to sit down and think about what is a 'tap' and what is a 'slap'. There's a real difference between a tap and a slap, but then, is there really?

This illustrates well the possibilities for confusion around the use of words, particularly emotive words such as those that tend to be used in the lexicon of safeguarding. However, early years staff must be conscious of such semantic misunderstandings, which can cause significant noise in communication. It is crucial to have this at the forefront of their minds when either presenting their own views or listening to those of others.

Psychological noise is present when one participant has a particular psychological reaction to a particular word, phrase or subject because of a preconceived idea or notion. For instance, the mention of a popular television series to some would spark a sudden interest in a conversation, whereas for others the same words might raise psychological barriers, both reactions possibly adding difficulty to the communication process. In the safeguarding arena, words such as domestic violence, abuse, neglect or children's social care often produce an obvious psychological response in those responsible for children – workers and parents alike. In addition to this, a person's feelings towards another person in a communication episode can also create psychological noise. As Practitioner A suggested, when reflecting on an incident that had occurred between two children:

> Sometimes it's people's backgrounds. That can create fear when staff are speaking to them. What are they going to threaten to do to me? I know you shouldn't judge a family but you can normally tell, can't you? You build a relationship with certain families, you know their extended families. You don't judge on wealth or anything like that, but you know this family are nice, pleasant; the kids will be in bed by seven. Whereas the other girl's mum has a new boyfriend every month. It can affect how you are when you're in that situation. It affects how you interpret what they say to you.

Therefore, the psychological nature of noise is predominantly personal in nature, and an awareness of such noise will often reveal personal distortions, biases and prejudices on the part of the receiver.

Key points: noise

Noise in this context is any phenomenon that prevents a message from being received in the way it was intended. It can also be referred to as a communication barrier. This chapter concentrates on three types of noise:

- Physical noise – where the environment or something in the environment has an effect on the communication process, for instance competing noise, an interruption or a threat of danger.

- Semantic noise – where people involved in communication have different interpretations about the meanings of words, phrases or gestures. This might include excessive use of abbreviations or slang, or a lack of clarity around wording, such as the difference between 'tapping' and 'slapping'.
- Psychological noise – a person's psychological response when they are discussing a particular subject, or hear a particular word or phrase. For instance, emotive words can 'turn a person off' from a conversation, in the same way that discussing a favourite artist or television programme might 'turn a person on' to a conversation.

Early years practitioners have to be aware of the impact of noise when communicating, as it can have a profound effect on the nature of the message received by the recipient. It is important to remember that all communication forms suffer from the effects of noise on some level, and practitioners should be conscious of the role of noise when reflecting on misunderstandings between themselves and others.

When the message has passed through the noise, it will be decoded by the receiver, who will often unconsciously apply their own understanding and appreciation of the non-verbal cues and the noise to the message, before offering feedback. Such feedback may be as complicated as a verbal response or as comparatively simple as a nod or a smile. However, it will pass back through the same route as the original message and be subject to the same distortions and complications.

To summarise, simple communication between two people can be considerably more multifaceted than anticipated, particularly with the additional stresses that an emotive subject such as safeguarding brings. An experienced practitioner with good metacommunicative competence should be conscious of the added complication of encoding, decoding and noise, and be able to use this appreciation to foster effective communication between themselves and parents or guardians, even when involved in a safeguarding episode.

Communicating with children

While being conscious of the factors that have been described in this chapter, such as noise and non-verbal communication, the early years practitioner must be mindful of additional factors when communicating with a child during a safeguarding episode. This section will propose a series of key ideas for use in such a circumstance:

- the *timing* and *location* of the communication;
- demonstrating sensitivity to *condition* and *situation*;

- ensuring a *calm introduction* to the communication;
- using *simple, clear language;*
- appreciating *facts, not feelings;*
- *sharing* the details of the communication appropriately.

Since responsibility for adherence to each of these areas lies with the practitioner, the simple model of communication focus proposed in Figure 9.2 demonstrates *where* the attention of the practitioner should be focused – either the child at the centre of the communication, the practitioner's self, the environment, or the external reporting mechanisms.

The timing and location of the communication

As has been suggested already in this chapter, revelations or realisations around safeguarding episodes can happen at any time in the setting. However, in consultation with the safeguarding lead practitioner, and following local setting policies and Local Safeguarding Children Board (LSCB) procedures, the practitioner can to some extent influence the timing and location of any communication with children in relation to the episode. In particular, practitioners can ensure that the child is not distracted by other activities taking place around them. That is, the child must feel secure that other people or children around them are not able to pry, but you also need to ensure that the child in question is not anxious to join others in playing a game or activity that they enjoy because of a conversation with you. In addition to this, consider the routines of the child, for instance mealtimes. Does the child have a regular toilet routine that you may be interrupting, or are the parents of the child likely to arrive imminently? These scenarios would all add unnecessary and unhelpful 'noise' to the communication, and thus impair the process.

It *may*, depending on circumstances, be rewarding to return the child to the scene of the original revelation. For instance, if a child was playing in the sandpit when they first made a comment that initiated your concerns, returning the child to the sandpit in order for you to explore the child's feelings may elucidate a more thorough response from them. Obviously, if you suspect that the safeguarding incident was geographically located within said sandpit, then the area should be avoided.

You should also give consideration where appropriate to examining any pertinent issues arising from the safeguarding episode with the other children in the setting, perhaps utilising a game or an outdoor activity, and obviously without making any reference whatsoever to the episode that acted as a catalyst for this action. For instance, Senior Practitioner A suggested, 'We often talk about secrets; we talk about how we don't keep secrets from each other, we just encourage the children in their honesty and openness. It hopefully makes them question if someone wants them to keep something secret.'

Demonstrating sensitivity to condition and situation

A key element alongside determining the appropriate location and timing for the communication is to deal with child's wellbeing initially. While this sounds like unnecessary advice, in pressurised situations we can often forget the obvious and leap straight into policies and procedures, bypassing the key element of ensuring the child's comfort and wellbeing. Therefore, dealing with the child's initial comfort and ensuring that they feel able to confide in you is paramount. Doing so may in extreme circumstances involve the application of first aid, the provision of sustenance or simply being a friend to play with for a little while, prior to any thought of exploring the safeguarding issue. The children's charity Barnardo's supports this commitment to the child's immediate mood and state, explaining that 'exhausted, hungry, ill or frightened children need to have their problems acknowledged before they can start talking with you. Don't press them for information or leave them with a sense of failure because they have not answered your questions' (2006: 15). This sensitivity also applies to your interactions with the child, as Room Leader S commented:

> You want to find out what's happened, but you can't just go and barge in with questions: how did this happen, who has done this? Sometimes you can alarm the child and make them feel different, so we would do it on a one-to-one with the child – keep them calm, and make sure that they know they are not in trouble. We just need them to know that we can help to make it better.

This advice resonated with Senior Practitioner J, who added:

> You don't probe with questioning. By making the child comfortable in that situation, you encourage them to talk to you, especially as their key person. If that wasn't working for some reason, but I wanted to hear the 'child's voice', I'd use some kind of activity that they could join in with, maybe some kind of role play or game that might hopefully encourage the child, rather than just questioning them.

Ensuring a calm introduction to the communication

A calm introduction to the communication is vital in allaying any fears the child may have in regard to talking with you. An introduction that does not arouse upset in the child and does not differentiate the child from others is key, as is maintaining a demeanour with the child that ensures they do not feel isolated or 'in trouble'. Practitioners should give thought to how the communication will be introduced, perhaps in the form of a game or activity, in order to ensure that the child is relaxed. In particular, practitioners should be conscious of their own metacommunicative competence, and the potential for unwanted messages that a child will interpret from non-verbal cues. An unnecessary grimace or wince, or even verbal outburst, could make the child far more conscious of the issue at hand, or even make them feel as though they themselves are now 'in trouble'. Therefore, a calm introduction to the communication with a complete absence of drama will elicit a more productive response from the child. It may be that you have already contacted other agencies or services, whose personnel are in attendance. If so, ensure that the child is introduced to and fully aware of everyone involved in the communication.

Using simple, clear language

Practitioners are incredibly skilled in the use of language appropriate to the individual child, often having spent years developing their craft through the relationships that they develop with each child that they support. Practitioners must be mindful that, despite the emergence of a possible safeguarding episode, the nature and design of their communication with individual children should not change, as this would only raise the suspicions and defences of the child and would be completely counter-productive to the communication episode.

The relationships that practitioners build with children also place them in an ideal position to identify when the child is not telling the truth. However, Barnardo's reminds us that 'when children lie they usually have good reason to do so. If you find they are lying don't show anger, press for the truth or interrogate them' (2006: 16). It is likely that the child is either not trusting of you or is unclear regarding your motives, or it may be that the child is attempting to balance loyalties to both yourself and other parties (Barnardo's 2006), with a perceived or instructed need to maintain secrets and confidentialities and perhaps a building discomfort with the situation at hand. This may well manifest itself in communication cues such as eye contact, a lack of which in the case of children will often mean discomfort in the situation or lack of trust in people involved in the situation, and should not be confused with the same observations in adults.

Appreciating facts, not feelings

When a safeguarding episode occurs, it is far too easy to become swept up in emotion and to try to become a combination of Sherlock Holmes and Florence Nightingale, not only tending to the child's immediate needs but hypothesising and conjecturing on likely causes and culprits. This is not appropriate, and in fact can be potentially quite damaging in some circumstances. as often suspicions can be groundless. As Room Leader A explained during her interview:

We once started making our own notes on a little boy who had a mark on him. It looked like a cigarette burn, but then one day he came in with this little toy that had an odd end and [laughs], you know, that was that.

While it is clear that the setting staff in this instance had shown appropriate diligence and followed procedures well, a 'cigarette burn' on further observation became a mark self-inflicted by playing with a favourite toy. This illustrates the necessity to include relevant external professionals as discussed later in this chapter. In this case a medical professional could have provided a useful diagnosis at an earlier stage.

This example also highlights the importance of observation and sound observational practice in the setting. This is particularly important in all aspects of a child's development (Palaiologou 2012), and its merits are equally prevalent in safeguarding situations, where observations of a child's behaviours or interactions may reveal the first clues as to the existence of an issue. As Senior Practitioner J revealed:

Sometimes the child doesn't have the language to be able to tell you something, so you have to use observation, and your own intuition to pick up on things. You'd look at their non-verbal communication, obviously their bodily appearance such as perhaps weight loss, or the expressions on their faces when they play – are they unusually solitary? When you work with children you quickly notice the differences.

Therefore, we can utilise casual observation, and also comparison of current behaviour against formal observation records in the child's personal file, to identify possible issues. In circumstances where the child has their voice and is able to talk to you effectively, other strategies can be utilised. As Senior Practitioner A explained:

We are very careful not to keep questioning, you know; we might *compare*,though, for instance 'Oh, I've got a poorly too' and encourage them to talk, rather than questioning them with 'How've you got that', 'Who did that?' We are open, we need the children to be open, so we don't make anything into a secret. That might be what *they've* been told to do by someone.

This approach of 'comparing poorlies' in the case of children having visible injuries can be utilised as a useful introduction into establishing the initial facts around a potential safeguarding situation. Of course, this example relies on the word 'poorlies' being a term used and understood by the child; the word can obviously be replaced with others that have meaning to other children.

In addition, the communication process must be recorded, verbatim. Practitioners and settings should identify a suitable document for recording such details. It may be that a form ordinarily used in setting for a narrative observation (Palaiologou 2012) will provide you with sufficient space and opportunity to record the conversation in a verbatim manner, together with descriptions of the child's demeanour, relevant body language cues, or other important observations such as the child's state of dress or reference to any injuries.

Sharing the details of the communication appropriately

Serious case reviews have historically revealed that it can often be the process of 'sharing information' among those with responsibility for the safeguarding and welfare of children that has failed children most seriously, sometimes with calamitous results. As Reder and Duncan confirm, 'since the 1970s, virtually all reviews of fatal child abuse cases in the United Kingdom report that there was evidence of communication failures between professionals' (2003: 82). This has resulted in increased pressure on those working with children to formulate a 'joined-up' approach to communication, best demonstrated by the commitment to multi-agency working, championed through the *Every Child Matters* agenda (DfES 2003a).

For this reason, it is essential that early years practitioners with concerns about a child's welfare share those concerns with others, in the first instance the member of staff in their own setting with overall responsibility for safeguarding, often designated the Safeguarding Lead Practitioner. This person will then take responsibility for collecting and collating all relevant records from the setting, and determining the extent to which outside authorities such as the LSCB are involved. This necessary and welcome addition of outside agency and structure places a great deal of importance on the quality of the records that we have maintained, as Bandele emphasises:

> Clear and accurate factual recording of all safeguarding concerns/incidents is vital to the effective safeguarding of children, and, in some cases, the apprehension and prosecution of perpetrators. It is important to realise that safeguarding records are kept until the child has reached their twenty-fifth birthday. Therefore, records must be as meaningful in 20 years time as they are at the time of writing.
>
> (2009: 41)

Despite the serious nature of Bandele's remarks, and the potentially worrisome thought for new staff of the implications of multi-agency working, the experience, training and spheres of influence of those outside our settings are a vitally useful tool for practitioners. This point is emphasised by Senior Practitioner A when discussing a child who had given her team cause for concern:

I'd be on the phone talking to the children's centre, or the safeguarding board. You're acting on instinct, but you must get that clarification from the people who, at the end of the day, are there to help you with this. We've even phoned the hospital in the past to ask advice.

Therefore, the practitioner must be mindful of the range of support and expertise available to them in such instances, in addition to legal, LSCB and organisational requirements to disclose information in a timely and detailed manner to their Lead Safeguarding Practitioner, or other agencies.

Key points: communicating with children

This section introduces a Simple Model of Communication Focus and recommends a series of key ideas for use by practitioners when communicating with children in the early stages of a safeguarding episode:

- Be mindful of the *timing* and *location* of the communication.
- Demonstrate sensitivity to condition and situation.
- Ensure a *calm introduction* to the communication.
- Use *simple, clear language*.
- Appreciate *facts, not feelings*.
- *Share* the details of the communication appropriately.

In order to fully comply with these steps, practitioners must familiarise themselves in detail with their setting's safeguarding policy, which may well be updated on a regular basis, such as following the release of a new EYFS standards document, or a serious case review.

Furthermore, practitioners must be aware of their personal responsibility in abiding by this policy, and have immediate knowledge of and access to their Safeguarding Lead Practitioner, and steps to follow in involving outside agencies, such as the Local Safeguarding Children Board.

Conclusion

Practitioners have a moral and professional responsibility for effective communication with children at all times during their careers, but that responsibility is never more acute than at the emergence of a potential safeguarding episode. Serious case reviews (Reder and Duncan 2003) have pinpointed communication as a consistently failing element in many high-profile child abuse cases, and only through acknowledging these failures and challenging ourselves at the grassroots level will the situation improve.

Communication is more than a cognitive concern. With it come significant emotional or other unexpected consequences, such as the emergence of sympathy for those accused during some safeguarding situations.

The concept of meta-communicative competence and the importance of clear, explicit, authoritative record keeping are central themes throughout the chapter. Shannon and Weaver's mathematical model of communication (1949) provides a framework with which to explore some of the issues inherent in communication, particularly communication in the emotionally charged arena of a potential safeguarding episode. This includes the often counter-productive nature of non-verbal communication, particularly in the form of kinesic, proxemic and haptic communication. Underpinning this is the practitioner's need to appreciate and understand their own metacommunicative competence, or ability to analyse and utilise the multitude of communication cues at their disposal during any face-to-face communication exchange.

It is to be hoped that this chapter has provided new or inexperienced practitioners with a realistic and relevant flavour of the impact that a safeguarding episode will have on them as individuals, and has provided practical tips to deal with such episodes in a manner that meets the needs of the child, themselves and their setting, and the wider community.

Further reading

Hargie, O. (2006) *The Handbook of Communication Skills*, 3rd edn, Hove: Routledge.

Owen Hargie is an internationally recognised author on the subject of communication. This book is essential for anyone wanting to understand more fully the communication that goes around them, and become more engaged with their own meta-communicative competence.

Reder, P. and Duncan, S. (2003) 'Understanding communication in child protection networks', *Child Abuse Review*, 12 (2): 82–100.

Written and published following Lord Laming's report into the death of Victoria Climbié, Reder and Duncan's paper provides a fascinating yet damning analysis of the role of communication within the context of multi-agency failure. Although it is particularly relevant to setting managers and local authority staff, all early years practitioners would benefit from the developmental approaches advocated.

10

Inter-agency working, observation and assessment

Frances Marsden, Samantha McMahon and Andrew Youde

This chapter explores the inter-agency approach to safeguarding children and considers the knowledge and skills of early years professionals involved in protecting children and young people through:

- the Common Assessment Framework (CWDC 2007), inter-agency working and the importance of their communications and relationships in these roles;
- the practice of observations and assessing children's needs to provide evidence that then informs the team around the child;
- the relevance of power in professional relationships.

Additionally, the role of advocate for the child is considered, alongside the roles and responsibilities of all childcare professionals.

An inter-agency approach to the protection and wellbeing of children is not new; the Children Act 1989 specifies duties and powers for co-operation between social services departments, education, housing and health. However, by 1997, when New Labour came to power, only a handful of local authorities had established services that were partially integrated, and an assessment of services by the Department of Health in 1998 suggested that co-operation was fragmented, inflexible and suited to institutional rather than individual needs. In order to reverse the trend of prioritising institutional needs, the Labour government set out to break down barriers between agencies and develop a policy strategy which meant that the welfare of children in need, including those requiring protection, was no longer seen to be the responsibility of a single agency. In order to speed up the radical institutional change required to ensure inter-agency co-operation, the government seized upon the Laming Report (2003) into the murder of Victoria Climbié. The report of the inquiry describes the case as a 'vivid demonstration of poor practice between services' (ibid.: 13) and recommends inter-agency co-operation. Around the same time, an inter-departmental review of early years services identified significant benefits of early interventions for disadvantaged children, and recognised weaknesses of multi-agency work in general (DfES 2003b). This provided more evidence of the need for a coherent multi-agency policy on children, leading to the Green Paper *Every Child Matters* (DfES 2003a). The Children Act 2004 followed, which provided the legislative framework for working in partnership; however, it went further than the 1989 Children Act by setting out new organisational configurations such as Children's Trusts and Local Safeguarding Children Boards to promote co-operation between agencies. Subsequent statutory and policy guidance issued in 2005 and 2006 by the DfES (2006), and then the Childcare Act in 2006, created a duty for all early childhood services to work together to deliver integrated early childhood services. In order to facilitate the translation of law into practice and overcome some of the barriers to integrated working, particularly in the assessment process, the Common Assessment Framework (CWDC 2007) was introduced to promote a single assessment process to identify children in need, co-ordinate provision and bring together a range of professionals in an inter-agency collaborative model. Fundamental to the policy and legislation included in this section is the need to safeguard and promote the welfare of children, through early identification, early intervention and inter-agency co-operation.

Policy and practice from 2010

Although the government changed in 2010, subsequent reviews conducted by Field (2010), Allen (2011a, b) and Tickell (2011) have reinforced the importance of early identification and early intervention to safeguard children. Further, Munro (2011a, b) stresses that early help for children and families does more to reduce abuse and neglect than reactive services do. The government has pulled together findings of these reviews to produce the policy document *Supporting Families in the Foundation Years* (DfE 2011a), which states that 'good early intervention in the foundation years relies on genuine integrated working' (ibid.: 53). Many children's centres are integrated within nurseries, infant and junior schools in an identified area of need and offer full day care, wrap-around care (care provided at either end of the school day that might include a breakfast club and an after-school club and that may be on the school premises, although not always owned or managed by the school) and after-school care facilities for children aged from birth to 11.

Early years practitioners need to work with a range of other individuals such as social workers, health professionals and educational specialists, many of whom will be housed within a children's centre. The close proximity of the varied agencies helps deliver closer links and therefore facilitates some shared understanding with inter-agency teams. In order to provide this integrated working, childcare professionals need to be aware of the need to communicate responsibly and effectively with each other. The early years professional's knowledge and skills when sharing information is key to a shared understanding of the concerns for and protection of children.

One obvious context for the sharing of information is in the assessment of a child's development. From September 2012, all nurseries and childminders are required to give parents a written summary of their child's progress at around the age of 2. The intention is to combine this with the Healthy Child Programme Review (DH 2009b), which will ensure families can access early support. To complete the child's progress review it is essential that the practitioner working in early years has in-depth knowledge and understanding of child development that are inclusive and culturally diverse (Nutbrown 2012). However, knowledge and understanding alone are not enough; the practitioner must be able to apply this knowledge to data they have gathered about the child. Practitioners gather data about the child through listening to and observing the child; therefore, the practitioner must be tuned into the child and a competent observer. Consequently, the practitioner has a responsibility to highlight any concerns arising from assessment of the data gathered but must be aware that the words they use are emotive and powerful. The child being observed has feelings; so do the parents and other professionals. It is important to be aware of the emotional dimension when communicating the findings. When time is short, it can be tempting to label children, to summarise, and in the process lose a more nuanced and sophisticated understanding. Understanding the impact of communications is of great importance to relaying the message to parents or carers and other childcare professionals.

As we learned in Chapter 9, when considering discussing something as emotionally charged as the behaviour of a child who is being cared for by a childminder or in a nursery setting, it is important to consider whether non-verbal communication supports or contradicts what is being said. Also, if there is sensitivity to non-verbal communications of others, it is possible to gain valuable feedback regarding their thoughts about messages being relayed.

The environment for communication with a parent or carer, or another professional, is important. Finding a quiet space to discuss a child's development, for example, is crucial to ensuring that the parent or carer is able to concentrate on the message being given. A noisy nursery with people coming and going and staff busying themselves with regular duties is distracting. It is important for early years practitioners to realise that at the end of a busy working day most parents or carers are mentally planning the next stage of their day and regularly rushing from one place to another in a short timeframe. In such cases it is often best to make a clear appointment time when the practitioner and the parent or carer can discuss the observations made and plan for an early intervention to be actioned if required. If the parent or

carer is given time to plan for the discussion, they will generally be more prepared to listen actively and to openly discuss issues and concerns and, often,
offer their own ideas for solutions and remedies. Most importantly, the child
is a key part of the process of discussing the observations and their emotions
should be appropriately considered too.

Conducting observations and assessing children's needs

Observing children is a fundamental aspect of all early years practice and
ensures that practitioners can match provision to children's needs in order to
support learning and development. Observation also underpins practice that
safeguards children. In this section it is not possible to discuss every aspect of
observation, including the range of methods available or the complex ethical
considerations. This is not to suggest that these are not important; it is simply to
say that they are not the focus of this chapter. This section considers some of the
knowledge and skills that have been highlighted in current policy developments linked to safeguarding, with particular reference to the progress check
and working with other professionals through inter-agency working.

To provide meaningful information that might be used by other professionals, practitioners need to be engaged in systematic and methodical observation and analysis (Papatheodorou and Luff 2011). In practice this means
that observations must be planned and carried out by an organised practitioner who is able to capture key aspects of the child's development.

While it is recommended that progress reviews should focus on three
prime areas, namely communication and language, physical development
and personal, social and emotional development (DfE 2012b), each child will
follow an individual path and may be more developed in some areas than
others (NCB 2012). Therefore, practitioners should be alert to all aspects of the
child's development and employ a range of observational methods at different points in the day. As was mentioned in Chapter 7, Bronfenbrenner (1979)
explained that the environment or context has a significant influence on a
child's behaviour and development, therefore practitioners must also be conscious of this and include relevant information in the observation – for example, is the setting particularly busy or noisy? Might the weather conditions
have changed the routine of the day? Papatheodorou and Luff (2011) describe
observation as a context of dynamic interaction in which the observer,
observed and setting are influenced by each other.

In this dynamic interrelationship the practitioner must be aware of the
context, know the child and family, and be aware of how these can influence
observations. The NCB (2012) recommends that the practitioner who prepares
the progress check and provides information to other professionals should
know the child well; they will normally be the child's key person. This is
important, because the key person is likely to know the family, which means
they can work with the parents on completing the progress check and will be

aware of any changes to family circumstances that might affect the child's development, for example, the birth of a sibling. While some changes to family life are not a major cause for concern, a trusted practitioner may find that parents confide in them about other, more sensitive issues that could adversely affect the child's welfare and development, for example, domestic violence.

In order to deal with such disclosures it is essential that the practitioner has knowledge of and fully understands the setting's safeguarding policy and their legal responsibilities. Furthermore, the practitioner must be aware of how their relationships with, and knowledge about, the child and family might influence judgements made in observations. They should also be aware that first impressions can have a lasting effect on observational findings, to the extent that the observer seeks out information which is consistent with those first impressions (Papatheodorou and Luff 2011). It can be very difficult for a practitioner to acknowledge, for example, that they may like or favour one child over another, which might lead them to selectively record information or interpret a child's behaviour in a certain way.

Case study: Max

At tidy away time, Max (age 4) throws the bricks into the box then runs to the carpet area. He sits down and in the process kicks Amy and hits Harley with his arm.

If your impression of Max is that he is a fun-loving and enthusiastic boy who is keen to get to the carpet to take part in story time because he enjoys stories with his parents, your interpretation of this scenario might be very positive. Consider how it might be if you perceive Max always to be where the trouble is, and you know that his father is in prison.

Activity

Consider how you would react to such a child in your care. Do you have a stereotypical view of fathers in prison or attitudinal bias against the upbringing of children in your care?

We all try not to be influenced by such information, but can we really say that it does not inform our behaviour towards the child?

Observational findings can be further compromised when reports are passed among concerned professionals. As Billington (2006) cautions, they can generate set responses and prejudice the way children are seen. To strengthen the validity and reliability of observations, practitioners should use different methods of observation and where possible cross-check their observations against another professionals. The practitioner must be prepared to confront their values, emotions and language, and ultimately their own beliefs about the best interests of the child (Willan 2010).

Case study: communication

Following a series of observations, the family support worker and the children's centre manager discussed the need for intervention for Ruby, whose mother was having problems managing her behaviour. The children's centre was about to start a 12-week behaviour management programme for families, and a meeting was scheduled between the three adults. The two early years professionals used their online calendars to arrange a time when they knew they could discuss the situation, and the family support worker phoned the mother to confirm she could make the meeting.

Holding a joint meeting like this ensures that all aspects of Ruby's behaviour and concerns are considered carefully before a programme is provided to help improve the situation. It also gives each person time to gather any necessary information that may need to be shared. There is a need to consider the relationship building that needs to take place before the mother can accept the help on offer; this can happen quickly only in face-to-face meetings, as reading body language and expressions helps to confirm relationships during communications.

The family support worker was able to offer information regarding social services' involvement with the family and the recent involvement by the health team. The mother confided that she was having great difficulty managing Ruby's behaviour, which often resulted in shouting matches between the two, with her other children being upset and the mother giving in to Ruby's demands. The children's centre manager offered a behaviour management course and, in particular, the expertise of the play and learning worker. The mother agreed.

The family support worker arranged a meeting at the family home with the play and learning worker. This ensured that the family's other children were aware of the behaviour management programme being considered and arrangements were made for them to be cared for appropriately while Ruby and her mother attended the sessions.

During the home meeting, the mother explained she felt she had no bond with Ruby, her youngest child, and gave a relevant history of the pregnancy and birth which highlighted an attachment formation issue. The play and learning worker suggested working one to one with the mother and Ruby, using a technique based on infant massage to help with attachment.

Questions

Was the best method of communication used in this case study?
What could have been done differently?
How many different agencies were involved in the case?
Who are the team around the child?

Active listening forms part of good communication

Ruby's case study shows why active listening is an important skill for all childcare practitioners communicating with a child, family or carer. If the individual is to fully understand a message, it is important that they are able to actively listen. With so many distractions in today's world, individuals appear to be listening when actually they are thinking about other things. Real listening is active and it ensures thoughtfulness and consideration of the message and often ensures a response, sometimes with the need for clarification of certain points. Active listening takes account of non-verbal messages given by body language and tone of voice.

Questions for reflection

Consider the last time you actively listened to a message given by a parent or carer. How did you show you were actively listening?

What non-verbal messages were being given?

Was the outcome successful? Why do you think this?

Good, clear communication and listening skills are required by all professionals in the inter-agency working environment when considering the needs of children. If the team around the child is to be successful, then every member of the team should be able to communicate their views in the best interest of the child.

Power and status in inter-agency working

Jane Osgood (2005, 2006, 2009) has repeatedly drawn attention to the low status of practitioners who work in early years, and Nutbrown (2012), in her review of childcare qualifications, points out that unfortunately this is still the case. This lack of status has implications for inter-agency working.

Case study: Lynn and Melanie

Consider the last time you actively listened to a message given by a parent or carer.

Lynn has been Jade's key person for six months and has worked closely with Melanie, her mother. Jade is 3 years old and has communication delays, and Melanie has struggled to manage some of her daughter's behaviour. They were referred to the setting by the health visitor when Melanie found she was pregnant with a second child. Lynn collected detailed evidence charting Jade's progress while at the setting and built a relationship with Jade and Melanie

---

based on respect and trust. When a recent inter-agency meeting was called, Melanie asked if Lynn could be present, along with the speech and language therapist, advisory teacher, health visitor and special needs co-ordinator. Lynn was asked to provide a summary of Jade's progress and Melanie added that Jade 'is really coming on' and 'things were better at home' thanks to the setting and Lynn's help.

The team felt that Jade and Melanie still needed ongoing support and monitoring and that someone needed to take responsibility as 'lead professional', acting as a single point of contact for Melanie and keeping the records. Melanie asked whether Lynn could take on this role as she knew her and Jade so well. At this point one of the other members of the team commented, 'Oh, we need somebody more qualified than Lynn.' No one objected, including Lynn and Melanie.

Consider the message communicated by this statement, to both Lynn and Melanie, about the role and status of the early years practitioner, and the parents.

Questions

Who holds the power in this situation?

Do you think status is important when working with other agencies? Why?

In the case study, neither Lynn nor Melanie felt able to challenge the often widely held view that working with young children is unskilled and of little worth. Such powerlessness is deeply ingrained, explained by Bourdieu (1977) as a process of socialisation whereby, as a result of many social and cultural factors, both Lynn and Melanie accept as legitimate their lack of power and status. Furthermore, established professions may feel threatened by a perceived loss of power to someone considered 'unqualified', particularly through loss of a formal power role, such as that of 'lead professional'. Thus, they seek to exert power and remain unchallenged. This is not surprising. For many years, working in early years was associated with low levels of qualification and only recently (in 2006) emerged as a graduate profession in the United Kingdom, one that needs time to become established.

Although the actions of the other professionals are, at best, ill-informed and might embarrass Lynn and Melanie, they could mean that Jade's needs are not met and that the effectiveness of the intervention is compromised. This contradicts Munro's (2011a) recommendation which calls for a system that values and develops professional expertise, and is focused on the safety and welfare of children and young people. The early years practitioner cannot immediately control or change the extremely complex interplay of social, cultural, professional and political factors that determine perceived levels of power in a multi-professional team. However, there are some things they can do which will strengthen their position in the team and help other professionals recognise the value of their work in safeguarding the child. These include:

- Focus on the child.
- Provide accurate evidence based on systematic observations and in-depth knowledge of child development.
- Be confident. Draw strength and confidence from being recognised by the government as being in a unique position in knowing the child and family.
- Build trusting, respectful and professional relationships.
- Pursue higher-level qualifications, as higher education improves levels of confidence and the ability to communicate effectively. This can help practitioners to assert themselves as knowledgeable professionals. Qualifications do matter; they confer status and help reduce power differentials between professionals.
- Remember why you work with young children. Most practitioners have a deep-rooted 'ethic of care' and want to make a positive difference to young children's lives. Young children can be vulnerable because of their age and life circumstances, and may not be able to say what they need.
- Be an advocate for the child, be their voice, or encourage them to find a voice.

Being an advocate for the child

Child advocacy applies to a range of individuals, professionals and advocacy organisations that watch over and promote the development of children. An individual or organisation engaging in advocacy aims to protect children and their rights. This includes safeguarding them from harm or harmful situations.

In 1991 the UK government agreed to ratify the UN Convention on the Rights of the Child (UNCRC) (United Nations 1989) and, while it is not UK law, there is a clear commitment to protect and promote children's rights by all means available. The government appointed a Children's Commissioner for England following the Children Act 2004 whose specific purpose was to 'promote the views and interests of all children in England, in particular those whose voices are least likely to be heard' (Office of the Children's Commissioner 2012: 3). The Munro Review (2011a, b) recommended putting the power of decision making back into the hands of local authorities and giving leading professionals more time with families while using their expertise to make life-changing judgements, rather than the emphasis being on recording targets and procedures.

The key to successful local government responsibility is to ensure flexibility in the roles and development of joint working practices for childcare professionals such as inter-agency working. This should ensure that the sharing of information and documentation is at least compatible across agencies, to speed reporting and prioritisation of cases. It is important for all childcare professionals that inter-agency help is available when a situation arises and that there is no delay when a child's needs must be met.

One way of being an advocate for children is to ensure that the child's voice is heard. An advocate will always try to prevent children from being harmed and may try to obtain protection for those who have already been injured in some way. They will also ensure that children have access to positive influences or services that will benefit their lives, such as appropriate child care and education.

Generally it is the parents of the child who advocate for their children, but schools and early years settings also work with social services, and occasionally the police, to advocate on behalf of children. A safeguarding officer is required in all settings as an advocate for the child for protection and to ensure that all children are nurtured. Advocacy should be the responsibility of everyone who can recognise harmful situations for children and young people.

Case study: a young childcare student

In 1977 I was a childcare student aged 16. I would spend a week in college being taught child care and a week in a nursery class or school. As a new student I was given all the jobs others did not want. A small boy called Brian needed changing. I was asked to take him to the loo and clean his soiled pants. He was a lovely boy with long blond hair and kept saying to me, 'I am a boy, you know, not a girl. I am a boy because my name is Brian.' I chatted away to him so he was not uncomfortable. After removing his trousers and pants and wiping him clean, I could see immediately he was covered in a chickenpox rash around his torso and legs (or so I thought). I managed to put underpants on him but asked him to wait for the teacher to come and see him.

One member of staff came, then another. Even the head came to see him. I was observed closely the rest of the day and felt I must have not cleaned him correctly and maybe had infected one of the very sore chickenpox blisters. However, the next day I was told that Brian did not have chickenpox and the poor child was covered in cigarette burns. I have never forgotten my first case of child abuse. He was immediately taken into care and we never saw him again at nursery.

Questions

How would you have helped Brian?

Which agencies should be involved in Brian's care?

Given this situation today, what procedures do you have in place for reporting and recording actions?

Being an advocate for the child is littered with difficult decisions and comes with enormous responsibility.

Inter-agency team working

With government proposals in the form of *Every Child Matters* (DfES 2003a) and the Children Act 2004, the need for teamwork within all childcare settings is paramount, with a view towards inter-agency working being more vital than ever before. The *Every Child Matters* agenda (DfES 2003a) promoted many benefits that collaborative working delivers in the interests of the child's family in improving their outcomes and general wellbeing. The benefit of inter-agency working does not solely impact upon the child and their family; as Halsey *et al.* (2005) argue, practitioners prefer not to operate as single agencies, but report increased levels of satisfaction with inter-agency working. This perhaps implies that practitioners within inter-agency teams find their sense of fulfilment being achieved, possibly through the less mundane routine of their customary place of work.

The *Every Child Matters* agenda (DfES 2003a) outlined models of effective inter-agency working, but unfortunately these are not always reflected in practice, often because of a lack of time. In reality there are many barriers to hinder inter-agency teams from working effectively together. The lack of understanding of, and respect for, other professional roles is a predominant factor in influencing the way in which a team works. The *Common Core of Skills and Knowledge for the Children's Workforce* (DfES 2005) states, 'To work successfully on a multi-agency basis you need to be clear about your own role and aware of the roles of other professionals.' The lack of time for practitioners to develop skills in being able to work across their professional boundaries is a major barrier (Hackett 2003). For this reason, inter-agency team meetings can regrettably fail, owing to a lack of understanding by those attending about each other's responsibilities. Often, a hierarchy can occur according to power and status rather than to knowledge and skills. However, inter-agency teams can make a difference to the lives of children and their families when they work together as a team around the child.

Case study: Alex

Alex lives with his grandparents, who have had legal custody of him since he was 9 months old. He was born at 26 weeks as a result of his mother's poor health and drug abuse, and spent three months in hospital before being discharged to the care of his mother, where he was subjected to severe neglect. He has very limited, or no, contact with his birth parents.

Alex is 4 years old. He attends a school nursery for five afternoons per week and the integrated child care of a children's centre for two mornings per week.

He has been attending the setting consistently for 14 months. From transition into the setting, Alex has displayed behavioural concerns. Through observation and the involvement of outside agencies, he has an Individual Education Plan enforced, has been placed on the Special Educational Needs Register and is currently on Early Years Action Plus. Through positive relationships built up with his grandparents, it has been possible to understand Alex's needs and why he displays such behaviours.

Questions

Distinguish the teams involved in the welfare of Alex.

Identify barriers that directly affect the way in which teams work effectively.

How might inter-agency communication be affected?

Case study: Joy

Joy was living with her mother in a dirty house overrun with pets. Joy did not have her own bed and, although she was almost 5, still slept with her mother. During a home visit the reception teacher and teaching assistant reported their concerns to the head teacher and continued to monitor Joy closely. During Reception and Key Stage 1, Joy's attendance was erratic, her learning and development were delayed, she was dirty with unwashed clothes, and she was often left uncollected at the end of school. Her mother would not talk to staff or attend meetings. The head was concerned about Joy's lack of friends and slow progress in school, and contacted social services. Joy's social worker explained that she was aware of Joy's circumstances, but it wasn't until her mother was arrested for a very serious offence that a case conference was called, and Joy was made the subject of a child protection plan.

At the age of 7, Joy went to live with her father. The head teacher and the learning mentor welcomed the father into the school and quickly realised that he was struggling to parent. He confided that Joy wanted to sleep in his bed with him, which made him uncomfortable. The head contacted social services and was able to source funding for a new bed; the learning mentor helped Joy to come to terms with sleeping on her own. The head worked with social services and the local authority to secure counselling for Joy, and throughout Key Stage 2 the teaching assistant and lunchtime supervisors worked with the head and Joy's father to make sure she had enough to eat, and was dressed appropriately. Within two terms Joy had made two years' progress in her learning and development, and her attendance was 100 per cent. She made friends and became a happy, confident child.

Unfortunately, Joy's mother and her case were well known in the community. Towards the end of Key Stage 2 she was to appear in court. The head was aware that publicity surrounding the case might leave Joy vulnerable to bullying when she started high school. She contacted the high school and worked with them, the social worker, the local authority, Joy and Joy's father to manage a smooth transition into high school. The social worker commented that she had never dealt with a case with such a positive outcome.

Questions

What are the key elements that contributed to the successful inter-agency approach in this case?

Do you have a clear understanding of your roles and responsibilities to an inter-agency approach in your setting?

When might you need to take the lead or provide support as part of a wider team?

Children's Services discuss the shared purpose and vision for integrated services but have difficulty in providing a formula to ensure truly integrated working is achieved by their teams. Although there is agreement that inter-agency team working is the best way to resolve childcare and safeguarding issues, they do not have an agreed policy or framework for its achievement.

The Children's Workforce Development Council (CWDC 2009) defines inter-agency working as 'an effective way of supporting children and families with additional needs', and Lord Laming (2009), quoting an unidentified social sorker, stated that 'relationships are crucial; it's not about structures, it's about making it work for children out there'. This suggests that different agencies should do what is necessary to work in the child's best interest and disregard the organisational structures that get in the way of being proactive. Inter-agency teams work best when a culture of honesty and understanding is created – when challenge and conflict are used within the group to produce different creative options and better strategies for a successful outcome.

Structure and culture of teams

Individuals from different childcare backgrounds work differently and fail to use a common language to communicate. For example, health professionals use a different language from that found in the educational sector, and childcare professionals working in local authority settings have different working practices as compared with those who work in privately run settings. When working across disciplines it is important to acknowledge these issues at the outset, otherwise misunderstandings cause problems. When professionals are working collaboratively in an inter-agency team there needs to be a team structure that enables clear communication and decision making. When they are working across agencies, team structure should be organised so each individual holds an equal status, providing a feeling of true collaboration. The leadership expert Adair (2009) states that a team leader will emerge, given time, and generally it is this person who will determine the culture of the collaborative work. Given that inter-agency team working is responsive and then the team disperses, this theoretical approach is a difficult one to follow.

Team formation

When inter-agency teams form, they need time for a settling-in period, as roles and practices are established. Tuckman (1965) describes this as formation, where each individual determines how they can best contribute to the team and the role they will play in the process. As inter-agency teams generally come together to resolve a problem, this formation needs to be achieved quickly. Inevitably there will be some conflict within the group of individuals as professionals, even though everyone is aiming to achieve their best for the child. At this stage a true professional will be able to put their differences in policy or procedure aside to concentrate on the child and issues at hand. Here a leader will emerge if one has not been appointed previously. For the team to work quickly and in the best interest of the child, its members need to perform as a team, working to each other's specialist expertise and accepting each other's specialist advice and guidance while considering all points of view. The leader can facilitate this process by gathering together information provided by the individuals in the team and ensuring that regular communications are maintained by agreed methods.

The main difficulty in working in inter-agency teams is they are short-lived: the problem is resolved or an intervention is put into place and a 'key person' is left to monitor the situation and keep communication channels open for feedback. This makes it difficult for a team ethos to emerge, but if different agencies are to be successful, they need to engage in exercises so that team working practices become the norm. If inter-agency teams practise working together, when the time arises for the team to be built around the child, it will become quick, efficient and successfully interdependent.

Conclusion

As has already been stated, this chapter, in common with Chapter 9, 'Communicating through a crisis', demonstrates that effective communication is at the heart of safeguarding practice, never more so than when professionals are engaged in inter-agency working.

While there are barriers to effective communication, focusing on the needs of the child should always be at the forefront of practice. Inter-agency teams may need to practise working together in order to develop good communication strategies. This practice will facilitate reflection on the unequal distribution of power and status within the team. It allows the team to rehearse true collaboration and build respect for, and understanding of, the varied roles and responsibilities of all the childcare professionals involved. Keeping the needs of the child at the forefront of this process should encourage professionals to negotiate the barriers to effective communication. For early years practitioners, their communication is underpinned by their knowledge and understanding of child development, together with their information gathered through observations and their role as advocate for the child.

Further reading

Jones, P. and Walker, G. (eds) (2011) *Children's Rights in Practice*, London: Sage.

An accessible book exploring children's rights in theory and practice, and in an effective inter-agency approach to safeguarding.

Knowles, G. and Holmstrom, R. (2012) *Understanding Family Diversity and Home–School Relations: A Guide for Students and Practitioners in Early Years and Primary Settings*, London: Routledge.

In today's constantly changing society this text helps students and early years practitioners understand theoretically and practically what may constitute a family, in order to facilitate good communications.

11

Supervision and reflective practice

Samantha McMahon and Julie Percival

In this chapter we consider the role of supervision in safeguarding children and staff, and draw upon the stories of early years practitioners as the basis for understanding the concept of safeguarding in practice.

Supervision is an essential process of professional communication to and from the practitioner, where the focus is on competence, accountability, continuing professional development and personal support. Supervision therefore serves a number of aims, including ensuring that staff are effective in everyday practice; an opportunity for support, encouragement and critical feedback; a forum for reflection on practice; and time to consider any personal issues that affect or are affected by practice. Overall, effective supervision aims to value and develop staff to ensure they are prepared and committed to high-quality, safe practice. By the end of this chapter you will understand:

- the status and role of supervision in early years settings;
- the importance of reflection for enhancing personal effectiveness and learning;
- supervision as a space to 'think better'.

Supervision and the early years

Since the launch of the National Childcare Strategy in 1998 and the subsequent implementation of *Every Child Matters* (DfES 2003a), Sure Start and children's centres, early years practice has changed irrevocably. With an emphasis on early intervention and the recent extension of the 2-year-old offer to the most disadvantaged children, early years practitioners are increasingly on the front line of supporting children and families with complex needs. The government suggests that all interactions are an opportunity to assess the child's and family's needs, and as such it accepts the importance of a well-qualified and motivated professional workforce to implement the policy of early intervention (DfE 2011a). However, early years practitioners, despite the introduction of Early Years Professional Status (EYPS), are still struggling to be recognised as professionals, and Osgood (2009) suggests that this is due to emphasis within EYPS on technical competence, rather than understanding what drives people to work with children. Furthermore, Mathers *et al.* (2011) and Hadfield *et al.* (2012) discovered that the roles and responsibilities of an early years professional lack clarity and definition. While this might be expected in any new profession, it can leave practitioners struggling to manage the demands of their work. Caring for young children is an emotional business, often very rewarding, affording the practitioner a sense of great satisfaction, but there can also be an emotional cost (Elfer 2012). Elfer (2007) draws upon research in nursing which shows that patients project their anxieties and fears onto those who care for them, and suggests that young children do the same. It is likely that this projection of feelings will be heightened when practitioners are working with vulnerable children, and they will have to deal with an array of conflicting and complex emotions.

In other caring professions – nursing, health visiting and social work – for practitioners who work on safeguarding and child protection cases there is an acceptance that strategies must be in place to support them in dealing with the emotional impact of their work. Supervision is an established strategy which can ensure that practitioners continue to safeguard children effectively, as it addresses emotions, ensures that the practitioner knows they are not alone, relieves stress, prevents burnout and can be problem-solving (Morrison 1993, 2005; Ward *et al.* 2012). At the moment, supervision is not an established part of professional life in early years; this may be explained in part by the newness of the professional status.

Case study 1: Suzie

Suzie is 3 years old and in her second foster placement. She attends Bright Days Nursery for 15 hours per week and Lucy is her key person. Lucy works closely with Suzie and her foster mother; they exchange reports on Suzie's progress almost daily. Suzie was very withdrawn when she started nursery but has made enormous progress in her social, emotional and language development. Suzie's foster mother has confided to Lucy that she would like to adopt Suzie.

On returning to work after the weekend, Lucy is informed by her manager that Suzie will not be returning to the setting. Her manager promises to try to contact the social worker to attempt to get some more information. All the social worker will say is that the foster placement has broken down but that she will call into the nursery to pick up some of Suzie's personal possessions. Lucy takes home photographs of Suzie at the setting, observations and examples of Suzie's work and puts together a memory book for Suzie. When the social worker calls in to collect Suzie's belongings, she decides that it would not be appropriate to take the memory book prepared by Lucy. Lucy is very upset and tries to speak to her manager about how she feels. Her manager suggests that it would be best for Lucy to forget about Suzie, put it down to experience and get on with her work.

In Suzie's case study the manager may not be aware of how distressed the practitioner is, or perhaps simply does not know how to deal with the situation, so that it seems easier to avoid talking about it and to move on. This strategy, described by Hawkins and Shohet (2006: 3) as 'institutional containment', is a traditional response to deal with stressful situations and may in part be explained by tacit organisational assumptions, which are unspoken rules that associate professional behaviour with the suppression of challenging emotions. Elfer (2007, 2012) draws on his earlier research to explain this behaviour by referring to practice in nursing, where a good nurse adopts a professional distance. In this case study it is extremely likely that the practitioner will indeed learn to keep her distance, yet this may be the very worst outcome for other vulnerable children in her care. Children, especially vulnerable children, require a key person to be emotionally available to them (Gerhardt 2004) – someone who knows them, who is responsive to their needs and notices any changes in their behaviour or developmental progress. In the case study the manager is not available for discussion and as a result a vital opportunity was lost to provide support, discover learning that might emerge, and search for ways of managing such situations in the future (Hawkins and Shohet 2006).

Practitioners who work with young children do so because they have a strong ethic of care (Osgood 2009), but they must be able to balance the emotional costs of caring with the rewards in order to be able to continue caring and to maintain their own wellbeing. It is recognised within the Early Years Foundation Stage (EYFS) that the best interests of children are served by staff who feel supported (DfE 2012b). The safeguarding and welfare requirements in EYFS expect all providers to put appropriate arrangements in place for the supervision of staff who have contact with children and families. The EYFS suggests that

> [s]upervision should provide opportunities for staff to:
>
> - discuss any issues – particularly concerning children's development or well-being;
> - identify solutions to address issues as they arise; and
> - receive coaching to improve their personal effectiveness.
>
> (ibid.: 17)

However, there is no guidance on how, or even how often, supervision should take place, and in many settings senior staff lack experience or understanding of the process.

Examples from practice

Gail is the owner-manager of a private day nursery where key responsibilities (e.g. special educational needs, equality, behaviour and safeguarding) are shared amongst the senior staff team. Gail has adopted a distributed leadership style which recognises that tasks may be too complex for one person to complete successfully (Leeson 2010). Furthermore, she recognises the need to set aside time for talking, so she schedules weekly meetings with the senior staff team at which each member of the senior team has the opportunity to discuss any issues arising, and the team can collaborate on creative solutions (Leeson and Huggins 2010). Gail has also initiated 'stay back meetings' for the rest of the staff. These meetings are not formal supervision; nevertheless, they provide staff with a vital opportunity to, as Gail puts it, 'clear the clutter'. The 'clutter' as identified by Gail tends to be unresolved issues between staff, so the meetings provide time and a safe space to address and renegotiate how the staff interact and communicate with each other. If the 'clutter' remains unchecked, effective working relationships might break down, thus compromising the welfare of the children in the nursery's care. Gail has established formal mechanisms for discussion that certainly meet some of the criteria for supervision as set out in EYFS.

Angela is the leader of a voluntary pre-school that is managed by committee. Her leadership style allows collaboration and teamwork, which fosters a culture of mutual support (DfE 2012b). The small team do not have formal supervision, yet they are encouraged to discuss and share ideas, and examine their practice collaboratively. Angela reaffirms that safeguarding children is everything they do – not just the big stuff, the small everyday stuff – and the staff support each other in this. For example, after one member of staff has spent two hours with a challenging child who refuses to leave the toilet, another member of staff steps in and the first practitioner takes a break. Later the team members reflect on the incident, and Angela encourages the team not just to share strategies to manage the situation but to explore feelings the situation has precipitated. Both managers have developed models of supervision which demonstrate that they are emotionally literate leaders, sensitive to the emotional needs of their staff (Goleman 1996). In both settings the leaders have, as per EYFS, fostered a culture of mutual support and teamwork, but neither formally uses strategies such as coaching to improve personal effectiveness.

Personal effectiveness, learning and supervision

Personal effectiveness is something early years practitioners strive for in one form or another as they go about their work. They are continually making sense of the actions of others, exercising choices and working out ways to cope with the unique situations presented to them. Practitioners enhance their personal effectiveness and build knowledge through formal learning and training, and through experience. However, such knowledge is most useful when it is integrated into practice and is fully known; yet often it can only become fully known when significant events requiring a response happen.

Dee's story

Effective practice starts with a questioning disposition and a workable policy; it is a constant and consistent tool. A young couple explained some injuries to their 11-week-old daughter Mayer in a way that just did not ring true. As I rang social services, the fear of the consequences of my actions made me doubt myself. It turned out that Mayer's father had caused the marks. Step by step we followed policies and procedures, but it was the talking things through as a staff that really helped us make sense of it all. Of course we could not talk to anyone outside our small staff team, so it was important that we did not just bury our feelings. We worked with Mayer's mother and father and the social worker, and for some of us it was really hard to be straight with them; all sorts of questions came to mind … We are a small team and talking it through was really important so that we could get back the unconditional regard that is so important – especially for the father. We planned specific confidential times to listen to each other – a kind of formal informality where we worked things through so we could do the best for all concerned. With all the staff and with the mother and father it was a case of saying, 'I'm not sure, but we can go back to policy and get some advice and then maybe we can make things better.' Sorting out your feelings, asking sensitive questions and deciding what things mean, having a plan and bit by bit you get there – things do get better.

In Dee's case study, despite her experience, training and qualifications, it was the very 'doing' of child protection that offered her the most powerful learning opportunity. As Edwards and Thomas (2010: 406) argue, 'reflection and action are indivisible aspects of the same process'. Dee's story illustrates the fundamental ethic of care for children and their families that lies at the heart of early years practice. She cares deeply about her own personal effectiveness and that of the setting. Supervision offers practitioners an opportunity to examine some fundamental values through the sharing of their version of events and the meanings they have made. When a critical incident occurs, it can be a dynamic learning opportunity.

Sometimes the kind of learning that evolves through supervision can be performative, associated with targets and specific outcomes, which is a firmly established part of working in early years, but it should also be much more. Hawkins and Shohet (2006: 16) ascribe three functions to supervision: it should improve the quality of the supervisee's work with the client, develop the competence and capacity of the supervisee and increase the supervisee's ability to resource and sustain themselves as an effective practitioner. Supervision should grow each practitioner's confidence to negotiate how they fulfil their aspiration to deal with practical issues in an effective way.

Supervision provides a space for reviewing understanding. It is not a time to be made accountable for actions in the way that appraisal might be. It is a form of social activity that gives practitioners space to inevitably reflect. It does not provide space for correction, but for thinking in a creative and constructive way, for checking that actions are in the best interests of the child and their family. In turn, when children's needs are being met, the early years setting is deemed a successful enterprise. For Dee, the practitioners' reactions to Mayer and her parents highlighted to her the need for a flexible routine of talking and listening as part of ongoing reflective practice. How do our actions and our feelings affect our personal effectiveness and understanding of practice? Just asking the question means you are open to different ways of thinking about practice.

Munro (2010, 2011a, 2012) consistently acknowledges the uncertainty of safeguarding work. It can be reassuring to know the procedures for referral, the textbook signs for neglect; and compliance with procedure is important, but it should not drive action. For Munro, effective and responsive safeguarding practice relies on leaders developing teams who have skills in helping people solve problems and make decisions. Supervision can build this problem-solving capacity within a team and reinforce the skills and techniques for reflective practice taught on graduate-level courses. It is important for early years practitioners to use their existing dispositions, their inevitable reflections on their work to, day by day, develop particular 'habits of conduct' (Edwards and Thomas 2010: 411, after Oakeshott 1962) that empower and enable them to use what they know. Anecdotally, in our discussions for this book with early years professionals it is apparent that experienced, effective practitioners intuitively know that knowing how to be with people is central to safeguarding practice. They know about their own community of practice and the children, families and colleagues who inhabit their world. Practitioners who spend time with children and families, and use their relationship-led knowledge in the best interests of the child, are more likely to 'make judgements and decisions that, on the evidence available, look the best' (Munro 2012: 6).

Storytelling, relationships and models of supervision

Safeguarding children relies on building a bank of knowledge and skills traditionally associated with being an early years practitioner, for example a sound knowledge of child development, curriculum frameworks and supporting families. Training and education courses also induct and further develop a series of dispositions and attitudes, socialising practitioners into ways of working that are important to the smooth running of the setting (Vincent and Braun 2011). Indeed, many of these routine, organisational matters are a necessary part of complying with the legal requirements placed on all those who work in early years. Favourable child:adult ratios, clean and physically safe environments – indeed, attention to all aspects of section 3 of the EYFS (DfE 2012b) – are associated with more attuned, responsive caregiving and the provision of a stimulating learning environment (Sylva and Roberts 2010). There can be no doubt that safeguarding practice relies on organisational matters such as a safe nappy-changing policy, arrangements for the use of mobile and internet technology, or indeed the child protection policy.

However, the meanings placed on these depend on how each and every policy is integrated into practice and how those policies help practitioners to cope and make sense of their interactions with children, families and colleagues. The stories told in staff rooms illuminate practitioner understanding. It is this understanding that forms the basis of supervision. Every practitioner, modern apprentice or graduate professional has stories to tell about their work, all of which are based on interaction with other people (both young and old). The stories offered in this chapter provide some insight into safeguarding narratives. They are presented to illustrate how powerful stories are in the lives of practitioners and managers who deal with safeguarding matters – not as examples of procedures that can be lifted and applied in other contexts.

Raj's story

Raj knows a thousand and one stories about the children and families in her care; she was the daycare manager and now as Children's Centre manager hears about the joys and the 'causes for concern' that crop up on a regular basis.

> I start with the facts, the paperwork, but then I purposely think about the history we have together – the children, the family and us – and I look for the intuitive feelings I have that are based on knowledge and trust. Basically they know we care about their child. When the children talk about you at home, you know you are a part of their lives!
>
> Jo's mum came and asked us to keep a special eye out as he was not himself. I was surprised because he had been with us for two years and was a regular, confident character in pre-school. Over the next few days a couple of incidents were reported to me until it became clear that one member of the staff had been correcting Jo's behaviour with stern words and slaps. Within the day the member of staff was required to leave and formal proceedings began. Working to policy was vital and we ensured that all the employment regulations were followed. Talking to the parents was so painful. How could this have gone unnoticed for weeks?
>
> One morning, as things were being sorted out, Jo sat with a friend drawing and chatting and casually told a part of his story – that the practitioner had hit him the other day. His friend was disapproving. 'That was not very kind; we don't do that at nursery, do we?' Jo agreed, 'No, we don't, but Raj knows and Mummy knows and it's going to be all right now.'
>
> Jo's story hit me like a ton of bricks. He had organised his ideas, talked to his parents and his friends, and talked so we could hear. His faith in me and his mum meant he could see a way forward.

When stories are told, the teller has already processed the events being recounted and reflection has taken place. The listener is looking for meaning – deciding on the effectiveness of the teller in covering essential elements, deciding whether the story adds up. Each and every practitioner has a story to tell – at least something! In conversation, questions arise for both the teller and the listener, and understanding is further developed. For Raj, there were very many pieces of the jigsaw to be discovered and made sense of. Members of the staff team came to share incidents with her that had seemed inconsequential before but that they needed to share. It is never ethical to talk freely in the rooms with the children, with students on placement or other parents, but daily safeguarding practice requires space in the working week to mention the small things that practitioners see and hear. The close ways in which practitioners know children can sometimes get lost in busy weeks. Raj wonders whether it was the close relationship with Jo's mother and the quieter week due to holidays that helped practitioners notice more about Jo and his relationships. By asking for an eye to be kept on Jo, Jo's mother handed direct responsibility to practitioners to reflect on his wellbeing.

Raj makes time for one-to-one supervision so that each person in the team feels able to take daily responsibility for safeguarding. They talk about their key children – their achievements and their niggles. They think creatively about practice and make plans for the children (and perhaps their parents). However busy the weeks seem to get, the small things and the potentially bigger things such as risk assessments and 'causes for concern' find their way into supervision meetings.

Lead practitioners resolve safeguarding issues in multi-layered and complex ways (Richmond 2009; Figure 11.1). This multi-layered approach to supervision, through the organisation of specific meetings with specific agendas, focuses on process reflection rather than end products and outcomes. Safer outcomes for children (and families) are the desired outcome, but the 'getting there' is important. For the practitioners in this chapter, their

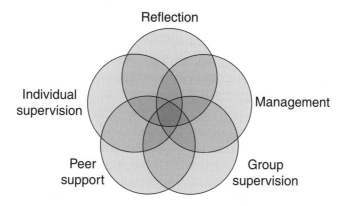

FIGURE 11.1 Essential elements of multi-layered supervision from Richmond (2009).

approaches to coping and to demonstrating personal (and setting) effectiveness evolved in tandem with their understanding of policies and procedures as matters were resolved. The team must trust that the lead practitioner will listen; the team must be willing to listen to themselves. The lead practitioner must establish clear boundaries and facilitate practitioners to practice and learn within those spaces. Managers need to use their power to facilitate reflection so that practitioners have the confidence to tell their stories – stories of difficult days and challenging feelings, of concerns for wellbeing and exactly why things went well (as well as not so well). It is through our stories that we make sense of our world and look forward to the future – as Jo did when playing alongside Raj and his friends.

Relationship-based, reflective supervision

There are other models of supervision, and Bernstein and Edwards (2012) make a strong case for a model adopted by early childhood practitioners working in Early Head Start programmes in the United States in the 1990s. For these practitioners the focus of their work is on supporting families to nurture their children in times of stress and anxiety. Mutual competence is a central concept, and parents are encouraged to see and acknowledge competence in their children, and to be responsive to their needs. For the child, the aim is to reduce behaviours associated with feelings of stress and increase trust in the parent. Practitioners help parents to recognise signs of reduced stress and co-ordinate their behaviour with the child's to maintain this cycle of mutual positive reinforcement. This work is based upon time spent together playing with children, retelling the event, then listening and responding with genuine interest. This model of practice is taken into the supervision room. The content of the sessions is protected reflection time; appraisal or administrative supervision (related to performance, meeting deadlines and organisational matters) does not form part of the reflective supervision approach.

Essentially, the practitioner is enabled to share accounts of their work in an environment that is safe and supportive. The supervisor listens, shares some past experiences for the practitioner to reflect on, asks open-ended questions designed to check understanding and acknowledges the complex range of feelings associated with the practitioner's chosen account.

This model of reflective supervision makes the distinction between disagreeable and unacceptable practice (Bernstein and Edwards 2012). Unacceptable behaviours relate to actions that break with policy or legal requirements, while disagreeable behaviours relate to actions that may not be deemed effective practice but do not directly contravene the setting's policies and procedures. According to Bernstein and Edwards, 'Outside the realm of the *unacceptable*, a nurturing relationship is unconditional' (ibid.: 290; emphasis added).

Acceptance and mutual trust allow practitioners to be open to sharing as honestly as possible how they work. In this way there is understanding. Neither party feels under pressure to discipline or to conform. The Plymouth Serious Case Review (Plymouth Safeguarding Children Board 2010) highlighted the need for managers to have greater understanding of the relationships, thoughts and feelings of the staff team. The review also highlighted how practitioners' uncertainty and discomfort could not be expressed in a safe and non-confrontational way. Complex feelings about children, families and indeed colleagues affect practice decisions. Talking things through helps to organise experiences and emotions, and while sharing what has worked before might help, it is not intended as a prescription. Practitioners should be encouraged by supervisors to try out ideas through talk and maybe in practice. The supervisor gives responsibility to the practitioner to set a course of action. This does not mean that the sole responsibility to 'fix' the problem rests with the practitioner, and in some situations the supervisor can help identify when immediate action is required. Patient, purposeful action and time bring about resolution in many cases. For reflective supervision to be effective, each party has a responsibility to prepare for the supervision session; it is important that both hold the best interests of the child and the child's journey (Munro 2012) in mind. Although safeguarding and child protection are rarely a source of joy, in general practice this model of supervision aims to 'search for the joyful area and zero in on what is working' (Bernstein and Edwards 2012: 301).

Accountability comes through a carefully drawn up agenda that is worked through flexibly. Supervisor and practitioner review past conversations (by using notes, diaries and specifically designed forms, for example). Each brings key points to be addressed to the meeting and they construct the agenda together. While the discussions should primarily focus on stories (accounts) of experiences with children and families, research by Elfer (2012) suggests that relationships between colleagues can also have a profound impact on practice. He found that the diaries compiled by nursery managers 'showed how each of the nurseries operated within closely networked communities … in this internal community, often referred to by the managers as the "nursery family", any tensions in staff relations also became easily magnified in their impact on nursery life'. Consequently, given the choice of topic for 'Work Discussions' (Elfer 2012: 134), staffing matters were repeatedly the concern of the research participants. Supervisors need to build trust and acceptance, and clear boundaries for discussions that deal with relationships between staff. There needs to be a forum for this, because relationships between the adults in the child's life can affect the child's wellbeing.

Supervisor and practitioner discuss specific issues, with the supervisor encouraging the telling of as complete a picture as possible. Together they explore different possible interpretations of the situation and look for positives as well as matters for concern. A plan of suggested actions is recorded and the child's needs are reconsidered. Before the session ends, the practitioner is invited to offer feedback on the session: what matters have been resolved or are being addressed? Are there other issues to consider? The cycle begins again because the next meeting begins with an update on the plan and the developments that have taken place since the last meeting. Over time, the practitioner opens up and feels able to discuss practice. If this form of supervision is embraced by the setting, the practitioner is likely to take ownership of their good practice; less confident practitioners become less defensive and more open to asking the supervisor to share their wisdom.

Thinking better

Some level of criticality and interrogation is needed. The aim, though, is to 'think better', not to adopt a prescribed role. Supervision cannot be therapy (Belton *et al.* 2011) or personalised 'off-line' mentoring (Megginson and Clutterbuck 2005). Stories or accounts of practice give us a way into understanding thoughts, feelings and actions. These can be set against the need (and aspiration) to work to professional boundaries, and within clear roles and responsibilities. The setting's priorities should be established, and clear for all who work and access the setting. To get to this point is no small piece of work. Establishing the principles of a 'safer cultures approach' (Powell and Uppal 2012: 61) to practice within a setting is part of the ongoing development and review programme for the whole learning community. Such work can be supported by but not led through supervision.

Supervision cannot be imposed on practitioners without the careful process of preparation outlined by Bernstein and Edwards (2012). The practitioner needs to draw on their self-examination and their knowledge of the children and families concerned, and to feel that through the process they are able to articulate the reasons for their actions. Using a reflective supervision model, the feedback or final reflections should consider the following:

- What understandings of practice have been developed?
- What response (emotionally and practically) is being planned?
- How does this affect the child and the family?

These questions are a matter of interpretation. Work in early years is a political and moral enterprise. Gender, culture and race, for example, can affect the supervisory relationship and the way in which accounts or stories of experiences are recalled. Knowledge is not absolute fact. Practitioners and children will benefit from pausing to consider whether practice is culturally responsive. People do not have fixed identities, yet we use our perceptions of their identity to inform our thinking and practice. Supervision provides practitioners and supervisors with an opportunity to explicitly consider whether the 'ideas, stories and narratives that identify individuals and communities are flexible, relational and co-constructed using multiple view points, different voices and various approaches to knowledge' (O'Donoghue and Tsui

2012: 75) or based on unchallenged assumptions. Supervision work must not be used to co-construct and 'silently endorse' (ibid.: 79) limited and limiting understandings of children, families and colleagues.

The process of reflective supervision should acknowledge the powerful feelings that working to safeguard young children can evoke. It should alleviate stress, and the process has the potential to bring about more specific, identifiable improvements to practice. However, for it to be effective, both the supervisee (practitioner) and the supervisor must be prepared and they should be able to use records to trace back how and why decisions were made. Of course, the provider must keep accurate and timely records to comply with the safeguarding and welfare requirements, and routine records ensure that on an ongoing basis the setting is safe and that the needs of all children are met (DfE 2012b). While safeguarding pervades all aspects of early years work and should be established as routine practice, incidences of child protection are, thankfully, not routine. Such critical incidents are rare, vital opportunities for learning from 'doing', as Dee and Raj found, and also subsequently for reflective supervision.

Critical incidents and supervision

The use of critical incidents (Butterfield *et al.* 2005) or critical events (Woods 1993) to inform practice in education is well established, especially for initial teacher training (Harrison and Lee 2011; Griffin 2003). Each can be used both to celebrate effective practice and to critically analyse more troubling events, with a view to learning and enhancing practice further. As a research method pioneered by Flanagan (1954), the critical incident technique is used to generate a functional description of a particular event or issue through a series of planned stages: first an aim is set and a plan of inquiry specified, then information is gathered and analysis undertaken, and finally conclusions are drawn and reported. A lead practitioner or researcher would collate information rather than directly provide information. The analysis rests on a detailed and accurate account of the event concerned set against a particular frame of reference – for example, safeguarding legislation, policies and procedures alongside the EYFS framework.

For any practitioner or manager involved in an incident, the focus is inevitably on resolving practical yet highly ethical dilemmas, and they are, quite rightly, not looking for opportunities for learning and research. They are immersed in careful negotiation of rules and regulations but also emotionally charged conversations with children, families, colleagues and local authority officers. Far from being a set of discrete stages of objective evidence gathering, the incident will be a complex interplay of information and existing relationships, which are being framed and understood, and then reframed, as new information comes to light. During this time it is essential that staff should have opportunities to discuss issues concerning the child's wellbeing and to identify solutions to the issues; however, in-depth reflection and learning to enhance practice may need to wait. Nevertheless, at a suitable time retrospective and systematic analysis of the incident can provide a framework for effective supervision and a chance to discover the learning that often emerges from the most difficult situations (Hawkins and Shohet 2006).

A critical incident is likely to bring enhanced scrutiny from external organisations, such as the local authority, Ofsted and possibly media organisations. Such external pressures and increased emphasis on compliance are likely to make practitioners feel vulnerable to being blamed and therefore wary of discussing inadequacies. Managers are likely to focus on tangible outcomes and, as a result, just when effective supervision is most needed, it is likely to be avoided. Therefore, supervision needs to become 'habit', a routine aspect of practice and professional development in early years. Supervision is not straightforward; there are considerable challenges to be overcome. Practitioners and managers need to understand that it is not selfish or self-indulgent to focus on the needs of the practitioner; rather, it is an essential tool to prevent 'burnout' (Hawkins and Shohet 2006: 27). Critical incidents bring to light some of the difficult choices and dilemmas practitioners face, which can seemingly challenge the fundamental principles that underpin their practice – for example, caring for children and supporting parents becoming monitoring children and policing parents. Supervision should allow a safe space to discuss such dilemmas and the powerful emotions they evoke.

Although the term 'critical incident' used in the preceding paragraphs refers more to major incidents of child protection, safeguarding children is bound up with routine tasks. As Angela said, 'It's everything we do.' The everyday encounters and routines associated with practice in early years can be equally valued as critical – critical because they offer an opportunity to advance in learning and for the acquisition of knowledge and the development of skills (Woods 1993). A major incident provides many obvious opportunities for reflection and supervision, whereas in daily practice it might be a fleeting feeling of unease, a niggle, something difficult to pin down. The practitioner as supervisee can maximise the potential for reflecting on these incidents by keeping a journal, and the supervisor should make time and space to discuss them on a regular basis. Dee is fully aware of how important this is. She describes the supervisor as developing a gentle awareness and the supervisee as feeling listened to, thus 'keeping things manageable'. Keeping things manageable encapsulates the philosophy of early intervention and is the best way to safeguard and ensure the welfare of children (Munro 2011a).

Conclusion

Supervision is here, it is part of EYFS, and at the outset it might appear to be little more than an opportunity to sit and chat, something of a luxury in a busy setting. However, effective supervision can tease out issues, address emotions, help solve problems, relieve stress and ultimately support high-quality care. It is likely that the process will take time to become established and a rigid model, or one-size-fits-all approach to supervision, will not work; it must grow and develop in the setting. There are many different models of supervision and we have only touched upon a few in this chapter. However, they all require the supervisee and supervisor to take joint responsibility for the process. Supervision is founded upon supportive, trusting and respectful relationships and flourishes when both parties co-construct stories and develop a mutual understanding. The process is reflective, culturally responsive and for the benefit of all who work in and use the setting.

Points for reflection

Why would we engage in supervision if it just time to sit and chat? Early years settings are busy places, where in some cases time away from babies and children is an additional cost to be borne by the business. How does supervision differ from appraisal or mentoring? If we must obey certain rules and regulations, surely ensuring that these are in place has to be the focus of the limited time available to us? Should supervision and appraisal be combined?

Safeguarding is such an important element of early years work – it affects everything we do – yet stories are full of personal perceptions and possible bias; they are influenced by life scripts and lapses in memory. How can this be the basis for supervision?

Further reading

Bernstein, V. J. and Edwards, R. C. (2012) 'Supporting early childhood practitioners through relationship-based reflective supervision', *NHSA Dialogue: A Research-to-Practice Journal for the Early Childhood Field*, 15 (3): 286–301.

A journal article rooted in practice, offering a specific model of supervision in the early years. The distinction between appraisal and developmental, reflective supervision is clear. Using this model, the uncertainty and the emotional nature of safeguarding can be worked through in ways that put the child's experiences at the centre of practice.

Read, V. (2010) *Developing Attachment in Early Years Settings: Nurturing Secure Relationships from Birth to Five Years*, London: Routledge.

This book contains a chapter that explores the web of relationships in the setting as part of an enabling environment. It asks who nurtures the nurturers and explores how to support practitioners who feel overwhelmed, and describes how supervision can work in practice.

12

Conclusion

Steven Burton

As the final stages of editing and concluding this book are being undertaken, the safeguarding landscape in the United Kingdom continues to develop.

The campaign End Child Poverty revealed in early 2013 that in 69 wards in the United Kingdom, more than half of the children live below the poverty line and that, nationally, one in five children live below said poverty line (2013: 8). Again in early 2013, the police have revealed that the detection rate of crimes relating to accessing illegal images of children has risen by 48 per cent between 2007 and 2011 (Cafe 2013). Meanwhile, the 'More Great Childcare' governmental response to the Nutbrown Review of 2012 has divided the early years workforce, with many practitioners predicting that the proposed changes to childcare ratios will put children in danger. Most crucially, in Birmingham a man and woman were arrested on suspicion of the murder of an 18-month-old boy in February 2013.

It therefore appears germane that we offer this text as a structured attempt to assist with the continued understanding of the area of safeguarding and protecting children in the early years.

The voice of the practitioner

Where appropriate, we have used practitioners' voices in our writing. At times this has been facilitated by primary research undertaken specifically for the book. At other times our privileged positions as lecturers in the field have enabled us to engage with members of the workforce in order to debate ideas, explore themes or test hypotheses. This way of working has given the book a tangible grounding in reality, which we hope will be recognised by the reader. Additionally, it is hoped that current practitioners will find comfort, support and validation from the voices within, and that students embarking on a career in the early years will find inspiration and encouragement in those same voices.

Recommended reading

Each chapter provides a small number of recommended texts to allow the reader to explore further either the subject matter of each individual chapter, or the authors that each contributor is inspired by in their field. What is apparent when one examines and analyses those texts is the variety, breadth and quality of work in this field that is available to the reader. We hope that this approach of celebrating and promoting other sources will act as a catalyst for extending knowledge among the children's workforce.

Areas for further specialist research

It is clear that a number of areas need to be considered in addition to the content of this book, and that as a society and a workforce we need to be more conscious of such areas. These areas include cultural understanding, for instance in areas around spirit possession, where guidance reminds us that associated abuse could be not only physical in nature, including 'beating, shaking, burning, cutting, stabbing, semi-strangulating, tying up the child, or rubbing chilli peppers or other substances on the child's genitals or eyes' (DfES 2007: 6–7), but emotional or sexual, and could also include neglect. When we are discussing the plight of abused disabled children, misunderstanding on the part of society leads to situations where '[p]rofessionals may find it more difficult to attribute indicators of abuse or neglect, or be reluctant to act on concerns in relation to disabled children' (DCSF 2009b: 47). This is a more prevalent issue in society than the previously mentioned spirit possession abuses, as disabled children are more likely to suffer sexual abuse than their non-disabled peers (DCSF 2009b). Furthermore, the DCSF reminds us that '[i]t has long been recognised that black and minority ethnic children have been disproportionally represented in the child welfare system' (2009c: 44), whereas Asian children tend to be under-represented in the same system.

Although these areas do not relate in their entirety to the early years age group, practitioners, like the rest of society, should be aware of 'what they do not know' – and while these themes in themselves have been beyond the remit of this book, it is clear that practitioners and settings must be aware of these additional cultural and sociological elements in the safeguarding arena.

Concluding thoughts

In his introduction to this book, James Reid detailed the contributions to be made by each individual chapter, and expounded on the duality of the content: Part 1 deals with the macro nature of societal and legislative conceptions of safeguarding, while Part 2 delves into the micro context of safeguarding at the 'coalface' of early years. In concluding the text, I offer an alternative yet complementary analysis of what we hope the reader will gain from the chapters herein.

Part 1 allowed James Reid, Nigel Parton and Neil Ventress to explore and present the structure inherent in the field of safeguarding, through a thorough and informative analysis of the historical framework, together with a critical eye cast over the legislative and policy framework guiding the sector.

Part 2 allowed the examination of agency within safeguarding, by focusing on the role of the practitioner in terms of the EYFS, health and wellbeing, online safeguarding, communication and multi-agency working, and developing reflective practice. This is pragmatically demonstrated by Frances Marsden, Samantha McMahon and Andrew Youde in Chapter 10, who when discussing the power and status of professionals involved in multi-agency working proposed a series of attributes to help other professionals recognise the value of their contribution when involved in a safeguarding episode. However, these attributes, when paraphrased, can be used as personal mores for all practitioners, and commitment to them will better support the practitioner should a safeguarding episode emerge in their arena:

- Focus on the child.
- Provide accurate, informed records.
- Be confident.
- Build trusting, respectful and professional relationships.
- Pursue continuing professional development such as higher education qualifications.
- Remember why you work with children.
- Be an advocate for the child.

These suggestions form vital guidance for early years practitioners in every aspect of their working lives, and are referenced either implicitly or explicitly throughout this book.

Therefore, it is our intention that, in the best Bourdieuian tradition, the cultural capital of the reader, irrespective of their position within the early years arena, will be enhanced by the collection of ideas and observations included here.

While the quotation used to launch this book may strike a solemn chord of acknowledgement among the various members of the children's workforce, it is hoped that by continuing to raise awareness of safeguarding in the early years, we will – as a society, as a state – get the message.

References

4Children (2011) '250 Sure Start Children's Centres face closure within a year'. London: 4Children. Online, available at: www.4children.org.uk/News/Detail/250-Sure-Start-Childrens-Centres (accessed 31 January 2011).

Acheson, D. (1998) *Independent Inquiry into Inequalities in Health*, London: The Stationery Office.

Action for Children (2011) *The Red Book: Impact of Government Spending Decisions on Children, Young People and Families*, London: Action for Children.

Adair, J. (2009) *Effective Teambuilding*, London: Pan Macmillan.

Ali, K., Ahmed, N. and Greenough, A. (2012) 'Sudden infant death syndrome (SIDS), substance misuse, and smoking in pregnancy', *Research and Reports of Neonatology*, 2012 (2). Online, available at: www.dovepress.com/getfile.php?fileID=14234 (accessed 26 February 2013).

Allen, G. (2011a) *Early Intervention: The Next Steps. An Independent Review to Her Majesty's Government*, London: The Cabinet Office.

Allen, G. (2011b) *Early Intervention: Smart Investment, Massive Savings: A Second Independent Review to Her Majesty's Government*, London: The Cabinet Office.

Alotaibi, N., Sammons, H. and Choonara, I. (2012) 'Methadone toxicity in children', *Archives of Disease in Childhood*, 97 (5): abstract.

Baldock, P. (2010) *Understanding Cultural Diversity in the Early Years*, London: Sage.

Bandele, F. (2009) 'The contribution of schools to safeguarding children', in L. Hughes and H. Owen (eds) *Good Practice in Safeguarding Children: Working Effectively in Child Protection*, London: Jessica Kingsley.

Bandura, A. (1977) *Social Learning Theory*, Englewood Cliffs, NJ: Prentice Hall.

Barnardo's (2006) *Say It Your Own Way: Children's Participation in Assessment*, Ilford: Barnardo's Publications.

Barnes, J., Katz, I. B., Korbin, J. E. and O'Brien, M. (2006) *Children and Families in Communities: Theory, Research, Policy and Practice*, Chichester: John Wiley.

Barry, A.-M. and Yuill, C. (2012) *Understanding the Sociology of Health*, 3rd edn, London: Sage.

Bate, E. (2005) 'The health and social needs of women who use illicit drugs', *Journal of Community Nursing*, 19 (4): 20–25.

BBC (2006) 'Third "have sex below legal age"', London: BBC, 13 August. Online, available at: http://news.bbc.co.uk/1/hi/4784939.stm (accessed 18 June 2012).

Beatbullying (2009) 'Truth of sexting amongst UK teens', London: Beatbullying, 4 August. Online, available at: www.beatbullying.org/dox/media-centre/press-releases/press-release-040809.html (accessed 18 June 2012).

Beck, U. and Beck-Gernsheim, E. (2002) *Individualization*, London: Sage.

Becta (2008) *Safeguarding Children in a Digital World*, Coventry: Becta.

Bee, H. and Boyd, D. (2006) *The Developing Child*, 11th edn, London: Pearson.

Bell, M. (2005) 'Community-based parenting programmes: an exploration of the interplay between environmental and organizational factors in a Webster Stratton project', *British Journal of Social Work*, 37 (1): 55–72.

Belton, B., Hill, J., Salter, T. and Peaper, J. (2011) *Supervision: Praxis and Purpose*, Lyme Regis: Russell House Publishing.

Beresford, P., Fleming, J., Glynn, M., Bewley, C., Croft, S., Branfield, F. and Postle, K. (2011) *Supporting People: Towards a Person-Centred Approach*, Bristol: Policy Press.

Bernstein, V. J. and Edwards, R. C. (2012) 'Supporting early childhood practitioners through relationship-based reflective supervision', *NHSA Dialogue: A Research-to-Practice Journal for the Early Childhood Field*, 15 (3): 286–301.

Billington, T. (2006) *Working with Children*, London: Sage.

Birmingham Safeguarding Children Board (2010) Serious Case Review (Khyra Ishaq). Online, available at: www.lscbbirmingham.org.uk/downloads/Case+14.pdf (accessed 22 February 2013).

Blundel, R. and Ippolito, K. (2008) *Effective Organisational Communication*, 3rd edn, Harlow: Pearson Education.

Bourdieu, P. (1977) *Outline of a Theory of Practice*, Cambridge: Cambridge University Press.

Bowlby, J. (1969) *Attachment and Loss*, vol. 1: *Attachment*, London: Hogarth Press.

Brandon, M., Sidebotham, P., Bailey, S., Belderson, P., Hawley, C., Ellis, C. and Megson, M. (2012) *New Learning from Serious Case Reviews*, London: Department for Education.

Brewer, M. (2010) 'The spending review and children', presentation to the All Party Parliamentary Group for Children, 29 November, House of Commons.

Bronfenbrenner, U. (1979) *The Ecology of Human Development: Experiments by Nature and Design*, Cambridge, MA: Harvard University Press.

Brooks, C., Brocklehurst, P. and Freeman, S. (2012) *Safeguarding Pressures Phase 3 Report*, Manchester: Association of Directors of Children's Services.

Bruce, T. (2001) *Learning through Play*, London: Hodder & Stoughton.

Butterfield, L. D., William, A. B., Amundson, N. E. and Maglio, A.-S. T. (2005) 'Fifty years of the critical incident technique: 1954–2004 and beyond', *Qualitative Research*, 5 (4): 475–497.

Cafe, R. (2013) 'Police detections of child porn images increases [*sic*] by 48%', London: BBC, 23 February. Online, available at: www.bbc.co.uk/news/uk-21507006 (accessed 24 February 2013).

Calder, M. C. (2003) 'The Assessment Framework: a critique and reformulation', in M. C. Calder and S. Hackett (eds) *Assessment in Child Care: Using and Developing Frameworks for Practice*, Lyme Regis: Russell House Publishing.

Cameron, D. (2009) 'The Big Society', Hugo Young Lecture, 10 November.

Canning, N. (2011) *Play and Practice in the Foundation Years*, London: Sage.

Cawson, P., Wattam, C., Brooker, S. and Kelly, G. (2000) *Child Maltreatment in the United Kingdom*, London: NSPCC.

Centers for Disease Prevention and Control (2012) 'Obesity and extreme obesity rates decline among low-income preschool children'. Online, available at: www.cdc.gov/obesity/data/childhood.html (accessed 8 August 2012).

CEOP (2009) 'What is online grooming?', London: CEOP. Online, available at: https://www.thinkuknow.co.uk/Parentsold/FAQ/Grooming/ (accessed 19 June 2012).

CEOP (2011) Annual Review 2010–11 and Centre Plan, London: CEOP.

Chowdry, H. and Sibieta, L. (2011) 'Trends in education and schools spending', IFS Briefing Note, London: Institute for Fiscal Studies.

Clark, A. and Moss, P. (2005) *Spaces to Play: More Listening to Young Children using the Mosaic Approach*, London: National Children's Bureau.

Claxton, G. (2002) *Building Learning Power: Helping Young People Become Better Learners*, Bristol: TLO.

Cleaver, H., Unell, I. and Aldgate, J. (2011) *Children's Needs – Parenting Capacity*, 2nd edn, London: The Stationery Office.

Clegg, N. (2010) 'Supporting families', speech to Barnardo's, 17 June. Online, available at: www.libdems.org.uk/speeches_detail.aspx?title=Nick_Clegg's_speech_on_supporting_families_and_children&pPK=6d739b75-08a1-4262-9309-39b0fc8fc45c (accessed 3 December 2012).

Colley, H. (2006) 'Learning to labour with feeling: class, gender and emotion in childcare education and training', *Contemporary Issues in Early Childhood*, 7 (1): 42–52.

Cooklin, A. (2004) Training pack to accompany *Being Seen and Heard: The Needs of Children of Parents with Mental Illness*, London: Royal College of Psychiatrists. Online, available at: http://familyandparenting.web-platform.net/item/document/1980/1 (accessed 24 February 2013).

Council of Europe (1950) *European Convention for the Protection of Human Rights and Fundamental Freedoms*, as amended by Protocols Nos. 11 and 14, 4 November, ETS 5. Online, available at: www.unhcr.org/refworld/docid/3ae6b3b04.html (accessed 9 August 2012).

Cowie, H. and Jennifer, D. (2008) *New Perspectives on Bullying*, Maidenhead: Open University Press/McGraw-Hill Education.

Creighton, S. J. and Russell, N. (1995) *Voices from Childhood: A Survey of Childhood Experiences and Attitudes to Childrearing among Adults in the United Kingdom*, London: NSPCC Research Policy and Practice Series.

Cremin, T., Burnard, P. and Craft, A. (2006) 'Pedagogy and possibility thinking in the early years', *Thinking Skills and Creativity*, 1 (2): 108–119.

Cross, E.-J., Richardson, B., Douglas, T. and Vonkaenal-Flatt, J. (2009) *Virtual Violence: Protecting Children from Cyberbullying*, London: Beatbullying.

Cross, E.-J., Piggin, R., Douglas, T., Vonkaenal-Flatt, J. and O'Brien, J. (2012) *Virtual Violence II: Primary-Aged Children's Experience of Cyberbullying*, London: Beatbullying.

Crossley, S. and Shildrick, T. (2012) 'Ending child poverty: a right or a responsibility?', London: Child Poverty Action Group. Online, available at: www.cpag.org.uk/sites/default/files/CPAG-Poverty142-ending-child-pov-right-responsibility.pdf (accessed 15 November 2012).

Cuthbert, C., Rayns, G. and Stanley, K. (2011) *All Babies Count: Prevention and Protection for Vulnerable Babies*, London: NSPCC Inform. Online, available at: www.nspcc.org.uk/Inform/resourcesforprofessionals/underones/all_babies_count_wda85568.html (accessed 22 August 2012).

CWDC (2007) *Common Assessment Framework for Children and Young People*, Leeds: CWDC.

CWDC (2009) *The Common Assessment Framework for Children and Young People: Early Identification, Assessment of Needs and Intervention: A Guide for Practitioners*, Leeds: CWDC. Online, available at: https://www.education.gov.uk/publications/eOrderingDownload/CAF-Practitioner-Guide.pdf (accessed 3 December 2012).

Daft, R. L. and Marcic, D. (2001) *Understanding Management*, 3rd edn, Stamford, CT: Thomson Learning.

Dahlberg, G., Moss, P. and Pence, A. (1999) *Beyond Quality in Early Childhood Education and Care: Postmodern Perspectives*, London: Falmer Press.

Dahlgren, G. and Whitehead, M. (2007) *European Strategies for Tackling Social Inequities in Health: Levelling Up Part 2*, Copenhagen: WHO Regional Office for Europe.

Dalgleish, L. (2003) 'Risk, needs and consequences', in M. C. Calder and S. Hackett (eds) *Assessment in Child Care: Using and Developing Frameworks for Practice*, Lyme Regis: Russell House Publishing.

Daniel, B., Wassell, S. and Gilligan, R. (2010) *Child Development for Child Care and Protection Workers*, 2nd edn, London: Jessica Kingsley.

Department for Children, Schools and Families (DCSF) *Safe to Learn: Embedding Anti-bullying Work in Schools*, Nottingham: DCSF.

Department for Children, Schools and Families (2008a) *Safer Children in a Digital World: The Report of the Byron Review*, Nottingham: DCSF.

Department for Children, Schools and Families (2008b) *Social and Emotional Aspects of Development: Guidance for Practitioners Working in the Early Years Foundation Stage*, Nottingham: DCSF.

Department for Children, Schools and Families (2008c) *Staying Safe: Action Plan*, London: DCSF.

Department for Children, Schools and Families (2009a) *Safeguarding Children and Young People from Sexual Exploitation*, Nottingham: DCSF. Online, available at: https://www.gov.uk/government/publications/safeguarding-children-and-young-people-from-sexual-exploitation-supplementary-guidance (accessed 10 June 2013).

Department for Children, Schools and Families (2009b) *Safeguarding Disabled Children: Practice Guidance*, Nottingham: DCSF.

Department for Children, Schools and Families (2009c) *Disproportionality in Child Welfare*, Nottingham: DCSF.

Department for Education (2011a) *Supporting Families in the Foundation Years*, London: The Stationery Office. Online, available at: https://www.education.gov.uk/publications/standard/publicationDetail/Page1/DFE-01001-2011 (accessed 3 January 2013).

Department for Education (2011b) *Childhood Neglect: Improving Outcomes for Children: Guidance for Trainers*. Online, available at: http://media.education.gov.uk/assets/files/pdf/c/childhood%20neglect%20improving%20outcomes%20for%20children%20%20%20guidance%20for%20trainers.pdf (accessed 2 May 2013).

Department for Education (2012a) 'Evidence based practice'. Online, available at: www.education.gov.uk/childrenandyoungpeople/families/b00203759/evidence-based-practice (accessed 28 August 2012).

Department for Education (2012b) *Statutory Framework for the Early Years Foundation Stage: Setting the Standards for Learning, Development and Care for Children from Birth to Five*, Runcorn: Department for Education.

Department for Education (2013) 'What is the difference between safeguarding and child protection?', London: Department for Education. Online, available at: www.education.gov.uk/popularquestions/a0064461/safeguarding-and-child-protection (accessed 23 February 2013).

Department for Education and Department of Health (2011) *Supporting Families in the Foundation Years*, Runcorn: DfE. Online, available at: http://media.education.gov.uk/assets/files/pdf/s/supporting%20families%20in%20the%20foundation%20years.pdf (accessed 7 August 2012).

Department for Education and Skills (DfES) (2001) *Promoting Children's Mental Health within Early Years and School Settings*, Nottingham: DfES.

Department for Education and Skills (2003a) *Every Child Matters: Change for Children*, London: DfES.

Department for Education and Skills (2003b) *Interdepartmental Childcare Review*, London: HMSO.

Department for Education and Skills (2005) *Common Core of Skills and Knowledge for the Children's Workforce*, Nottingham: DfES.

Department for Education and Skills (2006) *Safeguarding Children and Safer Recruitment in Education*, Nottingham: DfES.

Department for Education and Skills (2007) *Safeguarding Children from Abuse Linked to a Belief in Spirit Possession*, Nottingham: DfES.

Department of Health (DH) (1988) *Protecting Children: A Guide for Social Workers Undertaking a Comprehensive Assessment in Cases of Child Protection*, London: HMSO.

Department of Health (1995) *Child Protection: Messages from Research*, London: HMSO.

Department of Health (2000a) *Assessing Children in Need and Their Families: Practice Guidance*, London: The Stationery Office.

Department of Health (2000b) *Studies Which Inform the Development of the Framework for the Assessment of Children in Need and Their Families*, London: The Stationery Office.

Department of Health (2001) *The Children Act Now: Messages from Research*, London: The Stationery Office.

Department of Health (2002a) *Complex Child Abuse Investigation: Inter-agency Issues*, London: The Stationery Office.

Department of Health (2002b) *Safeguarding Children: A Joint Chief Inspectors' Report on Arrangements to Safeguard Children*, London: Department of Health.

Department of Health (2009a) *Healthy Child Programme: Pregnancy and the First Five Years*, London: Department of Health.

Department of Health (2009b) *Healthy Child Programme: The Two Year Review*, London: The Stationery Office. Online, available at: http://webarchive.nationalarchives.gov.uk/20130107105354/http://www.dh.gov.uk/prod_consum_dh/groups/dh_digitalassets/documents/digitalasset/dh_108329.pdf (accessed 14 January 2013).

Department of Health (2009c) *The National Child Measurement Programme Guidance for PCTs: 2009/10 School Year*, London: Department of Health. Online, available at: http://webarchive.nationalarchives.gov.uk/+/www.dh.gov.uk/en/Publicationsandstatistics/Publications/DH_086724 (accessed 3 December 2012).

Department of Health and Cleaver, H. (2000) *Assessment Recording Forms*, London: The Stationery Office.

Department of Health and Department for Children, Schools and Families (2007) *Healthy Lives, Brighter Futures*, London: Department of Health.

Department of Health, Home Office and Department of Education and Employment (1999) *Working Together to Safeguard Children: A Guide to Inter-agency Working to Safeguard and Promote the Welfare of Children*, London: The Stationery Office.

Department of Health, Cox, A. and Bentovim, A. (2000a) *The Family Assessment Pack of Questionnaires and Scales*, London: The Stationery Office.

Department of Health, Department of Education and Employment, and Home Office (2000b) *Framework for the Assessment of Children in Need and Their Families*, London: The Stationery Office.

Department of Health and Social Security (DHSS) (1970) *The Battered Baby*, CM 02/70, London: DHSS.

Department of Health and Social Security (1972) *Battered Babies*, LASSL 26/72, London: DHSS.

Department of Health and Social Security (1974) *Non-accidental Injury to Children*, LASSL 74/13, London: DHSS.

Department of Health and Social Security (1976a) *Non-accidental Injury to Children: Area Review Committees*, LASSL 76/2, London: DHSS.

Department of Health and Social Security (1976b) *Non-accidental Injury to Children: The Police and Case Conferences*, LASSL 76/26, London: DHSS.

Department of Health and Social Security (1978) *Child Abuse: The Register System*, LA/C396/23D, London: DHSS.

Department of Health and Social Security (1980a) *Child Abuse: Central Register Systems*, LASSL 80/4, HN(80), London: DHSS.

Department of Health and Social Security (1980b) *Inequalities in Health* (the Black Report), London: DHSS.

Department of Health and Social Security (1986) *Child Abuse: Working Together: A Draft Guide to Arrangements for Inter-agency Cooperation for the Protection of Children*, London: DHSS.

Department of Health and Social Security (1988) *Working Together: A Guide to Inter-agency Co-operation for the Protection of Children from Abuse*, London: HMSO.

Diggins, M. (2011) *Think Child, Think Parent, Think Family: A Guide to Parental Mental Health and Child Welfare*, London: SCIE.

Dowler, E. and Spencer, N. (2007) *Challenging Health Inequalities: From Acheson to Choosing Health*, Bristol: Policy Press.

Downie, R. S., Tannahill, C. and Tannahill, A. (1996) *Health Promotion: Models and Values*, Oxford: Oxford University Press.

Dykes, K. and Stjernqvist, K. (2001) 'The importance of ultrasound to first-time mothers' thoughts about their unborn child', *Journal of Reproductive and Infant Psychology*, 19 (2): 95–104.

Early Education (2012) *Development Matters in the Early Years Foundation Stage*, London: Early Education.

Edwards, G. and Thomas, G. (2010) 'Can reflective practice be taught?', *Education Studies*, 36 (4): 403–414.

Elfer, P. (2007) 'What are nurseries for? The concept of primary task and its application in differentiating roles and tasks in nurseries', *Journal of Early Childhood Research*, 5 (2): 169–188.

Elfer, P. (2012) 'Emotion in nursery work: work discussion as a model of critical professional reflection', *Early Years: An International Journal of Research and Development*, 32 (2): 129–141.

Elfer, P., Goldschmied, E. and Selleck, D. V. (2003) *Key Persons in the Nursery: Building Relationships for Quality Provision*, London: David Fulton.

Elliott, M. (2002) *Bullying*, 3rd edn, Harlow: Pearson Education.

Ellison N. (2011) 'The Conservative Party and the "Big Society"', in C. Holden, M. Kilkey and G. Ramia (eds) *Social Policy Review 23: Analysis Debate in Social Policy*, Bristol: Policy Press.

End Child Poverty (2013) *Child Poverty Map of the UK*, Loughborough: Centre for Research in Social Policy, University of Loughborough.

Evangelou, M., Sylva, K., Kyriacou, M., Wild, M. and Glenny, G. (2009) *Early Years Learning and Development: Literature Review*, Research Report DCSF-RR176, London: DCSF/University of Oxford.

Evans, S. (2008) 'Consigning its past to history? David Cameron and the Conservative Party', *Parliamentary Affairs*, 61 (2): 291–314.

Falkov, A., Mayes, K. and Diggins, M. (1998) *Crossing Bridges: Training Resources for Working with Mentally Ill Parents and Their Children: Reader for Managers, Practitioners and Trainers* (commissioned by the Department of Health), Brighton: Pavilion Publishing.

Field, F. (2010) *The Foundation Years: Preventing Poor Children Becoming Poor Adults: The Report of the Independent Review on Poverty and Life Chances*, London: The Cabinet Office. Online, available at: www.bristol.ac.uk/ifssoca/outputs/ffreport.pdf (accessed 10 June 2013).

Finkelhor, D. (2008) *Childhood Victimization: Violence, Crime, and Abuse in the Lives of Young People*, New York: Oxford University Press.

Fisher, D. and Gruescu, S. (2011) *Children and the Big Society*, London: Action for Children and ResPublica.

Flanagan, J. C. (1954) 'The critical incident technique', *Psychological Bulletin*, 51 (4): 327–358.

Frost, N. and Parton, N. (2009) *Understanding Children's Social Care: Politics, Policy and Practice*, London: Sage.

Garrett, P. M. (2009) 'Transforming' Children's Services? Social Work, Neoliberalism and the 'Modern' World*, Maidenhead: Open University Press/McGraw-Hill Education.

Gerhardt, S. (2004) *Why Love Matters: How Affection Shapes a Baby's Brain*, Hove: Brunner-Routledge.

Gill, C., La Ville, I. and Brady, L.-M. (2011) *The Ripple Effect: The Nature and Impact of the Children and Young People's Voluntary Sector*, London: National Children's Bureau.

Goleman, D. (1996) *Emotional Intelligence: Why It Can Matter More than IQ*, London: Bloomsbury.

Gove, M. (2010) 'Munro Review of Child Protection: better frontline services to protect children', letter to Professor Eileen Munro, 10 June, London: Department for Education.

Gray, C. and MacBlain, S. (2012) *Learning Theories in Childhood*, London: Sage.

Griffin, M. L. (2003) 'Using critical incidents to promote and assess reflective thinking in preservice teachers', *Reflective Practice*, 4 (2): 207–220.

Hackett, S. (2003) 'A framework for assessing parenting capacity', in M. C. Calder and S. Hackett (eds) *Assessment in Child Care: Using and Developing Frameworks for Practice*, Lyme Regis: Russell House Publishing.

Hadfield, M., Jopling, M., Needham, M., Waller, T., Coleyshaw, L., Emira, M. and Royle, K. (2012) *Longitudinal Study of Early Years Professional Status: An Exploration of Progress, Leadership and Impact: Final Report*, Wolverhampton: University of Wolverhampton/DfE. Online, available at: https://www.education.gov.uk/publications/eOrderingDownload/DfE-RR239c%20report.pdf (accessed 3/1/2013).

Halliwell, E., Main, L. and Richardson, C. (2007) *The Fundamental Facts: The Latest Facts and Figures on Mental Health*, London: Mental Health Foundation. Online, available at: www.mentalhealth.org.uk/publications/fundamental-facts/ (accessed 23 February 2013).

Halsey, K., Gulliver, C., Johnson, A., Martin, K. and Kinder, K. (2005) *Evaluation of Behaviour and Education Support Teams*, Research Report no. RR706, Nottingham: NfER/DfES Publications.

Hargie, O. (ed.) (2006) *The Handbook of Communication Skills*, 3rd edn, Hove: Routledge.

Harrison, J. K. and Lee, R. (2011) 'Exploring the use of critical incident analysis and the professional learning conversation in an initial teacher education programme', *Journal of Education for Teaching: International Research and Pedagogy*, 37 (2): 199–217.

Harrison, S. and McDonald, R. (2008) *The Politics of Healthcare in Britain*, London: Sage.

Hawkins, P. and Shohet, R. (2006) *Supervision in the Helping Professions*, 3rd edn, Maidenhead: Open University Press/McGraw-Hill.

Hart, B. and Risley, T. R. (1995) *Meaningful Differences in the Everyday Experience of Young American Children*, Baltimore: Paul H. Brookes.

Henricson, C. and Bainham, A. (2005) *Human Rights Obligations and Policy Supporting Children and Families*, York: Joseph Rowntree Foundation.

Higgs, L. (2011) 'Exclusive survey: youth services and children's centres worst hit as cuts average 13 per cent', *Children and Young People Now*, 25 January: 6–7.

HM Government (2006) *Working Together to Safeguard Children: A Guide to Inter-agency Working to Safeguard and Promote the Welfare of Children*, London: The Stationery Office.

HM Government (2007a) *Safeguarding Children from Abuse Linked to a Belief in Spirit Possession*, London: DfES.

HM Government (2007b) *Safeguarding Children Who May Have Been Trafficked*, London: DCSF.

HM Government (2008a) *Safeguarding Children in Whom Illness Is Fabricated or Induced*, London: DCSF. Online, available at: https://www.gov.uk/government/publications/safeguarding-children-in-whom-illness-is-fabricated-or-induced (accessed 10 June 2013).

HM Government (2008b) *The Right to Choose: Multi-agency Statutory Guidance for Dealing with Forced Marriage*, London: Foreign and Commonwealth Office. Online, available at: https://www.gov.uk/government/uploads/system/uploads/attachment_data/file/35532/fmu-right-to-choose.pdf (accessed 10 June 2013).

HM Government (2009) *The Protection of Children in England: Action Plan: The Government Response to Lord Laming*, Cm 758, London: DCSF.

HM Government (2010a) *Working Together to Safeguard Children: A Guide to Inter-agency Working to Safeguard and Promote the Welfare of Children*, London: DCSF.

HM Government (2010b) *Working Together to Safeguard Children: Government Response to Public Consultation*, London: DCSF.

HM Government (2010c) *Safeguarding Children and Young People Who May Be Affected by Gang Activity*, London: DCSF and Home Office.

HM Government (2013) *Working Together to Safeguard Children: A Guide to Inter-agency Working to Safeguard and Promote the Welfare of Children*, London: DfE.

HM Treasury (2010) *Spending Review 2010*, London: The Stationery Office.

Hobart, C. and Frankel, J. (2005) *Good Practice in Child Protection*, 2nd edn, Cheltenham: Nelson Thornes.

Hoghughi, M. and Speight, A. (1998) 'Good enough parenting for all children: a strategy for a healthier society', *Archives of Disease in Childhood*, 78: 293–300.

Holland, S. (2004) *Child and Family Assessment in Social Work Practice*, 2nd edn, London: Sage.

Home Office (1999) *The Stephen Lawrence Inquiry: Report of an Inquiry by Sir William Macpherson of Cluny*, Cm 4262-I. Online, available at: www.archive.official-documents.co.uk/document/cm42/4262/4262.htm (accessed 26 February 2013).

Home Office (2002) *Statistics on Women and the Criminal Justice System*, London: Home Office.

Home Office, Department of Health, Department of Education and Science, and the Welsh Office (1991) *Working Together under the Children Act 1989: A Guide to Arrangements for Inter-agency Co-operation for the Protection of Children from Abuse*, London: HMSO.

Horwath, J. (2007) *Child Neglect: Identification and Assessment*, Basingstoke: Palgrave Macmillan.

Howe, D. (1992) 'Child abuse and the bureaucratisation of social work', *Sociological Review*, 40 (3): 491–508.

Howe, D. (2011) *Attachment across the Lifecourse*, Basingstoke: Palgrave Macmillan.

Hughes, L. and Owen, H. (eds) (2009) *Good Practice in Safeguarding Children*, London: Jessica Kingsley.

Internet Watch Foundation (2012) *2011 Annual and Charity Report*, Waterbeach, Cambridgeshire: Internet Watch Foundation.

Kempe, C. H, Silverman, F. N., Steele, B. F., Droegemueller, W. and Silver, H. K. (1962) 'The battered-child syndrome', *Journal of the American Medical Association*, 181: 17–24.

Laming Report (2003) *The Victoria Climbié Inquiry: Report of an Inquiry by Lord Laming*, Cm 5730, London: The Stationery Office.

Laming Report (2009) *The Protection of Children in England: A Progress Report*, London: The Stationery Office.

Lancaster, Y. P., Kirby, P. and Coram Family (2010) *Listening to Young Children*, 2nd edn, Maidenhead: Open University Press/McGraw-Hill Education.

Laxton-Kane, M. and Slade, P. (2002) 'The role of maternal prenatal attachment in a woman's experience of pregnancy and implications for the process of care', *Journal of Reproductive and Infant Psychology*, 20 (4): 253–266.

Lazenbatt, A. (2010) 'The impact of abuse and neglect on the health and mental health of children and young people', Leicester: NSPCC, February. Online, available at: www.nspcc.org.uk/Inform/research/briefings/impact_of_abuse_on_health_wda73372.html (accessed 24 September 2012).

Leeson, C. (2010) 'Leadership in early childhood settings', in R. Parker-Rees, C. Leeson, J. Willan and J. Savage (eds) *Early Childhood Studies*, 3rd edn, Exeter: Learning Matters.

Leeson, C. and Huggins, V. (2010) 'Working with colleagues', in R. Parker-Rees, C. Leeson, J. Willan and J. Savage (eds) *Early Childhood Studies*, 3rd edn, Exeter: Learning Matters.

Lindsay, G., Strand, S., Cullen, M. A., Cullen, S., Band, S., Davis, H., Conlon, G., Barlow, J. and Evans, R. (2011) *Parenting Early Intervention Programme Evaluation*, London: Department for Education.

Livingstone, S. and Haddon, L. (2009a) *EU Kids Online: Final Report*, London: London School of Economics.

Livingstone, S. and Haddon, L. (2009b) *Kids Online: Opportunities and Risks for Children*, Bristol: Policy Press.

Lloyd, E. (2012) 'Childcare markets: an introduction', in E. Lloyd and H. Penn (eds) *Childcare Markets: Can They Deliver an Equitable Service?* Bristol: Polity Press.

Lord, P., Southcott, C. and Sharp, C. (2011) *Targeting children's centre services on the most needy families.* Slough: NFER.

McLeod, S. A. (2011) *Albert Bandura | Social Learning Theory.* Online, available at: www.simplypsychology.org/bandura.html (accessed 23 February 2013).

Mac Naughton, G. and Williams, G. (2009) *Teaching Young Children: Choices in Theory and Practice*, 2nd edn, Maidenhead: Open University Press/McGraw-Hill Education.

Manning-Morton, J. (2006) 'The personal is professional: professionalism and the birth to threes practitioner', *Contemporary Issues in Early Childhood*, 7 (1): 42–52.

Manning-Morton, J. (2011) 'Not just the tip of the iceberg: psychoanalytic ideas and early years practice', in L. Miller and L. Pound (eds) *Theories and Approaches to Learning in the Early Years*, London: Sage.

Markel, H. (2009) 'Case Shined First Light on Abuse of Children', *New York Times*, 14 December. Online, available at: www.nytimes.com/2009/12/15/health/15abus.html (accessed 8 August 2012).

Marmot, M. (2010) *Fair Society, Healthy Lives: A Strategic Review of Health Inequalities in England Post-2010*, London: UCL Institute of Health Equity.

Martellozzo, E. (2012) *Online Child Sexual Abuse: Grooming, Policing and Child Protection in a Multi-media World*, London: Routledge.

Mathers, S., Ranns, H., Karemaker, A., Moody, A., Sylva, K., Graham, J. and Siraj-Blatchford, I. (2011) *Evaluation of the Graduate Leader Fund: The Final Report* London: DfE. Online, available at: https://www.education.gov.uk/publications/standard/publicationDetail/Page1/DFE-RR144 (accessed 3 January 2013).

Megginson, D. and Clutterbuck, D. (2005) *Techniques for Coaching and Mentoring*, Oxford: Elsevier Butterworth-Heinemann.

Mehrabian, A. (1972) *Nonverbal Communication*, Chicago: Aldine Atherton.

Melhuish, E., Belsky, J. and Leyland, A. (2010) *National Evaluation of Sure Start Local Programmes: An Economic Perspective*, Bristol: Policy Press.

Millar, M. and Corby, B. (2006) 'The framework for the assessment of children in need and their families: a basis for a "therapeutic" encounter?', *British Journal of Social Work*, 36 (6): 887–899.

Milner, J. and O'Byrne, P. (2002) *Assessment in Social Work*, 2nd edn, Basingstoke: Palgrave Macmillan.

Morgan, J. (2010) 'Frameworks for understanding development', in R. Parker-Rees, C. Leeson, J. Willan and J. Savage (eds) *Early Childhood Studies*, 3rd edn, Exeter: Learning Matters.

Morris, S. (2009) 'Vanessa George jailed for child sex abuse', *Guardian*, 15 December.

Morris, S. (2010) 'Methadone given repeatedly to baby by parents, court told', *Guardian*, 11 June. Online, available at: www.guardian.co.uk/society/2010/jun/11/cruelty-case-baby-methodone (accessed 26 February 2013).

Morrison, T. (1993) *Staff Supervision in Social Care: An Action Learning Approach*, Harlow: Longman.

Morrison, T. (2005) *Staff Supervision in Social Care: Making a Real Difference for Staff and Service Users*, Brighton: Pavilion.

Moynihan, R. (2006) 'Expanding definitions of obesity may harm children', *British Medical Journal*, 332 (7555): 1412.

Munro, E. (2004) 'The impact of audit on social work practice', *British Journal of Social Work*, 34 (8): 1075–1094.

Munro, E. (2010) *The Munro Review of Child Protection: Part One: A Systems Analysis*, London: Department for Education/London School of Economics and Political Science.

Munro, E. (2011a) *The Munro Review of Child Protection: Final Report: A Child Centred System*, London: The Stationery Office.

Munro, E. (2011b) *The Munro Review of Child Protection: Interim Report: The Child's Journey*, London: Department for Education.

Munro, E. (2012) *Progress Review: Moving towards a Child Centred System*, London: DfE.

Munro, E. and Calder, M. (2005) 'Where has child protection gone?', *Political Quarterly*, 76 (3): 439–445.

Murray, L., Sinclair, D., Cooper, P., Ducournau, P., Turner, P. and Stein, A. (1999) 'The socioemotional development of 5-year-old children of postnatally depressed mothers', *Journal of Child Psychology and Psychiatry and Allied Disciplines*, 40 (8): 1259–1271.

Naidoo, J. and Wills, J. (2005) *Public Health and Health Promotion: Developing Practice*, 2nd edn, London: Balliere Tindall.

Naidoo, J. and Wills, J. (2009) *Foundations for Health Promotion*, Oxford: Elsevier.

Nazroo, J. Y. (2003) 'The structuring of ethnic inequalities in health: economic position, racial discrimination, and racism', *American Journal of Public Health*, 93 (2): 277–284.

NCB (2012) *A Know How Guide: The EYFS Progress Check at Age Two*, London: NCB. Online, available at: www.foundationyears.org.uk/wp-content/uploads/2012/03/A-Know-How-Guide.pdf (accessed 17 June 2013).

NSPCC (2012) 'Child protection registers statistics – UK', London: NSPCC Inform. Online, available at: https://www.nspcc.org.uk/Inform/research/statistics/unitedkingdom_wdf81294.pdf (accessed 3 December 2012).

NSPCC and University of Sheffield (2000) *The Child's World: Assessing Children in Need. Training and Development Pack*, London: NSPCC.

Nutbrown, C. (2012) *Foundations for Quality: The Independent Review of Early Education and Child Care Qualifications*, London: Crown Publications.

Oakeshott, M. J. (1962) *Rationalism in Politics and Other Essays*, London: Methuen.

O'Connell, R. (2003) *A Typology of Child Cybersexploitation and Online Grooming Practices*, Preston: University of Central Lancashire.

O'Donoghue, K. and Tsui, M. (2012) 'Towards a professional supervision culture: the development of social work supervision in Aotearoa New Zealand', *Social Work*, 55 (1): 5–28.

OECD (2011) 'The protection of children online: risks faced by children online and policies to protect them', OECD Digital Economy Papers no. 179, Paris: OECD Publishing.

Ofcom (2007) *Ofcom's Submission to the Byron Review, Annex 5: The Evidence Base – The Views of Children, Young People and Parents*. Online, available at: http://stakeholders.ofcom.org.uk/binaries/research/telecoms-research/annex5.pdf (accessed 10 June 2013).

Ofcom (2009) *UK Children's Media Literacy: Interim Report*, London: Ofcom.

Ofcom (2010) *UK Children's Media Literacy*, London: Ofcom.

Office of the Children's Commissioner (2012) *'They never give up on you': Schools Exclusions Inquiry – Full Report*, London: Office of the Children's Commissioner. Online, available at: www.childrenscommissioner.gov.uk/content/publications/content_561 (accessed 4/1/2012).

Office for National Statistics (ONS) (2011) *Life expectancy at birth and at age 65 by local areas in the United Kingdom, 2004–06 and 2008–10*, Newport: Office for National Statistics. Online, available at: www.ons.gov.uk/ons/dcp171778_238743.pdf (accessed 19 March 2012).

Office for National Statistics (2013) *Focus on: Violent Crime and Sexual Offences, 2011/12*, Newport: Office for National Statistics. Online, available at: www.ons.gov.uk/ons/dcp171778_298904.pdf (accessed 17 June 2013).

Ofsted (2005) *Healthy minds: promoting emotional health and well-being in schools*, Manchester: Ofsted.

Osborne, G. (2010) Spending Review Statement, London: HM Treasury. Online, available at: www.hm-treasury.gov.uk/spend_sr2010_speech.htm (accessed 19 March 2012).

Osgood, J. (2005) 'Who cares? The classed nature of childcare', *Gender and Education*, 17 (3): 289–303.

Osgood, J. (2006) 'Professionalism and performativity: the feminist challenge facing early years education', *Early Years: An International Journal of Research and Development*, 26 (2): 187–199.

Osgood, J. (2009) 'Childcare workforce reform in England and "the early years professional": a critical discourse analysis', *Journal of Education Policy*, 24 (6): 733–751.

Ottawa Charter for Health Promotion (1986) Geneva: World Health Organization. Online, available at: www.who.int/healthpromotion/conferences/previous/ottawa/en/ (accessed 3 December 2012).

Page, R. M. (2010) 'David Cameron's modern Conservative approach to poverty and social justice: one nation or two?', *Journal of Poverty and Social Justice*, 18 (2): 147–159.

Paige-Smith, A. and Craft, A. (2008) *Developing Reflective Practice in the Early Years*, Maidenhead: Open University Press/McGraw-Hill Education.

Palaiologou, I. (2012) *Child Observation for the Early Years*, 2nd edn, London: Learning Matters.

Papatheodorou, T. and Luff, P. (2011) *Child Observation for Learning and Research*, Harlow: Pearson Education.

Parekh, A., MacInnes, T. and Kenway, P. (2010) *Monitoring Poverty and Social Exclusion 2010*, York: Joseph Rowntree Foundation. Online, available at: www.jrf.org.uk/sites/files/jrf/poverty-social-exclusion-2010-full.pdf (accessed 12 December 2012).

Parton, N. (1985) *The Politics of Child Abuse*, Basingstoke: Palgrave Macmillan.

Parton, N. (1991) *Governing the Family: Child Care, Child Protection and the State*, Basingstoke: Palgrave Macmillan.

Parton, N. (ed.) (1997) *Child Protection and Family Support: Tensions, Contradictions and Possibilities*, London: Routledge.

Parton, N. (2006a) *Safeguarding Childhood Early Intervention and Surveillance in a Late Modern Society*, Basingstoke: Palgrave.

Parton, N. (2006b) '"Every child matters": the shift to prevention whilst strengthening protection in children's services in England', *Children and Youth Services Review*, 28 (8): 976–992.

Parton, N. (2011) 'Child protection and safeguarding in England: changing and competing conceptions of risk and their implications for social work', *British Journal of Social Work*, 41: 854–875.

Parton, N. (2012) 'The Munro Review of Child Protection: An Appraisal', *Children and Society*, 26: 150–162.

Parton, N., Thorpe, D. H. and Wattam, C. (1997) *Child Protection: Risk and the Moral Order*, Basingstoke: Macmillan.

Penn, H. (2008) *Understanding Early Childhood: Issues and Controversies*, 2nd edn, Maidenhead: Open University Press.

Penn, H. (2011) *Quality in Early Childhood Services: An International Perspective*, Maidenhead: Open University Press.

Perkins, M. (2006) 'Genetic and biological influences', in J. Aldgate, D. Jones, W. Rose and C. Jeffery (eds) *The Developing World of the Child*, London: Jessica Kingsley.

Plymouth Safeguarding Children Board (2010) *Serious Case Review: Overview Report. Executive Summary in Respect of Nursery Z*. Online, available at: www.plymouth.gov.uk/serious_case_review_nursery_z.pdf (accessed 13 August 2012).

Porter, L. (2003) *Young Children's Behaviour: Practical Approaches for Caregivers and Teachers*, London: Paul Chapman.

Powell, J. and Uppal, E. L. (2012) *Safeguarding Babies and Young Children: A Guide for Early Years Professionals*, Maidenhead: McGraw-Hill/Open University Press.

Pugh, G. (2010) 'The policy agenda for early childhood services', in G. Pugh and B. Duffy (eds) *Contemporary Issues in the Early Years*, 5th edn, London: Sage.

Putnam, R. D. (1995) 'Bowling alone: America's declining social capital', *Journal of Democracy*, 6 (1): 65–78.

Radford, L., Corral, S., Bradley, C., Fisher, H., Bassett, C., Howat, N. and Collishaw, S. (2011) *Child Abuse and Neglect in the UK Today*, London: NSPCC.

Reder, P. and Duncan, S. (2003) 'Understanding Communication in Child Protection Networks', *Child Abuse Review*, 12 (2): 82–100.

Rees, C. (2010) 'Promoting children's emotional wellbeing', *Paediatrics and Child Health*, 20 (9): 439–446.

Reilly, J. J., Armstrong, A., Dorosty, A. R., Emmett, P. M., Ness, A., Rogers, I., Steer, C. and Sherriff, A. (2005) 'Early life risk factors for obesity in childhood: cohort study', *British Medical Journal*, 330: 1357.

Richmond, D. (2009) 'Using multi-layered supervision methods to develop creative practice', *Reflective Practice: International and Multidisciplinary Perspectives*, 10 (4): 543–557.

Rinaldi, C. (2006) *In Dialogue with Reggio Emilia: Listening, Researching and Learning*, London: Routledge.

Roberts, R. (2002) *Self-Esteem and Early Learning*, London: Paul Chapman.

Roberts, R. (2010) *Wellbeing from Birth*, London: Sage

Rogoff, B. (1990) *Apprenticeship in Thinking*, Oxford: Oxford University Press.

Royal College of Psychiatrists (2012) 'Domestic violence – its effects on children: the impact on children and adolescents: information for parents, carers and anyone who works with young people', London: RCPsych. Online, available at: www.rcpsych.ac.uk/expertadvice/youthinfo/parentscarers/parenting/domesticviolence.aspx (accessed 26 February 2013).

Royal College of Psychiatrists (2013a) 'Postnatal depression', London: RCPsych. Online, available at: www.rcpsych.ac.uk/mentalhealthinformation/mentalhealthproblems/postnatalmentalhealth/postnataldepression.aspx (accessed 25 February 2013).

Royal College of Psychiatrists (2013b) 'Parental mental illness: the impact on children and adolescents: information for parents, carers and anyone who works with young people', London: RCPsych. Online, available at: www.rcpsych.ac.uk/expertadvice/youthinfo/parentscarers/parenting/parentalmentalillness.aspx (accessed 25 February 2013).

Royal Society for the Prevention of Accidents (2012) 'Accidents to children'. Online, available at: www.rospa.com/homesafety/adviceandinformation/childsafety/accidents-to-children.aspx#injuries (accessed 1 November 2012).

Rudolph, M. (2009) *Tackling Obesity through the Healthy Child Programme: A Framework for Action*, Leeds: University of Leeds Leeds Community Healthcare.

Schön, D. A. (1987) *Educating the Reflective Practitioner: Toward a New Design for Teaching and Learning in the Professions*, San Francisco: Jossey-Bass.

Scottish Intercollegiate Guidelines Network (2005) *Prevention and Management of Dental Decay in the Pre-school Child*. Online, available at: www.sign.ac.uk/pdf/sign83.pdf (accessed 30 October 2012).

Scriven, A. (2010) *Promoting Health: A Practical guide*, 6th edn, Oxford: Balliere-Tindall/Elsevier.

Secretary of State for Social Services (1974) *Report of the Committee into the Care and Supervision Provided in Relation to Maria Colwell*, London: HMSO.

Secretary of State for Social Services (1998) *Report of the Inquiry into Child Abuse in Cleveland*, Cm 412, London: The Stationery Office.

Shannon, C. and Weaver, W. (1949) *The Mathematical Theory of Communication*, Chicago: University of Illinois Press.

Siraj-Blatchford, I., Sylva, K., Muttock, S., Gilden, R. and Bell, D. (2002) *Researching Effective Pedagogy in the Early Years* (REPEY), Research Report RR356, London: DfES/HMSO.

Smale, G. and Tuson, G., with Brehal, N. and Marsh, P. (1993) *Empowerment, Assessment, Care Management and the Skilled Worker*, London: National Institute of Social Work.

Smart, C. and Neale, B. (1999) *Family Fragments?* Cambridge: Polity Press.

Smith, C. and Pugh, G. (1996) *Learning to Be a Parent: A Survey of Group-Based Parenting Programmes. Family and Parenthood: Policy and Practice*, London. Family Policy Studies.

Smith, K. (ed.), Coleman, K., Eder, S. and Hall, P. (2011) *Homicides, Firearms Offences and Intimate Violence 2009/10: Supplementary Volume 2 to Crime in England and Wales 2009/10*, London: Home Office.

Smith, K. P., Cowie, H. and Blades, M. (2003) *Understanding Children's Development*, 4th edn, Oxford: Blackwell.

Smith, R. (2008) 'From child protection to child safety: locating risk assessment in the changing landscape', in M. C. Calder (ed.) *Contemporary Risk Assessment in Safeguarding Children*, Lyme Regis: Russell House Publishing.

Social Work Task Force (2009) *Building a Safe, Confident Future: The Final Report of the Social Work Task Force: November 2009*, London: DCSF.

Solihull NHS PCT (2004) *Solihull Approach Resource Pack*, Solihull NHS PCT/Jill Rogers Associates.

Spencer, N. (2003) 'Parenting programmes', *Archive of Diseases in Childhood*, 88: 99–100.

Stalker, K., Green Lister, P., Lerpiniere, J. and McArthur, K. (2010) *Child Protection and the Needs and Rights of Disabled Children and Young People: A Scoping Study*, Glasgow: University of Strathclyde.

Stanley, N. and Cox, P. (2009) *Parental Mental Health and Child Welfare: Reviews of Policy and Professional Education*, London: Social Care Institute for Excellence.

Stevenson, O. (2007) *Neglected Children and Their Families*, 2nd edn, Oxford: Blackwell.

Stewart, K. (2011) 'A treble blow? Child poverty in 2010 and beyond', in C. Holden, M. Kilkey and G. Ramia (eds) *Social Policy Review 23: Analysis and Debate in Social Policy*, Bristol: Policy Press.

Strauss, R. S. and Knight, J. (1999) 'Influence of the home environment on the development of obesity in children', *Pediatrics*, 103 (6): 85.

Sullivan P. M. and Knutson, J. F. (2000) 'Maltreatment and disabilities: a population-based epidemiological study', *Child Abuse and Neglect*, 24 (10): 1257–1273.

Sylva, K. and Roberts, F. (2010) 'Quality in early childhood education: evidence for long-term effects', in G. Pugh and B. Duffy (eds) *Contemporary Issues in the Early Years*, London: Sage.

Tickell, C. (2011) *The Early Years: Foundations for Life, Health and Learning: An Independent Report on the Eearly Years Foundation Stage to Her Majesty's Government*, London: Department for Education. Online, available at: http://media.education.gov.uk/assets/Files/pdf/F/Foundations%20for%20life%20health%20and%20learning.pdf (accessed 4 January 2012).

Tuckman, B. W. (1965) 'Developmental sequence in small groups', *Psychological Bulletin*, 63 (6): 384–399.

UKCCIS (2009) *Children's Online Risks and Safety: A Review of the Available Evidence*, Slough: NFER.

UNICEF (2007) *Child Poverty in Perspective: An Overview of Child Well-being in Rich Countries*, Florence: Unicef Innocenti Research Centre.

United Nations (1989) *United Nations Convention on the Rights of the Child* (UNCRC), Geneva: United Nations.

Urban, M (2008) 'Dealing with uncertainty: challenges and possibilities for the early childhood profession', *European Early Childhood Education Research Journal*, 6 (2): 135–152.

Vincent, C. and Braun, A. (2011) ' "I think a lot of it is common sense…" Early years students, professionalism and the development of a "vocational habitus"', *Journal of Education Policy*, 26 (6): 771–785.

Viner, R. M., Roche, E., Maguire, S. A. and Nicholls, D. E. (2010) 'Child protection and obesity: framework for practice', *British Medical Journal*, 341: c3074.

Vygotsky, L. S. (1978) *Mind in Society: The Development of Higher Psychological Processes*, Cambridge, MA: Harvard University Press.

Ward, H., Brown, R. and Westlake, D. (2012) *Safeguarding Babies and Very Young Children from Abuse and Neglect*, London: Jessica Kingsley.

Wardle, J. (2005) 'The impact of obesity on psychological well-being', *Best Practice and Research Clinical Endocrinology and Metabolism*, 19 (3): 421–440.

Wardle, J., Guthrie, C.A., Sanderson, S. and Rapoport, L. (2001) 'Development of the Children's Eating Behaviour Questionnaire', *The Journal of Child Psychology and Psychiatry*, 42 (7): 963–970.

Whalley, M. and the Pen Green Centre Team (2007) *Involving Parents in Their Children's Learning*, London: Paul Chapman.

Willan, J. (2010) 'Observing children', in R. Parker-Rees, C. Leeson, J. Willan and J. Savage (eds) *Early Childhood Studies*, 3rd edn, Exeter: Learning Matters.

WiredKids (2012) 'What is cyberbullying, exactly?', New York: Wiredsafety.org. Online, available at: www.stopcyberbullying.org/what_is_cyberbullying_exactly.html (accessed 14 June 2012).

Wolak, J., Finkelhor, D., Mitchell, K. J. and Ybarra, M. L. (2008) 'Online "predators" and their victims', *American Psychologist*, 63 (2): 111–128.

Women's Aid (2009) Domestic violence statistics, Bristol: Women's Aid. Online, available at: www.womensaid.org.uk/domestic_violence_topic.asp?section=0001000100220041&sectionTitle=Domestic+violence+%28general%29 (accessed 26 February 2013).

Wood, J. T. (2010) *Interpersonal Communication: Everyday Encounters*, 6th edn, Boston, MA: Wadsworth.

Woods, P. (1993) 'Critical events in education', *British Journal of Sociology of Education*, 14 (4): 355–371.

Working Party in the Department of Child Health, University of Newcastle upon Tyne (1973) 'Non-accidental injury to children: a guide to management', *British Medical Journal*, 4 (5893): 657–660.

World Health Organization (WHO) (1948) 'WHO definition of health'. Online, available at: www.who.int/about/definition/en/print.html (accessed on 3 December 2012).

Z and Others v. *United Kingdom (Application 29392/95)* [2001] 2 FCR 246, *European Court of Human Rights (Grand Chamber)*; Judge L. Wildhaber (President), E. Palm, C. Rozakis, J.-P. Costa, L. Ferrari Bravo, L. Caflisch, P. Kuris, J. Casadevall, B. Zupancic, N. Vajic, J. Hedigan, W. Thomassen, M. Tsatsa-Nikolovska, E. Levits, K. Traja, A. Kovler JJ, Arden LJ (Ad hoc Judge) and P. Mahoney (Deputy Registrar); 10 May 2001.

Index

Page numbers in *italics* denote tables, those in **bold** denote figures.